GROVER SALES

JAZZ
America's Classical Music

A SPECTRUM BOOK

Prentice-Hall, Inc.,
Englewood Cliffs, N.J. 07632

Library of Congress Cataloging in Publication Data

Sales, Grover.
  Jazz : America's classical music.

  "A Spectrum Book."
  Bibliography: p. 231.
  Discography: p. 227.
  Includes index.
    1. Jazz music—United States—History and criticism.
  I. Title.
ML3508.S26 1984   781'.57'0973   84-4703
ISBN 0-13-509126-8
ISBN 0-13-509118-7 (pbk.)

10 9 8 7 6 5 4 3 2 1

ISBN 0-13-509126-8

ISBN 0-13-509118-7 {PBK.}

Editorial/production supervision
and book design: Joe O'Donnell Jr.
Cover design: Hal Siegel
Manufacturing buyer: Frank Grieco

This book is available at a special discount when ordered in
bulk quantities. Contact Prentice-Hall, Inc., General
Publishing Division, Special Sales, Englewood Cliffs, N.J. 07632.

The photograph of Cootie Williams on the title page was
taken at the 1963 Monterey Jazz Festival. It is by Grover Sales.

Prentice-Hall International, Inc., *London*
Prentice-Hall of Australia Pty. Limited, *Sydney*
Prentice-Hall Canada Inc., *Toronto*
Prentice-Hall of India Private Limited, *New Delhi*
Prentice-Hall of Japan, Inc., *Tokyo*
Prentice-Hall of Southeast Asia Pte. Ltd., *Singapore*
Whitehall Books Limited, *Wellington, New Zealand*
Editora Prentice-Hall do Brasil Ltda., *Rio de Janeiro*

Contents

Foreword   v

Preface   vii

1   Who this Book Is for   1

2   The Nature of Jazz   9

3   The Growth of Jazz   47

4   Jazz Today   205

5   Where Is Jazz Going?   213

Chronology   223

Discography   227

Selected Bibliography   231

Jazz Magazines
    and Publications   237

Index   238

Foreword

It occurred to me some time ago that I have, by accident, known most of the major figures in jazz history, some of them slightly and some of them intimately. Whatever I know of the subject I learned from them, not from books. Countless hours of conversations with them have long since sunk into my subconscious and shaped my thinking not only about jazz but about art in general and life itself.

One consequence of this experience is a skepticism toward histories of jazz, some of which are too technical for the layman, some of which reveal a limited technical grasp by the writer, some of which are at odds with the reminiscences of those who made it, and all too many of which have been political, serving one partisan purpose or another.

It is no surprise to me that Grover Sales has written a sensible, useful, and, to the best of my knowledge, accurate introduction to jazz, because that is a reflection of his character. His approach to the music has always been informed with the humility of the scholar. And in his various capacities as writer, lecturer on jazz history at San Francisco State University, and—at one time—publicity director of the Monterey Jazz Festival, he too has had the opportunity to know many of the major figures in jazz.

A few months before he completed work on this book, Grover did a program at San Francisco State on the career of Dizzy Gillespie, using photographic slides and records to trace the life of this remarkable musician. The participants in this presentation included an audience of 300 students and faculty members, and the object of the exercise, Mr. John Birks Gillespie himself. At several points in the proceedings there was a suspicious mist in the eyes of Mr. Gillespie, a man in whom lives not only a brilliant musical mind and a vast sense of the world's humor but also a deep gentleness. Yes, I would say that Grover Sales is well qualified to describe and discuss the music of Dizzy Gillespie.

Jazz is a living music, not only in the sense that it is still evolving in our time, but in the sense that as a music that is substantially improvised, its emphasis is on the performance rather than on the writing. In jazz, the creator and performer are one. It is a music that has evolved through recording, and indeed it seems likely that had the phonograph not been invented, jazz might not have come into being. Certainly it could not have had its phenomenal rapid development from a folk music into an art music requiring enormous knowledge and skill. (During that seminar with Grover, Dizzy said that no question annoyed him more than the one about whether he ever played any "serious" music. "Men have died for this music," Dizzy said, and added with his customary dry wit, "You can't get more serious than that.") Much of its history is preserved on records, albeit in the early days records with poor sound quality. And so the emphasis in an approach to jazz history must be on listening rather than reading. And it seems to me that if anyone were to follow this book very carefully, acquiring the records Grover recommends and then listening to them as he reads, he (or she) would come out at the other end with a rather considerable familiarity with the art, equipped now to appreciate and enjoy it on his own. I think this is an important point about this book: It is meant to be a linked listening-and-reading experience.

I believe this book does a major service for the art, particularly for the young, whether they intend to be players or appreciators, who will carry it into the future.

Gene Lees is a former editor of down beat *and a long-time contributor to* Stereo Review, High Fidelity, *and other major publications, as well as a composer and lyricist whose songs have been recorded by Ella Fitzgerald, Sarah Vaughan, and most of the major singers in jazz and popular music. He is the publisher and editor of* The Jazzletter, *whose subscribers include almost all the major jazz musicians.*

Preface

The term *jazzman* is used interchangeably with *jazz musician* with no offense intended or implied to women, in jazz or out. Jazz in its early days developed a male-dominated community whose players were steeped in a super-macho ethic reflected in their stance, attitude, slang, in the titles of jazz compositions, and in the nature of the music itself. With rare exceptions, women's role in jazz, until quite recently, was restricted to the piano and, most of all, to singing. The increasing role of women in jazz during the past decade as band leaders, composers, guitarists, and horn players is but one of the welcome byproducts of the current liberation movement.

I feel it does no service to the women's movement to concoct such a trendy contrivance as *jazzperson*, which strikes me as foolish and would seem all the more so ten years from now—or perhaps even less.

Acknowledgments

With thanks to my editor, Mary E. Kennan, whose faith and guidance made the book possible; Gene Lees, for editing the manuscript, monumental support, and feeding of ideas; Richard B. Hadlock, for further exhaustive editing and generous consultation; Leonard G. Feather, without whose *Encyclopedias of Jazz* all jazz writers would start from scratch; Max Harrison of the London *Times*, who first gave me the idea for the book; Bruce Kennan, for warm encouragement and expert Ellingtonia; Norma Teagarden, for priceless photos of the First Family of Texas; Dan Morgenstern, director, Institute of Jazz Studies, Rutgers University, for making their photo library available; Jean R. Gleason, for making available the

Ralph J. Gleason photo library; Larry Septoff, for sharing his research on Ornette Coleman; Don Asher, for much-needed technical advice; Bob Houlehan, whose Sunday night programs on KJAZ-FM, Alameda, California, are a continuing source of information and joy; Dizzy Gillespie, whose life and work have been an inspiration to all of us for four decades; my colleagues at San Francisco State University—Dr. Carolynn A. Lindeman, Dr. Richard Webb, Mark Radice, and William Hopkins—and to the memory of Jim Harris, who hired me; and most of all, to Georgia Sales, without whose love, direction, and infallible eye and ear, this book would not exist.

I am grateful to the following for material used in this book:

Excerpts from *The Making of Jazz*, by James Lincoln Collier, are reprinted by permission of Houghton Mifflin Company. Copyright © 1978 by James Lincoln Collier.

Excerpts from *The New Encyclopedia of Jazz*, copyright © 1960; *The Encyclopedia of Jazz in the Sixties*, copyright © 1966; and *The Encyclopedia of Jazz in the Seventies*, copyright © 1976, are reprinted by permission of the author, Leonard Feather, and of the publisher, Horizon Press, New York.

Extracts from Leonard Feather's "Blindfold Tests" are reprinted by permission of *down beat* magazine.

The excerpts from "An Interview with Louis Armstrong," by Richard Meryman, are reprinted by permission of *Life* magazine. Copyright © 1966 by Time, Inc.

The extracts from *Death of a Music?* by Henry Pleasants, are reprinted by permission of the author.

Excerpts from *Early Jazz*, by Gunther Schuller, are reprinted by permission of Oxford University Press.

Excerpts from *Hear Me Talkin' to Ya*, edited by Nat Shapiro and Nat Hentoff, are reprinted by permission of Holt, Rinehart and Winston, Publishers. Copyright © 1955 by Nat Shapiro and Nat Hentoff.

Extracts from *Four Lives in the Bebop Business*, by A. B. Spellman, are reprinted by permission of Pantheon Books, a division of Random House, Inc.

The photograph of Gunther Schuller and John Lewis on page 36 is by Vestal Photography.

The photograph of "Jelly Roll" Morton on page 55 is reprinted by permission of Sidney C. Martin.

The photograph of Billy Strayhorn and Duke Ellington on page 82 is by Rothschild Photo.

The photograph of Muggsy Spanier on page 95 was taken by Art Hoyt.

The photograph of Coleman Hawkins and Gerry Mulligan on page 124 is reprinted by permission of Peter Breinig.

The extract on page 169, from *Notes & Tones*, by Arthur Taylor, is reprinted by permission of Perigree Press. Copyright © 1981.

The photograph of Bill Evans on page 179 is reprinted by permission of Helen Keane.

The extract on page 215, from *Against the American Grain*, by Dwight Macdonald, is reprinted by permission of Gloria Macdonald and Da Capo Press. Copyright Gloria Macdonald.

Jazz critic **Grover Sales** has produced jazz concerts and helped promote the Monterey Jazz Festival in its formative years. For more than a decade he headed his own entertainment and theater publicity office whose clients included many jazz greats, such as Duke Ellington and Louis Armstrong. He teaches in the Jazz Studies programs at San Francisco State University, the San Francisco Conservatory of Music, and Dominican College in California.

1

Who this Book Is for

(overleaf)
Lester Young: His sleepy heavy-lidded
stance was the essence of "cool" — as
was his lazy, unforced way of
combining total muscular relaxation with
complete control over the tenor sax.
(Photograph courtesy of the Rutgers
Institute of Jazz Studies.)

This is an introduction to jazz intended for—but not limited to—those who cannot read a note of music and do not know the name of a single chord. Jazz became a universal language, not because Charlie Parker modulated from B flat to A–minor 7th, but because America's classical music seized people regardless of age, nation, or class in a unique emotional grip and urged their bodies and minds to move in very special ways.

Professional and amateur musicians of all persuasions, as well as the nonplaying listener, will, I hope, find this book useful. Though the condition is not as widespread as a generation ago, classical musicians through ignorance and prejudice often misunderstand the nature of jazz and tend to judge it by the standards they apply to Mozart or Schoenberg, unaware that jazz artists pursue vastly different but equally valid goals.

Jazz musicians and enthusiasts will discover the background of the music they love. To the eternal detriment of jazz as an evolving art form, many contemporary players remain unaware of early giants who shaped their styles, just as Haydn shaped the work of Beethoven: James P. Johnson, Sidney Bechet, Fletcher Henderson, Bix Beiderbecke, Coleman Hawkins, Duke Ellington, Louis Armstrong, and Earl Hines. All jazz musicians today, regardless of instrument or style, stand on these shoulders, whether they realize it or not.

Serious rock performers and listeners will find the deeply buried roots of their music and may learn, often to their surprise, how rock 'n' roll developed as an offshoot of jazz.

This book examines a crucial phenomenon of the twentieth century: how the music of black America began as a primitive folk entertainment and grew with amazing speed into a complex and varied art form that interacted with classical music; the ethnic musics of Latin America, the Middle East, Europe, Africa, and the Orient; and with jazz's offshoots, rhythm 'n' blues and rock, and became an international language. Thanks to a burgeoning technology—railroads, the automobile, player piano rolls, radio, and, most of all, the phonograph—in less than a century, jazz made changes that roughly correspond to the transition from the Gregorian Chant in the early Middle Ages to contemporary avant-garde music.

This book shows how the music of black America, beginning with ragtime at the turn of the century, sent successive shock waves throughout the white mass culture, and how these continuous explosions left lasting marks on our social landscape.

Readers will learn how jazz flowered into a unique art form in spite of (though some may insist because of) appalling racial and musical prejudice and hysterical attacks by the press, the pulpit, and the "proper" music schools who regarded this body-based music, with ironic accuracy, as a sexual-cultural threat—the lewd, degenerate noise of a despised and impoverished subculture. Readers will also discover how jazz music served as a fulcrum to overturn centuries-old fears and misunderstandings between white and black America that poisoned our national life.

This book attempts to show how jazz not only reflected but also anticipated radical social change within the United States, and how major shifts in the attitudes and behavior of black Americans and the white counter-culture first took root among the community of jazz musicians.

Whenever appropriate, the book will relate the continuous development of jazz to other concurrent art forms, particularly European concert music.

A book as brief and as general as this cannot hope to offer a comprehensive history of so varied and prolific a music. For this readers are directed to James Lincoln Collier's *The Making of Jazz*, the most complete and best-written single-volume survey in print.

Much of this book may seem elementary to jazz scholars, since it was prompted by encounters with students of all ages and backgrounds who had never heard of Art Tatum or Lester Young, who thought Benny Goodman played the trumpet, and who could not distinguish the sound of a tenor sax from that of a trombone. One still finds numbers of cultivated, well-traveled Americans whose table talk resounds of Pinter, Warhol, Fassbinder, Stoppard, Sondheim, Merce Cunningham, Twyla Tharp, and Jasper Johns but who have never heard of the Mozarts, Chopins, and Stravinskys of American music: Bud Powell, Billy Strayhorn, Eric Dolphy, Coleman Hawkins, James P. Johnson, Clifford Brown, and McCoy Tyner.

Although thousands who came of age in the 1960s now show signs of gravitating toward jazz, many believe that jazz started with Miles Davis, or even Keith Jarrett, just as they assume that the black movement began with Martin Luther King Jr., the women's movement with Betty Friedan, and the anti-war protest movement with Bob Dylan. As Cicero warned the citizens of ancient Rome, "To know no History is to remain a child all one's life."

For these reasons, much of this book is addressed to a general audience, although I hope that jazz specialists may see some of the material as breaking sparsely worked ground.

Making no technical demands on the reader, this book is meant as a manual in the *discipline* as well as the joys of listening to jazz. The word *discipline* is used deliberately. The finest jazz is not the mindless distraction of elevator or supermarket musak. Charlie Parker, Duke Ellington, and John Coltrane demand the same single-minded concentration and repeated hearings as the Beethoven Quartets and Bach's *Goldberg Variations*. Readers who listen often and with care to the records mentioned throughout this book will discover vast and surprising realms, rich in musical and emotional rewards that illuminate the American past and present in wondrous ways no textbook could hope to provide.

Jazz, like any other music, must be listened to in its historical context. No one expects Bach to sound like Bartók any more than one looked to Bartók to compose in the style of Bach. All major composers "wrote their time," like Haydn, whose music was a social and artistic mirror of Europe on the eve of the French Revolution, when Haydn was an "employee" of an Austrian count and as such was required to wear the uniform of a liveried servant. His pupil Beethoven developed a freer, more tumultuous music as befitted the radical changes wrought by the revolution when the composer was no longer beholden to the Church and the Aristocracy for his livelihood. This is not to say that one *ought* to prefer Haydn to Beethoven or vice versa, any more than one ought to favor Louis Armstrong over John Coltrane or Charlie Parker over Coleman Hawkins, even though most of us tend to gravitate toward one historical period or style more than others. But it is important to relate music to the society that spawned it. You cannot grasp the impact of Louis Armstrong and Earl Hines in the 1920s unless you compare them with their forebears as well as their immediate contemporaries, taking into account the social, economic, and psychological demands made on jazz artists of that time. The same is true of Charlie Parker in the 1940s and John Coltrane in the 1960s.

Finally, a word of advice so well put by James Lincoln Collier in his splendid survey *The Making of Jazz:* "We have to divest ourselves of the idea that the history of jazz has always been toward better and better. In no art has this ever been the case." If this *were* the case, *Garfield* would be a better comic strip than *Pogo*, John Belushi a better standup comic than Lenny Bruce, and Stephen Sondheim a better composer of show tunes than George Gershwin. "As jazz advanced," Collier continues, "it frequently discarded the valuable as well as the useless. There are things in the older forms worth exploring. Jazz has always been obsessed with the new, with experimentation, and the result has been that it has rarely paused to exploit its discoveries before leaping out to make fresh ones."

You may be enraptured with jazz of the 1930s and become an avid collector of Lester Young, Duke Ellington, and Django Reinhardt. Or it may be the bebop era of the 1940s that holds a special appeal. You may be repulsed or even angered by the "free jazz" of Ornette Coleman and Cecil Taylor in the 1960s, or you may feel that these revolutionaries speak to you of your time, making it hard for you to "relate" to earlier forms of jazz. If so, remember that you'll never know "where it's at" until you learn where it's *from*.

The house of jazz has many mansions. Visit all of these mansions, old and new, with open ears and open mind. This book attempts to guide those who will listen through these vast and varied chambers that honeycomb the miraculous cathedral that houses America's classical music.

Notes on the Recordings

The book makes continual reference to the *Smithsonian Collection of Classic Jazz*, the most complete and least costly anthology yet released. This boxed set of six LPs is not available in record stores, but it may be purchased directly from:

Smithsonian Performing Arts
P.O. Box 10230
Des Moines, Iowa 50336

The package includes a forty-page booklet with Martin Williams's excellent concise history of jazz and a useful guide to each of the eighty-six selections.

Records in the *Smithsonian Collection* (Smic) referred to throughout the book will be noted as follows:

"Lester Young solos on Count Basie's
Doggin' Around (Smic 5/7)"

This means that *Doggin' Around* is on Side 5, track 7 of the *Smithsonian Collection*.

Readers are reminded that the *Smithsonian Collection* is merely an *hors d'oeuvre* in the feast of jazz, and they will be referred to other available records, since the *Smithsonian* package is brief and marred by serious omissions. Most albums in the splendidly produced and annotated Time-Life *Giants of Jazz* series are recommended, especially Louis Armstrong, Duke Ellington, Lester Young, Count Basie, Billie Holiday, Benny Goodman, Jack Teagarden, Earl Hines, Coleman Hawkins, James P. Johnson, Johnny Hodges, and Teddy Wilson. Unfortunately, Time-Life limited its output to music before the advent of Charlie Parker and "modern jazz" in the mid-1940s. The *Giants of Jazz* packages are not available in record shops and must be ordered by mail from:

Time-Life Records
541 North Fairbanks Court
Chicago, Illinois 60611

A basic record library recommended for beginning listeners is listed in the back of this book.

2

The
Nature
of Jazz

(overleaf)
Miles Davis: "Something's wrong with my
lip tonight." A jazz improvisor's style
is often a direct expression of
his temperament.
(Photograph by Grover Sales.)

Jazz is an improvisor's art. Excepting Jelly Roll Morton, Duke Ellington, Thelonious Monk, Charles Mingus and very few others, the seminal figures who made revolutionary and permanent changes in jazz were not composers, but great improvisors: Louis Armstrong, Lester Young, Charlie Parker, John Coltrane. In jazz, the improvisor is the counterpart of the composer in classical music. It is child's play for an experienced jazz listener to tell Louis Armstrong and Dizzy Gillespie from all other trumpet players, or Johnny Hodges and Charlie Parker from all other alto saxophonists, just as it is routine for a steady concertgoer to recognize the work of Beethoven and Bartók, for an art connoisseur to distinguish El Greco from Rembrandt, or for a rock fan to identify the Beatles and the Rolling Stones.

A jazz improvisor's individual style, tone, ideas, and structure express that player's personality, just as the compositions of Beethoven and Wagner reflected their temperaments. A solo by Dizzy Gillespie (Smic: 7/5, 7/6) tells you he is uninhibited, outgoing, gregarious, funny, and at the same time, reflective and lyrical. Improvising on the same instrument, Miles Davis (Smic: 9/1, 10/2, 11/3) reveals a persona that is introspective, convoluted, intense, and fretful. The uncluttered, immaculate piano style of John Lewis (Smic: 8/3, 10/4) is the hallmark of an intellectual and worldly sophisticate equally at home with classical music and jazz. Fats Waller's face and carriage reflect his joyous, rollicking yet tender and romantic piano style (Smic: 4/1). When Fats ambled his three hundred and eighty pounds into a nightclub or recording studio he instantly spread a feeling of "let the good times roll!" and this showed up in his music.

The spontaneous creation of performed music did not begin with jazz; Bach and Mozart were both celebrated for their abilities to improvise at the keyboard, and flamenco music has been improvised at least since the early nineteenth century. But in jazz improvisation is not an adjunct to composing, but the very essence, the lifeblood of the art itself.

11

Dizzy Gillespie: "Did you hear that *beautiful* thing I just played!" A jazz improvisor's style is often a direct expression of his temperament. (Photograph by Grover Sales.)

In addition to reading complex written scores, something nearly all of today's competent jazz players can do with ease, the jazz soloist takes daring public risks nightly, with no scores to fall back on. One musician told critic Nat Hentoff:

> It's like going out there naked every night. Any one of us can screw the whole thing up because we're out there *improvising*. The classical guys have their scores, but we have to be creating, or trying to, anticipating each other, taking chances every goddam second. That's why when jazz musicians are really putting out, it's an exhausting experience. It can be exhilarating too, but there's always that touch of fear, that feeling of being on a very high wire without a net. (Hentoff, *Jazz Is*.)

Jazz musicians must improvise on a wide variety of materials: thousands of popular songs, slow romantic ballads, strictly jazz compositions, up-tempo flagwavers, and the blues—a black folk music dating from the nine-

John Lewis: His immaculate piano style is the hallmark of a dignified, worldly sophisticate. (Photograph by Grover Sales.)

teenth century that has survived and developed and whose structure we will explore in a moment.

Jazz soloists must improvise at breathtaking tempos that would challenge, and on some instruments excel, the technique, let alone the imagination, of top symphony musicians; for example, Art Tatum on *Too Marvelous for Words* (Smic 5/2), Charlie Mingus on *Hora Decubitus* (Smic 10/5), and Charlie Parker's incredible outpouring on *Ko-Ko* (Smic 7/7). It was said that Parker, like a chess Grand Master, could "think ahead" a dozen moves, knowing even at such a furious pace as *Ko-Ko* what he could fit to the forthcoming chord progressions of *Cherokee*, the popular tune on which *Ko-Ko* was based.

Chord Changes
or Progressions

Until the late 1950s, chord changes or progressions formed the blueprint for nearly all of jazz improvising. It is essential to grasp this concept of improvising on chord changes, not only because of its importance to jazz development, but also because adventuresome players like Miles Davis,

Fats Waller: Dizzy Gillespie said: "Fats did what I've always been trying to do: he played good music while himself and his audience were having fun." (Photograph by Ray Avery of Rare Records.)

Cecil Taylor, Ornette Coleman, and John Coltrane made self-conscious decisions to abandon chord changes and improvise on radically different frameworks or no framework at all.

Those unfamiliar with the rudiments of music need not be frightened off by the following oversimplified explanation of chord changes and can rest easy that this is, by far, as technical as this book is going to get. (Professional musicians may find this rudimentary, and may want to skip ahead.)

In grade school we all learned the do-re-mi's of the *diatonic* scale—the white keys on the piano starting with C (see Figure 1).

This is the diatonic scale in the key of C *major*, as determined by the note—C or "do"—on which the diatonic scale begins.

Figure 1: The diatonic C-major scale.

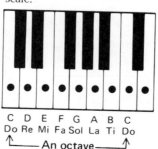

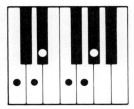

Figure 2: The diatonic
C-minor scale.

In addition to the diatonic *major* scale, every key has a *minor* scale, where the third and sixth notes are flatted or lowered by a half step, that is, to the next adjacent key (see Figure 2).

Regardless of your musical background, or lack of it, you sense the dramatic change from major to minor because of the contrasting emotions they evoke. *Minor* tends to suggest impending doom or tragedy—the opening strains of Schubert's *Unfinished Symphony*—or death as in Chopin's *Funeral March*. Ellington's *Blue Serge* (Smic 7/3) is a blues in minor that casts a spell of eerie, brooding melancholy. At the opposite end of the emotional spectrum is another Ellington blues, only this time in *major*, *Harlem Air Shaft* (Smic 6/7) that evokes jubilant airborn dance.

In addition to the diatonic major and minor scales, there is the *chromatic* scale that is sounded when you start on any given note on the keyboard and play in sequence all of the twelve white and black keys. In our system of Western music, there is a key for each of the twelve notes in the *diatonic* scale in *major* and another twelve keys for each of the twelve notes in *minor*, making a total of twenty-four different keys: C major, C minor, C–sharp major, C–sharp minor, and so on. We have all seen music written in sharps and flats, like Rachmaninoff's famous *Prelude in C-sharp Minor* (see Figure 3).

When various notes in any one of these twenty-four keys are combined they are called *chords* (see Figure 4).

Chords are groups of notes played simultaneously to form *harmonies* over which related melodies can be played that sound right and pleasing to our ears as conditioned by the traditions of Western music.

It is obvious that the mathematical possibilities of combining the notes of twenty-four keys into chords—and selecting the sequence in which these chords may "change" or "progress" from one to another

Figure 3: The C-sharp minor staff.

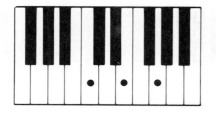
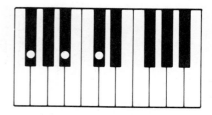

I chord in key of C   I chord in key of F-sharp

Figure 4: A chord in C and a chord in F-sharp.

(B–flat to C minor 7th to F 7th as in *I Got Rhythm*) are astronomical. This endless series of combinations is one reason why music, all kinds of music, is so varied and appealing. You might not know a note of music, but if you went to a jazz club, band concert, or Hawaiian luau where the musicians played every piece in the same key, you would soon find it boring even if you didn't know why.

Sometimes the jazz soloist improvises on a simple and limited series of chord progressions, as in Louis Armstrong's *West End Blues* (Smic 2/9) or the Gil Evans-Miles Davis version of *Summertime* (Smic 10/2). Sometimes the chord progressions are more complex and challenging as in Miles Davis's *Boplicity* (Smic 9/1) or Tadd Dameron's *Lady Bird* (Smic 9/2). Later we find they are not improvising on a series of chord changes at all, as in Ornette Coleman's *Free Jazz* (Smic 12/3)—but more of that later.

To understand this concept of chord changes in the most immediate way, look at perhaps the most simple and widely used series of progressions, something you've heard all your life (see Figure 5).

These three familiar chords form the foundation of songs like *Yankee Doodle, Swanee River*, and many church hymns: *Rock of Ages, Silent Night, I Walked in the Garden Alone.* Play these chords in sequence and pick out on the keyboard or sing the melody of any of these tunes, and you'll hear how everything fits. But if you try to fit these same chords to *I Got Rhythm, The Star-Spangled Banner* or *Norwegian Wood* they sound ludicrous, because each of these melodies is based on a different series of chord changes.

The Blues

There is one form of jazz music that fits the series of *Silent Night* chord changes shown in Figure 5, and that's the blues, hardly surprising when you consider how black religious and secular music, from the earliest times, constantly interacted with each other. Listen to Bessie Smith sing

Figure 5: Four simple chord progressions.

the opening two stanzas of *St. Louis Blues* (Smic 1/4) and play these *Silent Night* chords along with her to hear how they fit. Notice that Bessie is backed by a small reed organ that gives this blues a "churchy" feeling. Sometimes this line between black church music and the blues is hard to define. Singer-lyricist Jon Hendricks, who came out of a church choir like so many jazz and blues vocalists, said that the difference between the gospel singer and the blues singer is that one sings "Jesus" and the other sings "baby." The primitive "down-home" black sanctified church uses singing, hand clapping, stomping, "testifying," speaking in tongues, and playing jazz instruments to put the preacher and his congregation in direct ecstatic touch with God. As the comic Richard Pryor said, "When you go to a black church, you gits a *show* for your money! Black preachers know God *personally*!" Gospel queen Mahalia Jackson said that although she wasn't supposed to listen to Bessie Smith records because good church people like her parents thought her music "sinful," she found herself caught up in the power and the emotion of Bessie, who was an obvious influence on Mahalia among countless other gospel singers.

There is a blues scale distinct from the diatonic scale, but it can only be approximated on a page of sheet music or on the keyboard. Though still open to controversy, many musicologists believe that the "blue notes" fall somewhere between the cracks of a piano and do not exist in Western music, but are quite common in African singing and chanting. The closest we can come to representing the blues scale on paper is to show the *third* and the *seventh* notes of the diatonic scale flatted (see Figure 6). (Later, the "modern jazz" pioneers during the bebop era of the mid-1940s began to flat the *fifth* note in the scale as well.) Early jazz pianists, perhaps in emulation of African singers and their blues offshoots, began to play "smashed notes" in an attempt to approximate the "bent" notes or quarter tones so widely used in African music, producing a "jazzy" harmony that staid classicists would decry as "dissonant" or "discordant"—which it certainly sounded to symphonic ears (see Figure 7).

Again, these "smashed notes" were as close as early jazz and blues pianists could get to those "blue notes" lying somewhere in between E and E flat, and between B and B flat. But it is a simple matter to hear these

Figure 6: A blues scale.

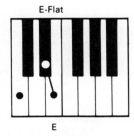
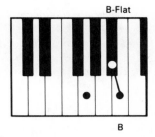

Figure 7: Dissonance, "smashed" notes.

"blue" or "bent" notes in Bessie Smith's classic version of *St. Louis Blues* (Smic 1/4) as she moans and draws out the word "sun" in the opening line. Her voice rises and falls to create notes that don't exist in the Western chromatic scale but which fall somewhere "between the cracks" of a properly tuned piano. Notice, also, how Louis Armstrong's cornet "responds" to Bessie's every cry by bending and sliding into his notes in the same way. This pattern of "cry and response," so essential a part of blues structure, comes out of the black sanctified church where the cry of the preacher is followed by the response of the choir or the congregation.

The poetry of classic folk blues often follows the metric pattern of iambic pentameter, something you've heard all your life. An *iamb* is two syllables, a short or "weak" one followed by a long or accented one. *Pent* is Greek for *five* (as in pentagon), and so *St. Louis Blues*, like much of Shakespeare, has five accented beats to each line, with the accent falling on the second syllable. Leonard Bernstein illustrates this in his highly recommended LP *What Is Jazz?* (Columbia 919) with a vocal version of *Macbeth's Blues*:

> I will not be a-fraid of death and bane,
> 'Til Bir-nam for-est come to Dun-si-nane.

You can sing these lines of Shakespeare to the tune of *St. Louis Blues* and they fit perfectly. The blues and iambic pentameter have a natural affinity because, as we will find, the jazz accent is an *iamb*, with the strong accents falling on the second and fourth beats of a measure—not on the first and third beats as is usual in Western music.

This folk tradition of declaiming a line, repeating it, and ending with a different line (AAB) is the classic structure of 12 bar blues like *St. Louis Blues* and *Lost Your Head Blues* (Smic 1/5). A *bar* refers to one musical measure of four beats in these cases. If Bessie and Louis were to collaborate on *Macbeth's Blues*, it would come out like this:

19

I will not be a - fraid of death and   bane   (cornet response)
(4 bars)   1 2 3 4   / 1 2 3 4   / 1234 /   1   2   3   4

(I said) I will not be a-fraid of death and bane.   (cornet response)
(4 bars)   1   2   3   4   / 1   2   3   4   /1234 /   1   2   3   4

'Til Bir-nam   for-est   come to Dun-sin-nane   (cornet response)
(4 bars)   1   2   3   4   / 1   2   3   4   / 1234 /   1   2   3   4

Blues lyrics reflect the yearnings and frustrations of a colonial sub-culture: lack of money, lack of love, cheatin' women, two-timin' men. "Romance without finance is a nuisance." Lil Green's *Why Don't You Do Right?* and Bessie Smith's *Cold In Hand Blues* spurn a man who brings no money into the house, while Bessie's *You've Been a Good Old Wagon* rejects a lover whose sexual prowess has waned. Billie Holiday's famous *Billie's Blues* complains about her mistreatin' man. Jimmy Witherspoon's *No Rolling Blues* laments, in turn, a woman who first cheats on him and then rejects him.

Billie Holiday: The startling contrast between the glamorous "on-stage" singer and the private grief-prone victim—when Billie sang the blues, it was something she had lived (see photo opposite). (Photograph from the Ralph J. Gleason Collection.)

Billie Holiday: The startling contrast between the glamorous "on-stage" singer and the private grief-prone victim—when Billie sang the blues, it was something she had lived. (Photograph from the Ralph J. Gleason Collection.)

There are other themes: Bessie Smith's *Backwater Blues* tells of the havoc unleashed by a Mississippi flood. Sometimes, though not as often as you'd expect, blues lyrics become the voice of social protest, as in Bessie Smith's *Poor Man's Blues*. Big Bill Broonzy's *Step Back* is a rare blues that deals with racial inequity. Still, the majority of blues are he-and-she songs laden with strong demands for sexual and financial satisfaction and fidelity.

The first blues singers to turn professional, who took the blues out of the cotton fields and railroad gangs to eke out a living with them, were wandering black men from the country, singing and playing primitive guitars and harmonicas on street corners for nickels and dimes: Blind Lemon Jefferson, his protegé Leadbelly, and their linear descendant from the Mississippi delta, Robert Johnson, whose *Hellhound on my Trail* (Smic 1/3) offers an accurate example of pure country blues. Suddenly, in the early 1920s, a blues craze mushroomed among southern blacks and newly uprooted emigrés in Northern ghettos who felt homesick for the down-home music. This fertile era is known as the age of classic women blues singers: Alberta Hunter, Ma Rainey, Victoria Spivey, Trixie Smith, Clara Smith, Maggie Jones, Sippi Wallace, and the Empress of the Blues, Bessie Smith, whose records sold out within hours of release to black record shops and whose unamplified cries and moans filled cavernous, many-balconied theaters in the ghettos of Chicago, Pittsburgh, Harlem, and Philadelphia, where people lined around the block to catch her. Guitarist Danny Barker recalled:

> Bessie Smith was a fabulous deal to watch. She was a pretty large woman and she could sing the blues. She had a church deal mixed up in it. She dominated a stage . . . she just upset you . . . If you had any church background, like people who came from the South as I did, you would recognize a similarity between what she was doing and what those preachers and evangelists from there did, and how they moved people . . . Bessie . . . could bring about mass hypnotism. When she was performing, you could hear a pin drop. (Hentoff-Shapiro, *Hear Me Talkin' to Ya*.)

With the onslaught of the Great Depression, the blues craze suddenly faded, a victim of radio, talking pictures, and changing tastes among urban blacks "movin' on up" who felt themselves too high-toned for the old-time music. Bessie Smith cut only four record sides from 1931 until 1937 when she was killed in a grisly car accident. Still, the blues survived throughout the depression and beyond. Even though record sales never climbed to the heights of the 1920s, dozens of blues singers continued to record for 35-cent labels like Decca and Bluebird: Bumblebee Slim, Peetie Wheatstraw the Devil's Son-in-Law, Big Maceo, Hound Head Henry, Robert Johnson, Big Boy Cruddup, Lonnie Johnson, Tampa Red, Memphis Slim, Blind Blake, Lil Green, Georgia White, Rosetta Howard, Rosetta Crawford, and Blue Lu Barker.

The blues continue to course through the history of jazz and rock like an ever-refreshing river. All the major and most of the minor figures in jazz have been rooted in the blues. Duke Ellington rarely got away from them, just as Bartók never cut his roots to the folk music of his native Hungary. For all his radical innovations, Charlie Parker was first and foremost a bluesman. One reason why the once-touted band of Stan Kenton left little imprint on jazz and seems destined for devaluation is that for all its technical gloss and the gifts of many superb sidemen, the Kenton Band rarely played the blues.

Hearing the Blues

Why do they call this haunting music the blues? Though no one can be sure, experts tend to agree that in its earliest times the blues were so called because they expressed the melancholy and despair of an oppressed and uprooted people. A common mistake is to label the blues solely a music of sadness and self-pity. The blues, like all of jazz, are capable of expressing every human emotion and can be played in every tempo from funereal slowness to breakneck speed. The following is a list of blues included in the *Smithsonian Collection*:

BLUES INCLUDED IN THE SMITHSONIAN COLLECTION

The Blues: Medium or Fast Tempo
Dippermouth Blues (King Oliver)
Honky Tonk Train (Meade Lux Lewis)
Blues Sequence from *Breakfast Feud* (Benny Goodman Sextet)
Harlem Air Shaft (Duke Ellington)
Ko-Ko (Duke Ellington)
Fantasy on Frankie and Johnny (Erroll Garner)
Bikini (Dexter Gordon)
Mysterioso (Thelonious Monk)
Blue 7 (Sonny Rollins)
Hora Decubitus (Charlie Mingus)
Django (Modern Jazz Quartet) Partially a blues.

The Blues: Slow Tempo
Hellhound on my Trail (Robert Johnson)
St. Louis Blues (Bessie Smith)
Lost Your Head Blues (Bessie Smith)
Dead Man Blues (Jelly Roll Morton)
Blue Horizon (Sidney Bechet)
S.O.L. Blues (Louis Armstrong)
West End Blues (Louis Armstrong)
Blue Serge (Duke Ellington)
Parker's Mood (Charlie Parker)
Blues Improvisation (Thelonious Monk)

The broad emotional range of these recordings includes the danceable joy of King Oliver's *Dippermouth Blues*, the brooding eeriness of Ellington's *Blue Serge*, the exuberant glee of Ellington's *Harlem Air Shaft* and Mingus's *Hora Decubitus*, the lonely yearning of Bessie Smith's *Lost Your Head Blues*, and the ferocious intensity of Bechet's *Blue Horizon*. The blues' infinite variety and their magical way of absorbing fresh material from the changing social landscape, decade after decade, have made this remarkable folk music the inexhaustible mother lode of jazz and rock. The Beatles's *Can't Buy Me Love* and *Say the Word* are mainly drawn from the blues. The Rolling Stones's *Love in Vain* and Cream's *Born Too Late* are British electrified rock translations of Robert Johnson's Mississippi delta blues of the 1930s. Bill Haley and the Comets' *Rock Around the Clock*, crucial in launching the initial thrust of rock 'n' roll in the 1950s,

came from the venerable sex-blues of the 1920s, *My Daddy Rocks Me*.
Elvis Presley's monster hit *Hound Dog* was lifted note for note from the
blues of Willie Mae Thornton.

Having the word *blues* in the title does not make it blues: *Singin' the
Blues* (Smic 3/5), *I Gotta Right to Sing the Blues* (Smic 3/3), and Jelly Roll
Morton's *Wolverine Blues* are not blues at all; neither is Armstrong's *Po-
tato Head Blues* (Smic 2/7).

You may have difficulty at first in realizing that all of the *Smithsonian*
selections listed are blues that share a common musical structure, but this
discovery will come with repeated hearings. Rock-oriented listeners
might hear the similarity between Oliver's *Dippermouth Blues* (Smic 1/6)
and the Beatles' *Can't Buy Me Love*, or between Bessie Smith's *Lost Your
Head Blues* (Smic 1/5) and the Rolling Stones' *Love in Vain*.

The blues infiltrated the work of Stravinsky, Milhaud, Leonard Bernstein, and many writers of Broadway shows and popular songs. The lovely
verse, or introduction, to Jerome Kern's *Can't Help Lovin' Dat Man* from
the long-running Broadway musical *Show Boat* is an undisguised 12-bar
blues, as is the beginning and end of *Blues in the Night* by Harold Arlen,
the most jazz-oriented of Broadway composers.

The Popular Song

Besides improvising on the blues at fast and slow tempos, the jazz soloist
must extemporize new melodies based on the chord changes of popular
songs not related to the blues, like Gershwin's *I Got Rhythm* (Smic 7/4).
Since it was written in 1930, this evergreen has served as an ideal "fast"
vehicle for improvisors and often crops up under a profusion of pseudonyms like *Shaw 'Nuff* by the Charlie Parker-Dizzy Gillespie Quintet (Smic
7/6) where the melody is so altered that only fellow musicians would suspect the source.

The structure of *I Got Rhythm* is common among popular songs:
AABA—a theme A is stated, then repeated, followed by a connecting
theme B—the "bridge"—before the A theme, usually varied at its close,
ends the piece. Sometimes popular songs are structured ABA or simply
AA. The *Smithsonian Collection* includes a number of these songs:

SMITHSONIAN POPULAR SONGS

AABA

I Got Rhythm (Shaw 'Nuff)
Sweethearts on Parade
Body and Soul
The Man I Love
He's Funny that Way

You're Drivin' Me Crazy (Moten Swing)
Too Marvelous for Words
Willow Weep for Me
I Can't Believe that You're in Love with Me
I Found a New Baby
I Can't Get Started
Somebody Loves Me
Smoke Gets in Your Eyes

AA
I Gotta Right to Sing the Blues
All of Me
You'd Be So Nice to Come Home To
In a Mellowtone
Dancing in the Dark
I Should Care
Summertime

The following is a list of selections from the *Smithsonian Collection* that are neither blues nor popular songs, but strictly jazz compositions.

JAZZ COMPOSITIONS

Black Bottom Stomp (Jelly Roll Morton)
Struttin' with Some Barbecue (Louis Armstrong)
Potato Head Blues (Louis Armstrong)
Hotter Than That (Louis Armstrong)
The Stampede (Fletcher Henderson)
Lunceford Special (Jimmy Lunceford)
When Lights Are Low (Benny Carter)
Taxi War Dance (Count Basie)
Doggin' Around (Count Basie)
Lester Leaps In (Count Basie)
East St. Louis Toodle-oo (Duke Ellington)
Creole Rhapsody (Duke Ellington)
Concerto for Cootie (Duke Ellington, later transformed by
him into the popular song, *Do Nothing 'Til You Hear from Me*)
Klactoveedsedsteen (Charlie Parker)
Little Benny (Charlie Parker)
Crosscurrent (Lennie Tristano)
Boplicity (Miles Davis)
Criss-Cross (Thelonious Monk)
Django (Modern Jazz Quartet) Partially a blues.
Pent-up House (Sonny Rollins)
Enter Evening (Cecil Taylor)

So What (Miles Davis)
Congeniality (Ornette Coleman)
Lonely Woman (Ornette Coleman)
Alabama (John Coltrane)

A gifted improvisor may depart so radically from the original melody of a well-known song (as in Parker's *Embraceable You* (Smic 7/8, 7/9) that listeners may be moved to protest, "But where's the melody?" This lament was so widespread that a 1939 Rodgers and Hart tune bore the wistful title *I Like to Recognize the Tune*. Feelings could run high. Songwriter Jimmy McHugh sued (without success) alto saxist James Moody whose brilliant recorded improvisation of McHugh's hit, *I'm in the Mood for Love*, so captivated the jazz fraternity that vocalists wrote words to fit and retitled it *Moody's Mood for Love*. McHugh claimed that Moody had debased his song; Moody thought he had improved it, and if you compare Moody's record to the original tune, you might agree.

Of course, variations on popular songs did not begin with jazz. Bach's Canonic Variations on *All Hail Thou Goodly Jesus* start with an unadorned organ statement of this traditional Protestant hymn that Bach proceeds to put through its paces until climaxed by a lofty fugue as removed from the original hymn as Notre Dame is from a one-room country shack. Haydn ended his 104th Symphony with variations on *Hot Cross Buns*, a well-known London Street song. When they are free to choose, jazz players pick tunes like *I Got Rhythm* and *Sweet Georgia Brown*, whose chord changes invite improvisations at fast tempos. Some of the more advanced musicians prefer the more complex and challenging chord changes of *Cherokee* (Parker's *Ko-Ko*, Smic 7/7), *How High the Moon*, and *Green Dolphin Street*. In the 1930s tunes were often picked by song pluggers and record executives. These hits-of-the-moment were thrust at Fats Waller, Teddy Wilson, and Billie Holiday, who never saw them before they entered the studio, and often ranged from the vapid to the frankly hideous. It became a supreme challenge for jazz artists to create music from such commercial popcorn. Many of the songs forced on Billie Holiday and Teddy Wilson survive today only because they wove timeless art from the ragged threads of *A Sunbonnet Blue*, *Me, Myself and I*, and *A Sailboat in the Moonlight*.

The Elements of Jazz

All music—Chinese, European, African, and jazz—is composed of four elements: rhythm, melody, harmony, and timbre (or tone color), the difference between middle C struck on the piano, bowed on a violin, sung by a baritone, or blown across the top of a pop bottle. At least two of these elements—rhythm and timbre—are used by jazz players in startlingly different ways than one hears in a symphony or string quartet. It was this very strangeness on so basic and immediate a level that aroused the fury of many classical musicians and concertgoers when ragtime and jazz first surfaced.

The rhythm of jazz sets it apart from other music, since rhythm has always been the most potent and body-based in the entire spectrum of sound. This is why jazz audiences always applaud the drum solo—even when it's bad. Even those who know nothing of jazz, and perhaps despise it, can instantly recognize this music because of its unique rhythm, first called *syncopation* during the ragtime era and then later known as *swing*. Swing defies literary analysis as well as strict musical notation. Once I gave a sheet music transcription of Meade Lux Lewis' *Honky Tonk Train* (Smic 4/2) to a concert pianist with no jazz background. After a few halting attempts she laughed, "I know that's not the way it should sound, but believe me, I'm playing it just the way it's written." I consoled her with the news that even top jazz pianists had failed to manage the subtle crossrhythms of this piece, and if *Honky Tonk Train* was impossible to copy from a phonograph record, it would be that much more difficult to transcribe into sheet music. What Lewis had achieved in this impressionist train ride was a much-simplified African device of keeping two or more different rhythms going at once. Even though its rhythmic complexity lies beyond even the best jazz pianists, a master African drummer, purely on a rhythmic level, would find this piece child's play, like comparing tic-tactoe to chess.

The complex phenomenon of African rhythm, and how it could have carried over into Afro-American music, lies outside the scope of this book. Musically advanced readers will find the best introduction in the opening chapter of Gunther Schuller's *Early Jazz* (New York: Oxford University Press, 1968). The specialist is directed to A. W. Jones's *Studies in African Music* (London: Oxford University Press, 1959). Schuller claims that African rhythm is, by far, the most complicated form of music that exists. Only in the last half of this century, and only with the aid of sophisticated electronic devices, has the non-African mind been able to measure and comprehend the complexity of African rhythm. We have learned that master African drummers can sense and create differences of *1/12 second* while engaged in ensemble playing that produces seven to eleven different musical lines. What is remarkable is not the number of lines, but, as Schuller notes: "in the case of a seven-part ensemble, *six* of the seven lines may operate in different metric patterns . . . staggered in such a way that the downbeats of these patterns rarely coincide." (Schuller, *Early Jazz.*) In Joplin's *Maple Leaf Rag* (Smic 1/1) Schuller finds "the American Negro was again asserting an irrepressible urge to maintain two rhythms

Figure 8: "Syncopation."

simultaneously *within* the white man's musical framework," and maintains that "jazz inflection and syncopation did not come from Europe, because there is no precedent for them in European 'art music'."

To put it simply, ragtime syncopation that started the world dancing at the turn of the century changed the marching beat into a dancing beat by accenting the normally weak beats in a measure—the second and fourth—and removing the stress on the normally strong beats—the first and third (See Figure 8).

Although syncopation had rarely been heard in Western music before the advent of ragtime, it was extremely common in African music. Ragtime developed as an Afro-American adaptation of the marching band music of German and Italian immigrants that still flourishes throughout the South and Southwest—"Music Man" territory—where piano ragtime took root. In march music, the strong count is on the first and third beats—the left foot (See Figure 9). In movies of black marching bands in the South, we notice the strong beat is on the *right* foot, breeding a different kind of marching, a shuffle closer to dancing with a decidedly unmilitary hunching of shoulders, and body english. Black church-goers, like jazz musicians, clap or snap their fingers on two and four, as do the "hip" (aware) members of the audience, while the "squares" are clapping on one and three.

Syncopation and swing are not all-or-none responses; there are varying degrees. Some musicians swing more than others, employing more subtle, complex rhythms that inspire a freer, less inhibited dance and embrace a wider emotional range.

Confining ourselves to the piano, listen to the following selections from the *Smithsonian Collection* to grasp the growing rhythmic complexity and *swing* that surfaced in jazz within a single generation:

Joplin: *Maple Leaf Rag* 1899 (1/1)	Stiff, unbending left hand oom-PAH oom-PAH derivative of marching band tuba or trombone.
Morton: *Maple Leaf Rag* 1938 (1/2)	Left hand is looser, more "loping" than Joplin's, generating more swing.
Johnson: *Carolina Shout* 1921 (2/4)	Ragtime structured, but using more left hand variety and broken rhythms that "swing" more than Morton.

HEP (right)   LEFT (right)

Figure 9: The marching beat.

Waller: *I Ain't Got Nobody*
1937 (4/1)

James P. Johnson's best pupil uses subtle dynamics and adroit placement of notes to generate tremendous "swing" at a lazy unhurried tempo.

Armstrong-Hines: *Weatherbird*
1928 (3/1)

With Hines, the vestigial trappings of ragtime oom-PAH give way to a free rhythmic form where the left hand suddenly leaps into some independent realm of its own, abandoning the timekeeping function of Johnson and Waller. Notice also how Hines's right hand octave lines closely resemble Armstrong's trumpet improvisations.

Basie: *Doggin' Around*
1938 (5/7)

Basie's piano was at first an imitation of Waller's "stride," as you can hear in Bennie Moten's *Moten Swing* (Smic 3/8). Here, with his own style fully developed, he abandons Waller's "striding" left hand timekeeping role whose function is now assumed by the modern rhythm section of bass, guitar, and drums. This frees Basie to "comp"—playing brief, staccato "fills" that get the maximum amount of swing from the barest minimum of notes: "Less is more."

Tatum: *Too Marvelous for Words*
1956 (5/2)

Inspired by both Waller and Hines, Tatum employs a phenomenal technique and imagination to invest this popular tune with a rich harmonic-rhythmic language far beyond Waller, even though vestiges of left-hand "stride" survive in this piece.

Though Art Tatum recorded this in 1956, he had been playing this style since the early 1930s. Now go back and replay Joplin's *Maple Leaf Rag* and realize, if you can, that only three decades separated Joplin from Tatum! Things happen quickly in jazz.

JAZZ TIMBRE (TONE COLOR)

From its earliest times, jazz was immediately recognizable by the unique timbres or tone colors of the wind instruments—trumpet, trombone, clarinet, saxes—and even stringed instruments like the guitar and fiddle. Classical wind players are schooled to produce the sound that "came with the instrument," a purity of tone free from vibrato and personal quirks. The aim of trumpeter Maurice André, who represents the art of classical brass playing at its highest form, is to serve the intentions of Vivaldi, Corelli, and Shostakovich, which he does to perfection. But jazz trumpeters like Armstrong, Gillespie, and Clifford Brown *are* the composers; their goals are not those of Maurice André, and neither is their emotional language. Jazz wind players, often unconsciously, conceive their instrument as extensions of the human voice, an expression of the musician's personality. They do not "play" Bach and Corelli—though many are capable of doing so—they play *themselves*. Benny Goodman, a classically trained jazz clarinetist, wears two hats. When he recorded Mozart's *Clarinet Quintet* with the Budapest String Quartet, Goodman wore his classical hat, using a pure conservatory-bred tone as Mozart intended. But when Goodman wears his more comfortable jazz hat, as in his sextet's recording of *I Found a New Baby* (Smic 6/2), his tone is ablaze with guttural cries, rasps, and bluesy smears no proper music conservatory would tolerate but which are right at home in jazz.

Although born poor, Goodman had access to "proper" training and jobs usually denied the black players who dominate jazz history. Black clarinetist Buster Bailey, whom Goodman insisted had a better technique than his own, held a chair in the Fletcher Henderson Band while vainly dreaming of a symphonic post. But symphony orchestras refused to hire blacks years after professional baseball was integrated. Cut off from the mainstream of white America, black musicians developed their own folk academy. There was no legitimate music school to tell them they could not hang a felt hat over a trumpet bell, or wave a toilet plunger over the bell of a trombone. No one told cornetist Rex Stewart it was improper to press a valve halfway down to produce a muted, cloudy effect. While classical reed players are encouraged to use "proper" fingering to produce "true" pitch, jazz clarinetists and saxophonists love to explore and master "false fingerings," producing sounds that strike symphony musicians as off, clunky, or weird but which intrigue jazz players because these "off" pitches seem closer to the human voice and its panorama of emotions, which interest them more than "true" pitch. Tenor saxist Lester Young was an acknowledged master of false fingering, a hallmark of his widely copied style heard on Basie's *Lester Leaps In* (Smic 6/1). The saxophones became dominant jazz instruments because musicians sensed they were akin to the human voice and that you could make these instruments *sing*.

The saxophone is an ideal instrument to begin our comparison of tone colors. Invented in the mid-nineteenth century by the Belgian Adolphe Sax, it was rarely used in symphony work except by more adventuresome tone colorists like Ravel in his famous *Bolero*. Listen to the sax

Al Grey: No "proper" music academy taught jazz musicians to explore strange and evocative sounds produced by mutes unknown to symphonic music. (Photograph by Ray Avery of Rare Records.)

solo in *Bolero* about one-third into the piece and hear the "pure" tone that came with the instrument. Now listen to Coleman Hawkins' *Body and Soul* (Smic 4/4) and you may have trouble believing this to be the same instrument. Hawkins is called "the inventor of the tenor sax" because in the late 1920s he was the first to coax genuine jazz out of this novelty vaudeville instrument famous for corny bloops and barnyard noises. He was also the first to adapt the instrument to an authentic ballad style. Now compare Hawkins to the tenor sax of Lester Young on Billie Holiday's *All of Me* (Smic 4/7) and *He's Funny That Way* (Smic 4/6), and it may not seem these two artists are playing the same instrument. This dramatic difference is a reflection of their contrasting temperaments as evident in their stance and expression while performing. Hawkins's huge-toned, bursting-at-the-seams sound seems wrenched up from the gut as he stomps his feet, bends his trunk, his face contorted in pained agitation. In contrast, Lester's light, airy sound was the essence of "cool" as he stood immobile and heavy-lidded, almost sleepy, combining complete muscular relaxation with absolute control of his horn, tilted to a flutelike angle. Master saxmen like Hawkins, Young, and Parker took fanatical pains to perfect their individual sounds, with endless hours spent in pursuit of the right reed, shaving and shaping it, sometimes even sculpting their own mouthpiece, as did some brass players. Trumpeters and trombonists have used anything as a mute—a tomato can, drinking glass, or silk stocking—to produce exotic and evocative sounds. The Smithsonian package includes a wondrous variety of tone colors produced by mutes utterly foreign to classical music. Listen to Joseph "Tricky Sam" Nanton use the "plumber's friend" to flush brazen and obscene yawps from the trombone

Ziggy Elman: Brass players have used anything as a mute—like a cut-up felt hat. (Photograph by Ray Avery of Rare Records.)

in Ellington's *Harlem Air Shaft* (Smic 6/7), *Ko-Ko* (Smic 7/2), and *Blue Serge* (Smic 7/3). After "Tricky Sam" died in 1945, Ellington urged a dozen successors, with little luck, to recapture his sound. But there was more to "Tricky Sam" than simply moving a toilet plunger in front of the bell. The mute was a mere handmaiden to his embrochure (the relationship between a wind player's lip and facial muscles and his mouthpiece), his throat and chest muscles, and most of all, his imagination and droll sense of humor. As Ellington's trombonist Lawrence Brown put it, "Tricky, he was just plain *dirty.*"

Using a cup mute, trumpeter Buck Clayton gets a warm, lyrical sound on Billie Holiday's *He's Funny that Way* (Smic 4/6). With a similar mute, Miles Davis produces a squeezed intensity on Gil Evans' *Summertime* (Smic 10/2). In Ellington's *Concerto for Cootie* (Smic 6/8), trumpeter Cootie Williams used a variety of mutes, and no mute at all, to create a variety of tone colors. Front-rank brass players need no mutes to be recognized but can be instantly identified by their style of playing "open." Compare the unmuted sound of Roy Eldridge on *Rockin' Chair* (Smic 5/4), whose buzzy, wide vibrato and upper register cries are poles apart from the clipped, detached "cool" of Miles Davis's open horn in *Boplicity* (Smic 9/1). To hear the trumpet as an extension of the player's singing, listen to any of the Louis Armstrong tracks in the *Smithsonian* package, particularly *West End Blues* (2/9) and *I Gotta Right to Sing the Blues* (3/3), and no one could fail to realize that the trumpet and vocal sound are as one.

For a player to produce an individual tone on the guitar and piano may seem unlikely, yet you can easily spot guitarist Django Reinhardt from his characteristic *sound* of a few plucked notes. Through some mysterious alchemy, a few pianists can summon identifiable *tones* with an elusive combination of touch, pedaling, and timing. Fats Waller does this in *I Ain't Got Nobody* (Smic 4/1), Ellington in *Blue Serge* (Smic 7/3), and Thelonious Monk in *I Should Care* (Smic 9/8). These pianists can strike two chords and everyone knows who it is.

Afro-American timbres and rhythms partly derive from the African heritage. Anthropologist Ernest Borneman's comments on African music-speech could as readily apply to much of jazz:

> While the whole European tradition strives for regularity—of pitch, of timbre, and of vibrato—the African tradition strives precisely for the negation of these elements. In language, the African tradition aims at circumlocution rather than at exact definition . . . no note is attacked straight; the voice or instrument always approaches it from above or below. The timbre is veiled and paraphrased constantly by changing vibrato, tremolo and overtone effects. (Borneman, *A Critic Looks at Jazz.*)

This African tradition of music-as-speech translates directly into the scat singing of Louis Armstrong, the sermons of singing preachers like Reverend Kelsey, the political speeches of Barbara Jordan and Jesse Jackson, the "I Have a Dream" of Martin Luther King, and the improvisational street raps of Richard Pryor. Gunther Schuller sees another carryover of the African tradition into jazz:

> Both originate in a total vision of life in which music, unlike the art music of Europe, is not a separate autonomous social domain. . . . It is not surprising that the word 'art' does not even exist in African languages. Nor does the African divide art into separate categories. Folklore, music, dance, sculpture and painting operate as a total generic unity, serving not only religion, but . . . birth, death, work, and play. (Schuller, *Early Jazz*.)

For musicians and devotees, jazz is a way of life. When a clumsy journalist asked Charlie Parker to name his religious affiliation, Bird replied: "I am a musician—that is my religion."

Jazz and Race

The Afro-American heritage, and not any inborn "natural sense of rhythm" as the racial cliché goes, is one reason why black players dominate the history and development of jazz. Music, show business, undertaking, hair-straightening, preaching, gambling, hustling, and much later, professional sports paved the restricted highways open to black Americans as alternatives to drudgery in the fields, factories, and domestic servitude. When jazz came of age in the 1920s, 1930s, and beyond, blacks, with few exceptions, were excluded from law, medicine, science, higher education, and allied professions open to whites. Guitarist Danny Barker said: "So many kids in New Orleans took up music because they heard it all the time. Gambling, race horses, being a pimp or playing music were the sports. If the kids were thick in the head, they'd end up doing stevedore work on the levee in the hot sun." (Hentoff-Shapiro, *Hear Me Talkin' to Ya*.) Drummer Art Blakey told Art Taylor he got into music "because I worked at the Carnegie Steel Mill in Pittsburgh, one of the things I would like to forget in my life. I started playing music to get out of the coal mine and the steel mill." (Taylor, *Notes & Tones*.) The jazz comic Lenny Bruce created a hilarious routine, "How the Negro and the Jew Got Started in Show Business" where "the Negro sang his ass right off the farm." In the same way, blacks predominate in boxing and, later, big league baseball and basketball, not because they are "natural born athletes," but because big-time sports, like music and entertainment, were among the few legitimate, glamorous, and non-drudge roles available. The overriding importance of music as a necessity for survival has long been a fixture in black American family life. In his 1901 autobiography, *Up From Slavery*, Booker T. Washington wrote of having dinner with a dirt-poor black family on an

Alabama plantation: "When I sat down at the table, I noticed that, while there were five of us, there was but one fork for the five of us to use. . . . In that same cabin was an organ for which the people were paying sixty dollars in monthly installments. One fork, and a sixty dollar organ!"

Jazz singer Babs Gonzales wrote in his autobiography, *I Paid My Dues*, "At the age of seven, my mother stressed the importance of knowledge and a profession to keep from being the white man's lackey. So she insisted I take music lessons." Dizzy Gillespie told Jon Hendricks on the Chevron School Broadcast, "My father was a brick mason in Cheraw, South Carolina, and spent all his extra money—aside from bringing up nine kids—on musical instruments. I was around music all my life." Tenor saxist Lester Young, "began as a child drummer in a band managed by his father, a Tuskeegee graduate, staffed entirely by members of the Young family. The children were taught to sing tunes as soon as they could walk. At the age of five or six they were able to read music and play at least one instrument. At the age of eight, Lester began making regular tours as the band drummer." (Russell, *Bird Lives!*)

Though the major innovators who altered the course of jazz have been overwhelmingly black, the music attracted many gifted whites, even non-Americans like Danish bassist Niels-Henning Orsted Pedersen and Belgian gypsy guitarist Django Reinhardt. Some of these players made a large impact on their cohorts, black as well as white. To claim that Bix Beiderbecke, Jack Teagarden, Benny Goodman, Stan Getz, and Bill Evans were of no consequence is to fly in the face of history. This was a widespread misconception spawned by the racial turbulence of the 1960s when black writer LeRoi Jones (Amiri Baraka), invading what had been an almost exclusively white domain of jazz critics, determined to write whites out of jazz with all the grim finality of Stalin writing Trotsky out of the Bolshevik Revolution. Jazz magazines were bombarded with angry letters and manifestos, all sounding variations on a single theme: "Jazz is our black music of protest. The white man cannot play it because he has no 'soul.' He can only rip it off and make millions on pale, gutless imitations while the black geniuses who created this music must exist on crumbs from the white man's table." This anger that spilled into the jazz press throughout the 1960s and after was sadly rooted in reality. With maddening regularity, white imitations of black music outsold the originals twenty to one. Still, this did not give the late critic Ralph J. Gleason the right to say: "It is possible to speculate that all the white musicians could be eliminated from the history of the music without significantly altering its development." Such "speculation" is a classroom example of what semanticists call the nonverifiable sentence. To prove it, the author would have to possess divine powers to rerun the course of jazz history.

Such statements were typical of the emotional heat radiated by the explosive subject of jazz and race. When black trumpeter Roy Eldridge said he could always tell a black from a white musician on record, Leonard Feather proved him wrong in a *down beat* Blindfold Test where Eldridge did not even score the fifty percent the law of averages entitled him to. Even during the most anxious period of racial tension in our history, the Watts Riot of 1965, black jazz leaders, more often than not, employed white sidemen in big bands and small combos. These not only included elder statesmen like Ellington, Basie, and Gillespie, but also the most racially outspoken among militant young blacks—Miles Davis, Charlie Mingus, Ornette Coleman, and Archie Shepp. It was during this troubled time that white pianist Bill Evans emerged as the undisputed keyboard influence on all jazz players, regardless of color. Again, this is not to deny that society has withheld its rewards from numbers of gifted black artists, while lavishing fame and money on a host of mediocre white imitators.

Jazz Is "Serious" Music

From its earliest times, "respectable" people, regardless of color, scorned jazz as low-class trash not to be mentioned in the same breath with "serious" music. This condescending posture still crops up in record catalogues, critical essays, and news columns that erect a mythical fence sepa-

Jazz is "serious" music: Gunther Schuller (left) and John Lewis prepare the score of *Portrait of Coleman Hawkins*, premiered at the 1959 Monterey Jazz Festival. (Photograph from the Ralph J. Gleason Collection.)

rating jazz from "serious" composition. Even jazz enthusiast Leonard Bernstein fell into this trap in 1947 when he wrote, "Serious music in America would today have a different complexion and direction were it not for the profound influence upon it of jazz." (*Esquire.*) This inference that jazz is not "serious" might have amused John Coltrane, who spent his days practicing and his nights on the bandstand. "No one," said Ellington, "is as serious about his music as a serious jazz musician." When a student asked Dizzy Gillespie during a band break if he ever played any "serious" music, the puckish trumpeter grew serious indeed: "Just what do you think we're doin' up here—foolin' around?" Bassist Ray Brown told the Chevron School Broadcast: "One of the great fallacies of all time is that the classical players felt the jazzman, if he were good, just rolled out of bed one morning and was able to do everything on his instrument. But if you want to play a two-octave D scale [he demonstrates] you have to study, practice, you don't luck up on it, and you spend the same amount of time a guy would who plays in a symphony orchestra."

It was difficult for the public, and impossible for the musical establishment, to take "seriously" a music played by a black subculture and white dropout rebels in dives and dance halls; whose leaders were hailed as "Satchmo'," "Prez," and "Bird"; whose recorded masterpieces bore such frivolous names as *Potato Head Blues*, *Taxi War Dance*, and *Shaw 'Nuff*. How could anyone be serious about a music bursting with such wild humor, parody, and lewd shrieks? A music wedded to sexy dancing and profane lyrics? A music that sent players and listeners alike into states of holy-roller ecstasy? How could you be "serious" and have such a screaming good time?

Another little-known aspect of jazz that renders its lack of seriousness all the more absurd is that jazz players have pushed the technical frontiers of many instruments far beyond classical boundaries, doing things on the string bass, drums, brass, and reeds that symphony players said couldn't—or shouldn't—be done. Left to their own devices with no music school to interfere, they experimented and, like most American inventors, became pragmatists: "If you plug it into the wall and it lights up, then it works." When Charlie Mingus found that classical string bassists rarely used the third finger of the left hand, "I started using the third finger all the time." This break-the-rules attitude does much to explain why jazz players often develop techniques that astonish symphony musicians. When I introduced a concert pianist to Art Tatum on records, his first reaction was, "All right—who *are* those guys?" On hearing a fast Charlie Parker solo, a symphony clarinetist insisted I was spinning a 33 rpm disc at 45 rpm. Classical musicians marvel at Niels-Henning Orsted Pedersen who strums the double bass like some giant guitar. The *Trombone Concerto* Rimsky-Korsakoff wrote as an endurance contest is something J. J. Johnson and the late Kai Winding could play in their sleep. This determination to play what the Academy considered unplayable is one reason why jazz blossomed with such richness and variety within an amazingly short time. But there were other catalysts of jazz's sudden growth that made it, in the words or composer Virgil Thomson, "the most astounding spontaneous musical event to take place anywhere since the Reformation."

Catalysts of Jazz

The speedy growth of jazz coincided with an exploding technology, the spread of literacy, and the written word. Electricity, steam power, and the internal combustion engine had compressed the American continent to the size of Ireland. Sheet music, the player piano roll, and, later, the radio spread the jazz gospel. But no device had more influence on the course of jazz than the phonograph record, that instantly transportable witness to the improvisor's art. Within weeks after Armstrong waxed his epochal *West End Blues* it was on record shelves—and quite soon in the homes of blacks and whites—in Dallas, San Francisco, New York, and Cleveland, inspiring hundreds of youths to enter the jazz life. The swift progress of tenor saxist Coleman Hawkins in the 1920s can be plotted on records almost month by month, in contrast to other types of folk music like country and bluegrass. It is not to disparage the solid musicianship and integrity of Jimmie Rodgers, Doc Watson, Hank Williams, Flatt and Scruggs, and Loretta Lynn to see that country music remained a rigidly stylized folk art with small capacity for growth and change. Aside from an occasional blend of jazz and bluegrass—Larry Coryell, Sandy Bull, Gary Burton, David Grisman—and despite Nashville's recent overlay of electronic hustle, country music stayed aloof from the radical changes that continuously altered the face of jazz.

The three minute limit imposed by the recording industry standard of the 10-inch, 78 rpm record imposed a benign discipline on soloists and bandleaders. The arrival of the LP in 1948 proved a mixed blessing: It gave Ellington and Gil Evans much needed room to stretch out but also gave mediocrities with nothing to say in one chorus the license to say nothing in a dozen choruses.

THE CUTTING CONTEST
VERSUS MEDIA HYPE

Fascinating tribal customs which are unique to jazz and whose crucial role in its development tend to be overlooked are the cutting contests, jam sessions, and "Battles of Music" that thrived throughout the 1920s, 1930s, and 1940s. These hornslinging marathon shootouts staged in after-hours clubs in Harlem, Chicago, and Kansas City provided jazz musicians with the toughest kind of music school. Bassist Gene Ramey, veteran of many such round-the-clock encounters, spoke of "difficult riffs set behind the soloist to throw him off balance, and transpositions into difficult keys at unnervingly fast tempi used to test newcomers and added to the pressures of waiting to go on and the humiliation that followed personal disasters." (Russell, *Bird Lives!*) When the as-yet unformed Charlie Parker rashly felt ready to jam with the top players in his native Kansas City, he recalled: "I was doing all right until I tried doing double tempo on *Body and Soul*, when everything became unglued." When this happened drummer Jo Jones glowered at the faltering youth, put down his sticks, unscrewed his top cymbal, and threw it with a hideous crash at young Bird's feet. "Everybody fell out laughing," said Bird, "and I went home and cried and didn't play again for three months."

Herman Pritchard, the bartender at Minton's Playhouse, scene of legendary Harlem jam sessions, said:

> Ben Webster and Lester Young used to tie up in battle like dogs in a road. They'd fight on those saxophones until they were tired out, and then they'd put in long distance calls to their mothers in K.C. and tell them about it. (Ellison, *Shadow and Act*.)

Guitarist Danny Barker recalled:

> It was dog eat dog. No place for the weakhearted. Here the men were divided from the boys. In Harlem during the thirties you were instantly classified, given a rating, once you were heard, and you soon found out your rating by who hired you. . . . Giants socialized with giants, lobs with lobs. You either upset New York or it upset you. It was keen competition. If you had greatness you had better keep alert—a young mind and forever on your guard because there is the new breed constantly snapping at your heels. (Liner Notes, *Chu Berry*, Epic EE 22007.)

The cutting contests had several functions. They were informal folk academies where new ideas were tested in the heat of battle. They separated competitors as champions, challengers, or chumps and served as hiring halls and means of building reputations at a time when jazz musicians were rarely if ever mentioned in print. Such lack of press coverage may be hard to envision for those who came of age when the sexual, sartorial, and pharmaceutical exploits of Janis Joplin, Gregg Allman, Bette Midler, and Elton John made instant splashes in *Rolling Stone* and *People*. Bix Beiderbecke, the mythic "Young Man With a Horn" who inspired a rash of romanticized fiction, films, and tributes long after his death in 1931, was mentioned briefly in print twice during his lifetime.

down beat, the first U.S. trade paper to report jazz news, did not debut until 1934 and, like its rival, *Metronome*, stressed white "name" bandleaders who topped reader's polls throughout the Swing Era: Goodman, Shaw, the Dorseys, Glenn Miller. The first U.S. journal devoted entirely to purist jazz did not appear until 1939, years after *Le Jazz Hot* was published regularly in Paris. Unsponsored late hours radio broadcasts "live" from supper clubs and dance halls built modest followings for Ellington, Basie, Chick Webb, and Jimmy Lunceford during the 1930s, but there was scant airplay of authentic black jazz and blues records until the early 1940s with the advent of Broadcast Music Incorporated (BMI) to fill a vacuum left by the staid, parochial American Society of Composers and Performers (ASCAP) that excluded most jazz and blues writers from membership.

Trumpeter Red Allen told the *New Yorker's* Whitney Balliett:

> Those cutting sessions were more than outblowing someone. They were the only way of getting noticed, they were our publicity. If you made a good appearance . . . the word got around, and that's where the jobs came from. If you lost out too often, you just wouldn't make it. There were challenges all the time. (Balliett, *Improvising.*)

Guitarist Danny Barker adds:

> The jam sessions were how reputations were made under fire in the thirties and forties, there was no big build-up in the press and news media. Rarely did the news columnists write up musicians—especially jazz. (Hentoff-Shapiro, *Hear Me Talkin' to Ya.*)

A companion ritual to the cutting contest was the "Battle of the Bands," a popular ballroom draw predating the Swing Era. Two competitive big bands would alternately slug it out at opposite ends of huge dance halls in New York, Chicago, and Pittsburgh: Count Basie vs. Chick Webb, Don Redman vs. the Savoy Sultans. There were even black-and-white battles: Gene Goldkette vs. Fletcher Henderson, the top-rated black band of the 1920s. Henderson's cornetist Rex Stewart recalled this 1926 confrontation in New York's famed Roseland Ballroom:

> We were supposed to be the kings, the greatest thing in New York. We had the best men, the best arrangements. Then suddenly up pops this band of Johnny-come-latelies out of the sticks—white boys on top of it—and they just *creamed* us. It was pretty humiliating, they were swinging like mad. And Bix—that *tone* he got! Knocked us all out. (Hentoff-Shapiro, *Hear Me Talkin' to Ya.*)

Ellington's baritone saxist Harry Carney told Stanley Dance:

> We battled Fletcher Henderson at the Savoy one night I'll never forget. Henderson played numbers in which Coleman Hawkins was heavily featured, and Hawk cut the whole Ellington band by himself. (Liner Notes, *Fletcher Henderson*, Decca DL9228.)

"Battle of the Bands": Chick Webb with his discovery Ella Fitzgerald and Count Basie with Billie Holiday would slug it out in Harlem's famed Savoy Ballroom—"The Home of Happy Feet." The Band that got the most dancers out on the floor was most likely to get booked for a return engagement.

The cutting contest carved out safe avenues for male aggression closed to blacks as husbands and fathers. Black psychiatrists Price M. Cobbs and William H. Grier wrote in *Black Rage*:

> The black male fights a never-ending battle for possession of his manhood [in a society where] he is powerless against the police or the white man who abuses, sexually, economically, socially, his daughter and wife. Male assertiveness becomes a forbidden fruit, and if it is attained, it must be savored privately.

The black asserted his manhood through the only channels the white man left open—the interrelated subculture of his pulpit, his hustle, his dance, comedy, his studhood—and his music. Jazzmen, pimps, numbers kings, and entertainers are much admired by lower class blacks as "men who are clever and talented enough to be financially well off without working," observed black sociologist Charles Keil in *Urban Blues*. Bassist Gene Ramey's description of the cutting contest is couched in such revealing terms as "tribal initiation rites, trials by fire, and constant tests of manhood." The language of the cutting contest resembles that of a knife fight or gang war. A jazzman's instrument, whether tenor sax, guitar, or piano, is his "ax." To best someone in a session is to "cut" him. A brash teenaged

Fats Waller challenged the elder Willie "The Lion" Smith in a Harlem piano club:

> "Hello, Lion—I come in to cut you."
>
> "You'll get your cuttin', son, 'cause I'm gonna cut you to a *gravy!*" (Memoirs of Willie "The Lion" Smith, RCALSP-6016.)

An "ambush" is when musicians of heavyweight stature make a surprise raid on the bandstand to gang up on weaker competition. In such a combative atmosphere a super-macho ethic arose among jazzmen. Women are "chicks" and men are "studs" in the argot that spells anathema to women active in the liberation movement. Jazzmen have long been preoccupied with the sexual conquest of women, many of whom find the jazz musician irresistible. In any cosmopolitan city you could always find the most exotic and uninhibited women where jazzmen performed. The titles of jazz tunes abound in reference to the joys of sexual congress: *Jazz Me Blues, Juicy Lucy, Poon Tang, My Daddy Rocks Me, I Aint Gonna Give Nobody None of My Jelly Roll, Warm Valley.* Since the early days of ragtime, musicians' flair for sharp dressing, colorful speech, and stance was calculated to enhance their sexual allure. James P. Johnson, king of the Harlem "ticklers" said:

> You had to have an *attitude*, a style of behaving that was your personal, professional trademark. When you came into a place you had a three-way play. First, you laid your cane on the music rack. Then you took off your overcoat, folded it and put it on the piano with the lining showing, then you took off your hat before the audience. Each "tickler" kept these attitudes designed to show a personality that the women would admire. With the music he played the tickler's manners would put the question in the ladies' minds: "Can he do it like he can play it?" It made for stance and attitude and made you strong with the gals. When Willie "The Lion" walked into a place his every move was a picture. (*The Jazz Review*, 1960.)

Given such a *macho* environment, it should be no surprise that of all the arts, performing or otherwise, jazz is unique for its remarkable absence of male homosexuality. There is far more evidence to support this than there is to buttress James Lincoln Collier's statement that "there are probably no more or no fewer homosexuals in jazz than anywhere else in society." (*Collier*, 1978.) Dizzy Gillespie wrote in his memoirs, "I don't even *know* of a jazz musician who's a homosexual—not a real jazz musician."

Cutting contests all but vanished in the early 1950s. Critic Nat Hentoff blames their decline on the nature of the new, free experimental jazz whose young players "separated themselves into tight intensely rehearsed units and began to neglect the old joys and hazards of jamming" while the older mainstream musicians found fewer opportunities for cutting sessions because they were not working regularly: "The newer audiences were focusing on modern jazz." (Hentoff, *Jazz Is*.)

Wynton Marsalis, brilliant new trumpet star of the 1980s said:

> It's just not cool to sit in now in New York. It's not like it was in the '50s. Cats have arrangements, and they don't really want you to sit in. It's not like when the guys were experimenting with bop, trying to figure out how to play. (San Francisco *Chronicle*, October 31, 1982.)

The cutting contest was finally killed off by the emergence of the mass media as a new means of gaining recognition. In the 1950s jazz suddenly flowered as big business with the Newport Jazz Festival, *Playboy* jazz polls, frequent airplay by disc jockeys, packaged concert and college tours, and *Time* cover stories—however error-ridden—on Dave Brubeck and Thelonious Monk. Such obvious differences between the old and the new ways of making a reputation had a profound effect on jazz. Players tested in battle speak with an exuberance and vitality that insured their artistic survival; the recordings of Lester Young, Art Tatum, Roy Eldridge, Ben Webster, Charlie Christian, Dizzy Gillespie, and Charlie Parker enjoy far greater sales today than when first released in the 1930s and 1940s. There is no question that the new media awareness created vast opportunities for the jazz musician. Still, for every Miles Davis and Dave Brubeck who got rich, there were dozens of media-hyped second-raters showered with record contracts and concert tours while many front-rank artists continued to scuffle for coffee-and-cake in obscure dives.

Jazz Is Not
Popular Music

The jazz musician's life and music were shaped by the conflicting demands of their art and the marketplace. How these commercial and social pressures changed over half a century, and how musicians adjusted to these changes, embrace and define major shifts in American culture.

To understand the jazzman's role in the culture requires an end to the confusion of "jazz" with "popular music" that has persisted since the so-called "Jazz Age" of the 1920s. It became natural for the media to link jazz and pop; jazz scarcely could have developed without the pop tune as a handy framework for improvising. The exchanges between jazz and pop had been frequent and often hard to see. Many jazz-tinged singers moved quickly into the more lucrative pop field. Bing Crosby began his career as a "scat" singer and devotee of Bix Beiderbecke during his tenure with the Paul Whiteman Orchestra in the 1920s. Frank Sinatra claims he learned to breathe and phrase by watching his trombonist-boss Tommy Dorsey. So thoroughly did Sinatra absorb the jazz idiom that in Leonard Feather's 1956 poll of 120 top jazz musicians, nearly half named him their favorite male singer, with Louis Armstrong a poor fourth. Glenn Miller, an early case of "crossover," switched to a bland version of jazz-flavored pop to become the biggest attraction of the Swing Era. Singer Ethel Waters, whose *double entendre* discs delighted the ghetto as well as Ivy League frat houses, made a quick transition to Broadway's musical and dramatic theater. Armstrong, Ellington, and Fats Waller clung to their jazz roots while making unprecedented inroads into the white mass market. Nat "King" Cole, once considered a piano threat to Art Tatum himself, literally gave up jazz to become the idol of black and white Americans as a singer of sugary pop ballads.

Aside from an occasional oddity like Teresa Brewer, the shift was rarely from pop to jazz but from jazz to pop where the big money is. With very few exceptions—Benny Goodman, Armstrong, Ellington, Miles Davis—premier jazz artists seldom reached the Himalayan peaks of money, power, audience, and notoriety enjoyed by Al Jolson, Bing Crosby, Guy Lombardo, Ethel Merman, Mary Martin, Judy Garland, the Andrews Sisters, Dinah Shore, Lawrence Welk, Frank Sinatra, Sammy Davis, Jr., the Kingston Trio, Peter, Paul, and Mary, Elvis Presley, the Beatles, the Rolling Stones, Bette Midler, Barry Manilow, Sonny and Cher, The Who, Led Zeppelin, John Denver, and Elton John. While Ellington was grossing $200,000 a year in the 1930s to meet an unheard of weekly payroll of $2500 for his all-star band, Kay Kyser, with his own sponsored weekly radio show, outgrossed Ellington better than six to one. Even at the end of his career, when Ellington's prestige was at its height, there were times when he could not fill half a theater in the United States. The Associated Press in September 1977 reported: "The three major television networks have rejected the proposal of a committee of black musicians to begin regularly-scheduled jazz programs, claiming the shows couldn't attract a mass audience."

When jazz made the quick transition from a folk entertainment to an art form still swathed in the trappings of the minstrel show, vaudeville house, and speakeasy, this foisted unusual problems on its players. Year by year their music grew more exacting, with the increased demands on its audience as well as its performers thrown into daily conflict with the business of making a living from the music they loved. An America lusting for casual diversion could patronize the old-time "darky" as a cavorting, bass-slapping, tapdancing fool to reinforce a comforting myth of white superiority. What white America could not abide was the notion of the jazz-musician-as-artist in a culture that disdained even the genteel, certified arts of the concert hall and art gallery. With a bitterness characteristic of the 1960s, LeRoi Jones wrote: "Art had become the dirtiest word in the American language." (LeRoi Jones, *Blues People.*)

In the mid-1940s the vigorous demands of the jazz musician's craft and his mounting self-image as a serious artist began to clash with white America's fixed image of the jazzman as an amoral underworld roustabout. During half a century, jazz players, both white and black, resolved this conflict in a variety of ways. Those few black jazz artists who made permanent inroads into white mass culture before World War II, when such forays required a caution and stealth hard to envision today, did so through avenues that bypassed their purely musical gifts. "The black musician," wrote Ben Sidran in his excellent study *Black Talk*, "has constantly had to maneuver around psychological misunderstandings that surround his music in order to present that music to mainstream America as a statement that speaks for itself."

The most successful of the pre-war jazzmen, by far, were Louis Armstrong, Duke Ellington, and Fats Waller (whose potential for mass appeal was cut short by an early death). With Janus-like guile all of them, in varying ways, wore a public and a private face. Their audience saw only the mask of the loveable entertainer. The private face of the artist was glimpsed only by fellow musicians and a hyperemotional cult of white critics and record collectors who mainly lived abroad where the relative freedom from racial and artistic prejudice better equipped them for an early embracement of American black music, not merely as an adjunct to dancing and partying but as the object of thoughtful listening and study.

3

The Growth of Jazz

When Miles Davis brewed his popular mix of jazz and rock in the late 1960s, the media hung a handy label on the product—"fusion." This was hardly new, since jazz from the beginning was fusion, a *bouillabaisse* of sound from every culture washed up on these shores: West African rhythms, German and Italian marching bands, Protestant hymns, European classical music, opera, English, Scottish, and Irish folk songs and their Appalachian and Ozark mountain derivatives, minstrel show tunes, "coon songs," French cotillion or country dance music, Spanish and Latin melodies and rhythms, and a profusion of black folk music—rural and urban, religious and secular—including slave chants, railroad gang songs, field hollers, "sanctified" church music, and the blues.

How such an intriguing merger took place, and when, is difficult to trace. Unlike today, when musicologists from every continent will eagerly track down the flimsiest of clues, jazz and the blues dawned unnoticed by scholars and professional folklorists. "Serious" music in the U.S. was dominated by Wagner, Beethoven, and Brahms, who reigned in its concert halls. Aside from Charles Ives, classical composers in America paid little mind to white folk music, while black folk music lay well outside the bounds of respectability. Rare exceptions were the Czech Antonin Dvořák, who worked themes from black spirituals into his compositions, and the New Orleans piano virtuoso Louis Moreau Gottschalk, one of the first classical composers to draw from authentic black folk music.

Delving into such an elusive mystery is beyond the scope of so general a book; readers are directed to Marshall Stearns' *The Story of Jazz* and Gunther Schuller's *Early Jazz* for excellent surveys on the origins of jazz and blues. Though much of these origins remain shrouded in legend and controversy, we do know that jazz and blues were born of the Afro-American's genius for survival through assimilation, his skill at adapting to white experiences, musical and otherwise. Stripped of tribal culture, families, language, and identities, even their names, black slaves had been left nothing to call their own except Jesus and their art—dance, comedy, and song. The "fusion" of the African heritage with the slaves' unique adaptation of the white man's religion and music flowered at the turn of the century into ragtime, the first in a continuing series of black shock waves to ripple through the white culture, here and abroad, unloosing an international dance craze that got people's bodies moving in surprising and sometimes shocking new ways.

Ragtime

In an era on the verge of kicking over Victorian restraints, ragtime burst on the scene as happy, infectious dance music. This kick-up-your-heels impulse that made dancers feel free and exalted coincided with the death of England's Queen Victoria, whose long reign (1837–1901) lent her name to an era synonymous with obsessive moral strictures regarding dress, conduct, and manners, with special regard to that unmentionable word—sex. Nor should it surprise us that Victoria was succeeded by her libertine 60-year-old son, Edward VII, "whose love affairs and extravagant living . . . often offended his mother's stern moral sense and distressed the proprieties of Victorian England." (*Columbia Encyclopedia*, 1963.) In our own age, the new king would have been called a "swinger," and while there is no ready evidence that he was a devotee of the new ragtime craze, we might assume him to be in agreement with the clairvoyant editorial in the London *Times* the year he acceded to the throne in 1901. "Ragtime is absolutely characteristic of its inventors. From nowhere but the United States could such music have sprung. Nor can there be any doubt about its vigor, brimming over with life. Here, for those who have ears to hear, are the seeds from which a national art may ultimately spring."

Though no one is certain, many suspect ragtime was named for the "ragged" rhythm of its unique syncopated beat that accented the normally weak beats in a measure of two-and-four. Like all of jazz to follow, ragtime was a synthesis of the Afro-American tradition and whatever white musical forms lent themselves to adaptation; plantation songs, minstrel tunes, and cakewalk music all went into classic piano ragtime. The "cakewalk" was a popular black folk entertainment that aped the fancy dress of the upper-class white. Black couples would compete in a high-stepping dance contest, decked in lavish finery—tall silk hats, spats, ascot ties, and cutaway coats for the men, large flowered hats, hoopskirts, and puff sleeves for the women. A multi-tiered wedding cake was awarded the couple that won the most applause. "Coon songs"—coon being slang for black—also contributed to ragtime. These popular tunes were of a flagrantly racist nature, with titles like *All Coons Look Alike to Me* and cartoons of blacks on the sheet music in the most degrading minstrel stereotype.

Ragtime also drew from classic piano concert music: Chopin and his American contemporary, Gottschalk. In some ways ragtime had more in common with Gottschalk than with what later became known as jazz. Some of Gottschalk's piano pieces, like the remarkably forward-looking *Pasquinade Caprice* Op. 59 of 1869, disported a left hand rhythm similar to Joplin's *Maple Leaf Rag* thirty years later.

The most dominant flavor of ragtime, aside from its infectious rhythm, was the black adaptation of German and Italian marching band music that thrived throughout the South and Southwest (and still does today). Sedalia, Missouri, the home of Scott Joplin and his publisher John Stillwell Stark, became the national capital of ragtime. Certain conventions of marching band music carried over into piano ragtime, like the "dogfight," a chromatic (key-changing) interlude and teaser that prefaced the all-out grand climax of favorites like Sousa's *The Stars and Stripes Forever*. You can hear a "dogfight" in the first rag ever published, *Mississippi Rag* by W. H. Krell, a white marching bandmaster. (*Original Ragtime*, Claude Bolling, piano, Columbia PC 33277.) The *Maple Leaf Rag* even bore the indication *Tempo di Marcia*. The "front-line" instruments of early dixieland jazz came out of the marching band: the cornet playing the lead, the clarinet playing trills in the treble (perhaps in imitation of the piccolo), and the trombone playing a "vamp" bass line.

Though ragtime was sometimes scored for a small band, it was most often conceived as solo piano music at a time when the piano was an invariable fixture in the American home, church basement, club, lodge, and the five-and-dime stores where sheet music was sold. Before the Great Depression of 1929 there were nearly 300 manufacturers of pianos in the United States alone. By 1932, their number was reduced to fewer than twenty, a result not only of the depression but of a change of taste toward the more passive entertainments of radio, talking pictures, and the phonograph.

Ragtime was a formally written-out music, almost never improvised, and contained four distinct though related themes in a prescribed order. Typical of this structure is *Maple Leaf Rag* (Smic 1/1).

A A B B A C C D D

When published in 1899 *Maple Leaf Rag* launched the ragtime craze, sold unprecedented hundreds of thousands of sheet music copies, and made Scott Joplin the undisputed "King of Ragtime." Although a form of black music, ragtime was first published in 1897 by the white composer W. H. Krell because it was unthinkable in those times, and in the decades to follow, for a black artist to slash his way unaided through the jungle of greed, avarice, and double dealing that infested the music publishing world of Tin Pan Alley. Joplin, the son of former slaves, formed an adhesive business and personal alliance with white publisher John Stark, who was utterly devoted to Joplin and shared his view that the Joplin rags would one day take their place alongside Mozart and Chopin as staples in the concert repertoire. (This became a recurrent pattern in the annals of Afro-American music; behind nearly all black artists who carved a niche in the white mass market—Joplin, Armstrong, Ellington, Erroll Garner—there stood a canny white business agent/manager.)

When the ragtime craze reached its fever pitch in the first decade of this century, hundreds of ragtime composers all over America were publishing, including dozens of women like May Aufderheide of Indianapolis. Besides Joplin, the other major figures were James Scott, whose *Grace and Beauty* and *The Ragtime Oriole* were stamped with an individual lyricism, and Joseph Lamb, an Irish-American from New Jersey whose stated ambition was "to write a real colored rag" like Joplin. (Some of the best work of ragtime's Big Three is played with the proper mixture of authenticity and bouncy good spirits on *Max Morath Plays Ragtime*, Vanguard VSD 83/84.)

Ragtime saw the birth of another recurrent pattern that runs throughout the course of jazz and rock—the arousal of livid opposition among the pulpit, press, and academy, which saw this danceable new music as a sexual threat and a flagrant assault on public morals. In 1901 the American Federation of Musicians passed a rule forbidding its members to play ragtime. Two years earlier, the American journal, *Musical Courier*, ran this scandalized editorial:

> A wave of vulgar, of filthy and suggestive music has inundated the land. Nothing but ragtime prevails. No seaside resort this summer has been without its ragtime orchestra, its weekly cakewalk. Worse yet, the fashionable idle folk of Newport have been the chief offenders. Society has decreed that ragtime and cakewalking are the thing, and one reads with amazement and disgust of historical and aristocratic names joining in this sex dance, for the cakewalk is nothing but an African *danse du ventre* [i.e., belly dance], a milder edition of African orgies, and the music is degenerate music. Ragtime rhythm's present usage and marriage to words of veiled lasciviousness should banish it from polite society. (Quoted in Feather, *The Book of Jazz*.)

Variations on this familiar theme, with a change of phrase here and there, were to crop up with regularity during the Jazz Age of the 1920s, the Swing Era of the 1930s, the Rock era of the 1950s, and beyond.

Cut off from the white establishment and its music schools, ragtime developed its own traveling folk academy. Piano "ticklers" prideful of dress and carriage wandered to bars, sporting houses, and expositions in St. Louis, Chicago, New Orleans, and Kansas City in search of ragtime contests, where prizes and trophies were awarded the winners. The fierce, independent pride of these black ragtime kings was embodied in Coalhouse Walker, Jr., the centerpiece of E. L. Doctorow's rich and splendid panoramic novel, *Ragtime*.

The craving for ragtime knew no bounds in England and the Continent where it spread to the courts of Europe. Sousa, the "March King," used cakewalk two-step syncopation when his band made a triumphal tour abroad. With the U.S. entry into World War I in April 1917, ragtime was spread by black orchestras touring Europe—Will Marion Cook's Southern Syncopated Orchestra and the Army band led by James Reese Europe. Ragtime intrigued classical composers, who used it in their work. Debussy wrote his *Golliwog's Cakewalk* in 1914, a frankly ragtime influenced piano piece. Young Stravinsky started his lifelong interest in American music in 1919 with his *Piano Rag Music* and the Ragtime Movement from *L'Histoire du Soldat*. New England aristocrat Charles Ives titled the astounding fourth movement of his *First Piano Sonata* (1902–10), "A Fastish Ragtime."

Following another well-known pattern, the decline of ragtime was hastened by commercial debasement as a legion of opportunists cheapened the art of Joplin and James Scott with furious tempos and flashy pianistic exploits. The Swiss conductor-critic Ernst Ansermet noted in his famous 1919 article for *Revue Romande*: ". . . hundreds of musicians are all applying themselves at this very moment to adapt this new art to the taste for the insipid and the sentimental, to the coarse and mediocre sensuality of their clientele."

Alarmed at the insensitive liberties taken with his work, Joplin published his *Book of Ragtime* in 1908 with the warning, "Play slowly until you get the *swing* [italics mine] and never play ragtime fast at any time." This might be the first time "swing" was used in print to describe this rhythm. The proud and driven Joplin prefaced his six ragtime études with this remarkable statement:

> What is scurrilously called ragtime is an invention that is here to stay. That is now conceded by all classes of musicians. That all publications masquerading under the name of ragtime are not the genuine article will be better known when these exercises are studied. That real ragtime of the higher class is rather difficult to play is a painful truth which most pianists have discovered. Syncopations are no indication of light or trashy music, and to shy bricks at hateful ragtime no longer passes for musical culture. To assist amateur players in giving the Joplin rags that weird and intoxicating effect intended by the composer is the object of this work.

Ragtime's eventual demise was further hastened because its rigid structure, limited rhythmic language, and narrow emotional range had painted this music into a corner. Joplin's last and in many ways his most arresting rags show him struggling to free himself from ragtime's built-in restrictions. In *Euphonic Sounds* (1909) he makes daring attempts to depart from the steady oom-PAH of ragtime's traditional left hand and imparts a spirit of melancholy, even tragedy, to what had long been a happy good-time music. Joplin's fatal misstep was to pour his final energies into the ambitious full-length folk opera *Treemonisha* in 1911. This ill-fated bid for "respectability" forced a miniaturist art into a grandiose mold—like the comic who dreams of playing Hamlet. Stark broke with Joplin by refusing to publish it. *Treemonisha's* dismal failure following one badly staged and received performance left Joplin crushed; he died in 1917 in a Manhattan hospital for the insane.

If ragtime did not die with Joplin, it went into a deep sleep that endured 50 years. The new improvisors' art of jazz found the complex many-themed structure of ragtime too unwieldy for embellishment and abandoned the AABBACCDD format for the simpler framework of the popular song. The ascendancy of the pop tune as the jazz musician's vehicle drove another nail into ragtime's coffin. As we will see, jazz improvisors burst the musical and emotional restraints against which Joplin vainly struggled in his later works.

After a full half-century of oblivion, ragtime suddenly came to life in the 1970s to enjoy a full-fledged revival. Millions were captivated by the Joplin rags that made up the movie score of *The Sting*, which swept the Academy Awards, including one for best film score. A new breed of concert pianists like Joshua Rifkin fulfilled Joplin's prophecy by including his rags in their public repertoire. *Treemonisha* enjoyed full-dress revivals in Houston and Atlanta to wild acclaim. People found ragtime too rich and beguiling a music to be killed off.

How Jazz
Emerged from Ragtime:
The "Fusion" of Jelly Roll Morton

In the late 1930s the jazz world was startled and amused by a *down beat* interview with a nearly forgotten pianist-composer-bandleader, Joseph Ferdinand la Menthe, known professionally as Jelly Roll Morton, who claimed to have "invented jazz in 1902." This boast, greeted with hoots of derision by younger musicians who had long written him off as a has-been, was typical of the flamboyant bragadoccio of this New Orleans creole whose calling card read: "Jelly Roll Morton: Inventor of Jazz & Stomps. World's Greatest Hot Tune Writer." When the "Father of the Blues" W. C. Handy called Morton's interview "the act of a crazy man," he replied, "Play some of Mr. Handy's music—and then play some of my own."

"Jelly Roll" Morton/1937: Self-styled "Inventor
of Jazz & Stomps. World's Greatest Hot Tune
Writer." (Photograph from the Ralph J. Gleason
Collection.)

Morton remains a figure of heated controversy to this day. Critic-en-
cyclopedist Leonard Feather insists Morton was a charlatan glorified by an
hysterical cult. Martin Williams, director of the Smithsonian jazz program,
regards him as a genius and assigned him more tracks in the Smithsonian
Collection than such towering figures as Earl Hines, John Coltrane,
Fats Waller, and Dizzy Gillespie. Ellington, who almost never had a harsh
word for a fellow musician, said Morton "played piano like one of those
high school teachers . . . his rhythm was unsteady." (Feather, *The Book of
Jazz*.) Morton's excellent clarinetist Omer Simeon claimed: "Jelly could
back up everything he said by what he could *do*." (Hentoff-Shapiro, *Hear
Me Talkin' to Ya*.) The key to this controversy lies in Morton's advice—
listen to his music, and compare it to his contemporaries.

Born in New Orleans in 1885, Jelly Roll Morton was an itinerant
musical folklorist and notetaker who meandered from St. Louis to California, New York, Memphis, Texas, and Chicago as a ragtime and blues pianist, bandleader, songwriter, gambler, pool shark, card manipulator,
pimp, nightclub operator, and master of ceremonies. He sported the fancy
clothes that became the badge of all "ticklers," a 24-carat diamond set in
his front tooth, a thousand-dollar bill tucked in his breast pocket. His art

55

was a synthesis of every kind of sound he heard around New Orleans and the Southwest territory at the turn of the century when he claimed to have "invented jazz" with the composing of *New Orleans Joys* which he called "the first playable jazz composition that was wrote on paper."

To compare *New Orleans Joys* and any number of other Morton pieces written or performed during the heyday of ragtime lends some credence to his seemingly extravagant claims. Morton may not have "invented" jazz any more than Louis Armstrong invented swing, Charlie Parker invented bebop, or Ornette Coleman invented free jazz. All these pioneers may have coalesced trends toward which their more adventuresome contemporaries had been moving. Morton may not have been either the first or the only jazz artist of his time to infuse formal ragtime with far-reaching changes. But to judge from the body of his published work, his recordings, the testimony of musicians more disinterested than himself, and from the extensive musical interview he waxed for the Library of Congress in 1938, there is much to support the widely-contested belief that Morton injected crucial elements into ragtime that nudged it further along the road to jazz.

The first of Morton's additions was continuous improvisation, the lifeblood of jazz. (As we have found, piano ragtime was almost never improvised.) This is proved easily by comparing Morton's various recorded versions of his compositions like *King Porter Stomp*, *The Pearls*, *Kansas City Stomps*, and *Wolverine Blues*. All these versions of the same tune reveal his unflagging urge to improvise.

A second innovation was to blend ragtime with folk blues, including "blue" notes and harmonies that had never surfaced in the rags of Joplin, Scott, Lamb, and other ragtime kings. *New Orleans Joys* and *Original Jelly Roll Blues* are prime examples of Morton's felicitous merger of ragtime, blues, and another addition to the stew, what Morton called "the Spanish tinge or seasoning," a variety of Latin rhythms replete with the click of castanets.

Fourth, Morton employed a much looser, more "loping" left-hand beat than the comparatively stiff syncopations of ragtime, pushing this beat closer to what we know as swing. This is evident when comparing Joplin's piano roll of *Maple Leaf Rag* (Smic 1/1) with Morton's gutsier version of the same piece (Smic 1/2).

Most of all, Morton expanded the narrow emotional vocabulary of ragtime, proving jazz and its inseparable handmaiden, the blues, capable of evoking every nuance of emotion from profound despair to the wildest joy.

Morton's bold injections of jazz rhythms and harmonies into ragtime can be plotted by comparing his Spanish-tinged *The Crave* (Time-Life *Giants of Jazz*, Jelly Roll Morton) with a similar piece of Joplin's, *Solace: A*

Mexican Serenade, available in any number of versions, and familiar as the lyrical background theme of *The Sting*. Both pieces were written at approximately the same time; both employ a somewhat similar ragtime structure of several distinct but related themes. Both are flavored with Spanish hot sauce, although *Solace* was Joplin's lone venture into the Latin idiom that Morton used all the time. But the differences are more striking than the similarities. Morton uses "breaks" in the right hand, while his left hand drops out altogether, and a variety of "blue" harmonies in his second chorus that lie well beyond the purview of classic ragtime. While both pieces are dance music, you would surely dance in a freer, less inhibited manner to *The Crave* than to *Solace*. It is also obvious that Morton *swings* more than Joplin—just as it will soon be obvious that Louis Armstrong swings more than Jelly.

In his interview with Alan Lomax for the Library of Congress in 1938—still the most extensive memoir yet recorded by a jazz musician— Morton, ever the theorist, claimed a jazz pianist cannot play jazz "unless he tries to give the imitation of a band." Morton put this idea into practice in 1926 with a magnificent series of small band recordings for Victor by Jelly Roll Morton and His Red Hot Peppers. With carefully chosen and sympathetic sidemen who could follow his precise instructions, Morton relentlessly rehearsed these sessions to produce the most widely-praised recordings of this enduring style of classic New Orleans collective improvisation. The instrumentation was the classic line-up of "dixieland" music, with the front line of trumpet, clarinet, and trombone carried over from marching bands and the rhythm section of piano, string bass, drums, and banjo, later giving way to the guitar, which remained the standard for decades to come. The Red Hot Peppers put into practice another of Morton's theories: "You cannot play crescendos and diminuendos when one is playing triple *forte*; you've got to be able to come down before you can go up. If a glass of water is full, you can't add any more water, but if you have half a glass, you can always put more water in it—and jazz music is based on the same principles." Morton kept the glass "half full" and filled it to the brim in the all-out rousing finales of *Grandpa's Spells* (Smic 1/7) and *Black Bottom Stomp* (Smic 2/1). Splendidly recorded by the advanced audio engineers at Victor, these definitive performances juggle what seemed to be incompatible—freedom and discipline, spontaneity and careful planning—to synthesize the variety of music available to Morton during the first decade of this century. It should be stressed that although Morton went unrecorded for the first twenty years of his active musical career, all evidence indicates that his style was fixed by 1902 and remained unchanged. It was this rigidity that did Morton in, that and his unceasing talk about his music and its greatness. By the time the Red Hot Peppers carried New Orleans collective jamming to its highest peak, this style was on its way to the junkpile, discarded as old hat by the new generation of musicians influenced not by arrangers or composers but by great soloists, mainly Louis Armstrong. By the late 1920s small combos like the Peppers gave way to the new fashion for big bands like Fletcher Henderson's, whose rehearsed brass and reed sections did not improvise collectively but played "riffs"—brief musical figures—either in a "cry and response" pattern or to provide brilliant soloists with an effective backdrop.

But with characteristic mulish pride, Morton clung to his outmoded ragtime-plus-blues formula, a lone holdout against the Swing Era of the 1930s. He went unrecorded from 1930 to 1937 but enjoyed a brief flurry of resurgence before he died in 1941, embittered, impoverished, and probably quite mad. Still, there was undoubtedly much truth in his insistent claim that his publishers made millions off his music and that very little of that money found its way to him. It would be hard to imagine what jazz might have been without him, for had he not added its essence to ailing ragtime someone else would have had to. Although his music is overdue for the major revival accorded Joplin's, Jelly Roll survives with pianists Dick Hyman, Dick Wellstood, Ralph Sutton, Bob Greene, Burt Bales, and young rock-eclectic Ry Cooder. And there remains the imperishable recorded legacy of his piano, the Red Hot Peppers, and his lovely warm vocals of blues and ballads that testify to his unfailing taste and sense of restraint, his logic and inventiveness, his passion, and his utter delight.

Louis Armstrong:
The Prometheus of Jazz

While Jelly Roll Morton stays a figure of contention, no controversy hovers over the legend of Louis Armstrong. Few would argue with drummer Gene Krupa's tribute: "There is no jazz musician regardless of instrument and no jazz singer today that does not owe their first debt of gratitude to Louis Armstrong. Louis did it all, and he did it *first*."

This may come as a surprise to the public that remembers Louis only as the loveable, grinning yuk-yukker of "yeaaaaaaaah man!," America's rags-to-riches "Ambassador of Happy Music," the gravel-voiced croaker of *Hello, Dolly* and *Mack the Knife*, which outsold the Beatles in their heyday, the master showman and purveyor of endless trumpet high Cs. These were but surface ripples on a river of intuitive genius that changed the course not only of jazz but of all American music.

The bare bones of the Armstrong ghetto-to-stardom saga—as Ellington eulogized, "Louis was born poor, died rich, and hurt no one along the way"—are well picked over. New Orleans around 1900, the place and approximate year of Louis's birth, was a wide-open cosmopolitan seaport that lured hustlers, tourists, big spenders, and musicians with its gaudy profusion of gambling, French and Creole cuisine, all-night cabarets, dance halls, saloons, riverboat excursions, ragtime piano contests, fancy hotels, the French Opera House, and the most lavish whorehouses America has ever seen. The city resounded with music. As Louis told Richard Meryman:

> Music all around you. The pie man and the waffle man, they all had a little hustle to attract the people. Pie man used to swing something on the bugle and the waffle man rang a big triangle. The junk man had one of them long tin horns they celebrate with at Christmas—could play the blues and everything on it. In those days in New Orleans there was always something that was nice, and always with music. (Meryman, *An Interview with Louis Armstrong*.)

Jelly Roll Morton recalled, "There were more jobs than musicians in New Orleans." (Lomax, *Mister Jelly Roll*.)

A product of New Orleans' teeming, violent red-light district—Storyville—Louis worked a coal wagon and unloaded bananas on the dock. He learned bugle and cornet in the Waif's Home, a reform school where he served eighteen months for shooting off a pistol outside a Rampart Street honky-tonk on New Year's Eve. A natural leader, he fronted a marching band of "twenty kids, and we played pretty good, not like Joe Oliver and Manuel Perez in that Onward Band. But we'd hire out to those big social clubs, and play in that hot sun and had to parade for miles and miles." (Meryman, *An Interview with Louis Armstrong*.)

> Marching band: The "front-line" instruments of the Oliver Band— cornet, clarinet, and trombone—came out of New Orleans marching bands to become the "front-line" of dixieland combos to this day (see photo on page 60). (Photograph by Ray Avery of Rare Records.)

King Oliver's Creole Jazz Band/1923: The "front-line" instruments of the Oliver Band—
cornet, clarinet, and trombone—came out of New Orleans marching bands to become
the "front-line" of dixieland combos to this day. (Standing, left—King Oliver, cornet;
bass player, unknown. Front, left to right—Baby Dodds, drums; Honore Dutrey,
trombone; Louis Armstrong, second cornet; Johnny Dodds, clarinet; Lil Hardin-
Armstrong, piano.) (Photograph by Ray Avery of Rare Records.)

      Louis's musical horizons expanded in Mississippi riverboat bands
led by Fate Marable, whose sidemen included advanced musicians soon
to form an historic alliance with Louis in the 1920s—bassist Pops Foster,
clarinetist Johnny Dodds, his brother Baby Dodds on drums, and banjoist
Johnny St. Cyr. In 1923, after three summers with Marable, Louis got the
telegram from his teacher and idol Joe "King" Oliver that was to change
the course of jazz: "I want you to come up [to Chicago] and join me." A
kindly cornet playing leader, Oliver had joined one of history's greatest
mass migrations during World War I when blacks by the tens of thousands
left the South in search of good-paying defense jobs, settling almost overnight in Chicago's South Side, which suddenly bloomed as an entertainment center to provide down-home music for the uprooted. King Oliver's
Creole Jazz Band had become a sensation at the Lincoln Gardens dance
hall, a magnet for young white musicians and dropouts like drummer
George Wettling who remembered: "Usually they'd dance the Bunny Hug
to a slow blues—and how the dancers would grind away!" New Orleans
trombonist Preston Jackson said: "That Oliver Band just went mad when
they played. Usually fast stuff. The Garden was a turmoil from the start of
the evening until the last note died away. Why, I thought they'd blow the

roof off the place, especially after Louis Armstrong joined the band." (Hentoff-Shapiro, *Hear Me Talkin' to Ya.*)

As the awestruck young Louis knew, Joe Oliver was the unchallenged master of this hell-for-leather, gutbucket, lowdown New Orleans jazz. Until Louis joined in 1923, the Oliver lineup was the classic "dixieland" combo derived from marching bands, identical to Morton's Red Hot Peppers: cornet, clarinet, and trombone frontline backed by piano, bass, banjo, and drums. Aside from brief arranged passages, Oliver's music was collectively improvised, especially in its grand climaxes. The band aimed for a collective rolling danceable beat with individuals subordinate to the group. There were featured solos like Oliver's much-copied choruses on *Dippermouth Blues* (Smic 1/6), but whether on fast stomps or slow blues Oliver's trademark was the rollicking rough-and-tumble jam that got dancers moving.

Oliver hired the 23-year-old Louis as second cornet to play harmony to Joe's lead. "When you saw Joe lean over towards Louis at the first ending," said Preston Jackson, "you know they were going to make a 'break' in the middle of the next chorus. And what breaks they made! Louis never knew what Joe was going to play, but he would always follow him perfectly." (Hentoff-Shapiro, *Hear Me Talkin' to Ya.*)

Aside from a few obscure sides by Kid Ory, King Oliver's Creole Jazz Band with Louis cut the first records of authentic black jazz in 1923, thirty-seven numbers "played into one big horn," Louis told Richard Meryman. "There were no mikes. And my tone was so much stronger than Oliver's that when we recorded I has to stand way over by the door so I wouldn't outblow him." Papa Joe kept his young stallion under wraps, but on those few records where he let Louis solo—*Chimes Blues* and *Frog-i-more Rag*—he burst through the tinny acoustical horn seething with passion and an irresistible drive that foretold of things to come. Louis was about to emerge from Oliver's cocoon as the first great soloist in jazz.

To understand how far Louis had outdistanced Oliver, compare Oliver's *Dippermouth Blues* (Smic 1/6) to *Cake Walkin' Babies From Home* by Clarence Williams Blue Five (Time-Life *Giants of Jazz, Armstrong*), where Louis's lead cornet has left Oliver light years behind. Louis is abetted in this explosive 1925 recording by the soaring soprano sax of New Orleans's Sidney Bechet, the first musician Louis ever recorded with who could drive and challenge him. There is no mistaking Louis's superiority over Oliver, playing the same kind of music, nor is there any mistaking the superiority of Louis and Bechet over their cohorts. Stunning performances of this kind were beginning to earn Louis a reputation among jazz musicians, white as well as black.

Without the prodding of Oliver's pianist, Lil Hardin, who became the second Mrs. Armstrong in 1924, easy-going Louis might have shared the lot of other New Orleans jazzmen like Oliver, who died in obscurity in 1938, or Henry "Red" Allen whose immense trumpet gifts were known only to fellow musicians and a coterie of critics and record collectors. A competent though indifferent pianist of the ragtime-plus-Jelly Roll school, Lil Hardin Armstrong was the most musically sophisticated member of Oliver's group. Early on she saw her shy husband's potential and urged him to better himself: "How long you gonna hang around Joe? It ain't doin' you no good." She pushed Louis to accept the challenging offer to play third trumpet with Fletcher Henderson, the most highly rated and advanced black orchestra of the day. This proved a momentous move for Louis, for the Henderson Band, and for the future of jazz.

Under Henderson's hand Louis faced complex arrangements in difficult keys rarely used in jazz at that time. Since Henderson was based in New York, Louis was thrown into contact—and vice versa—with technically proficient white players like cornetist Red Nichols and trombonist Miff Mole. "Louis was as impressed by their technical command and polish as they were by his extraordinary power and blues feeling." (Hadlock, *Jazz Masters of the Twenties*.) During his fourteen-month tenure with Henderson, beginning in 1924, Louis also came under the spell of high-note trumpet virtuosi in Manhattan's popular white hotel dance bands.

To the Henderson crew Louis gave as good if not better than he got. His charging solos had galvanized the band and had made him the talk of New York's jazz players. Ellington said: "The guys never heard anything like it. There weren't words coined to describe that kind of kick. Louis carried his horn around and sat in and played anywhere he happened to drop in. Everybody on the street was talking about the guy." (Hentoff-Shapiro, *Hear Me Talkin' to Ya*.)

Even a casual hearing of Henderson's *Copenhagen* (Time-Life *Giants of Jazz, Armstrong*) shows how Louis towered above the band with the shock of encountering the Parthenon in the Great Gobi Desert. To grasp the immense impact Louis had on this band, listen to Henderson's *Stampede* (Smic 3/6) recorded a mere eighteen months later. Coleman Hawkins unveils a stomping chorus of pure Armstrong that was to earn him the title of "inventor of the tenor sax," although his pathetic solos with Henderson during Louis's stay were grotesque blooperies rooted in vaudeville. Rex Stewart, cast in the terrifying role of replacing Louis, his idol, climaxes *Stampede* with screaming jubilance. It took Rex six months to work up the nerve to take Louis's chair in the band; his reverence of Louis was typical of the jazz community. As James Agee wrote of Chaplin, "His peers were no more jealous of him than they were of God."

Save for his diminutive height, everything about Louis was cast in an heroic mold. He was blessed with a rugged physique that he took pains to maintain and endowed with what Richard Hadlock called "a perfect physiological trumpet-playing mechanism." His tone was open, spacious, and impassioned, the daring escapades in the high register as generous and unforced as the throbbing low notes. His occasional use of a cup mute lent a clouded beauty to the warm vibrato. His unerring sense of time and placement of subtle accents got the most swing from the fewest notes. This was his far-reaching contribution, of the utmost importance to jazz development. He possessed the grace and self-assurance of a born leader who never lost touch with his earthy roots no matter how high he rose, and he rose to the top. His expansive love of good food, high times, and broad humor would light up a room. His entrance into a club spread joy among the patrons and panic among the band, especially trumpet players.

.Aside from a coterie of Bix Beiderbecke followers, and admirers of Henderson's Joe Smith—he takes the exquisite mid-register solo in the middle of *Stampede*—most trumpeters felt there could be no other way to play the instrument. Ellington's Cootie Williams, on first hearing a Louis record, vowed: "I don't know what he's playing, but whatever it is, I'm going out and buy me one of *them*!" His solos bristled with flourishes, rips, flares, and explosions that unavoidably cropped up in the work of his

Louis Armstrong: What Louis played applied, not only to the trumpet, but to all the instruments of jazz—including the voice. (Photograph from the Richard Hadlock Collection.)

successors—Roy Eldridge, Dizzy Gillespie, Miles Davis, Clifford Brown. This influence was not limited to trumpeters but extended to all of the instruments, including the voice. His final chorus on *Hotter Than That* (Smic 2/8), a single repeated staccato note, may have been an early lesson for the nonswinging drummers of the mid-1920s.

Louis's tenure with Henderson coincided with the classic age of women blues singers who craved his matchless accompaniment on records, giving him a chance to stretch out that Henderson did not provide. Musicians began to marvel at his passionate backing of Maggie Jones, Trixie Smith, Ma Rainey, Alberta Hunter, Sippi Wallace, and the Empress herself, Bessie Smith, who soon took an ugly view of Louis's habit of turning these sessions into trumpet solos with vocal obbligáti. Their final duet, or clash of wills, was aptly named *I Ain't Gonna Play No Second Fiddle*, for Bessie never used Louis again.

After little more than a year with Henderson, Louis reluctantly struck out on his own at Lil's urging: "You still playing third trumpet with Fletcher." Louis told Richard Meryman:

> I left Fletcher for a band of Lil's back in Chicago at the Dreamland Ballroom. That was the only time in all those years I played lead. I played second at the Vendome Theater when Erskine Tate had a fifteen-piece pit band playing overtures and everything to go with silent pictures. Well, I didn't know if I could do it. Never played any classical music—*Cavalleria Rusticana*, reading music, turning pages and all that, but Lil said I could, and she was a full-fledged musician, studied it and everything, graduate of Fisk University, and I couldn't argue with her.

In Chicago, bustling Louis worked several jobs at once and signed a contract with Okeh Records, the blues and "race" label. ("Race" was the actual designation in the catalogue and was even on some labels like Paramount and Brunswick.) Under the name of Louis Armstrong and his Hot Five, and later the Hot Seven, Louis was joined by Lil on piano and three other New Orleans veterans: Kid Ory, trombone; Johnny Dodds, clarinet; and Johnny St. Cyr, banjo. The Hot Fives and Sevens became the most important and influential series of records in the history of classic jazz and firmed up the leader's mounting repute among jazz artists as, far and away, the greatest soloist of the day.

With Okeh's promotion behind their rising new star, the Hot Fives sold well at seventy-five cents in urban ghettos. His career took an ominous turn when he waxed his "scat" (wordless) vocal on the 1926 *Heebie Jeebies*, the debut of Louis the master showman-to-come. His gutteral cries, a perfect counterpart to his trumpet flights, delighted audiences used to the syrupy falsetto vocals of pop male singers and made Louis an overnight sensation among black audiences. As Okeh executives soon discovered, Louis's rough-house vocals and comedy hokum far outsold

OKEH Records "Race" Catalog in the 1920s: Note the title of Reverend Gates's sermon (first listing), "Kinky Hair is no Disgrace," an early portent of the "black is beautiful" movement in the 1960s. (Photograph from the Richard Hadlock Collection.)

the instrumental numbers, and they urged more of the same. So did Joe Glaser, manager of the Sunset Cafe where Louis was nightly grabbing the dancers with rowdy clowning on *Big Fat Ma and Skinny Pa* and *I Want a Big Butter and Egg Man*. Glaser added to the marquee: "Louis Armstrong—World's Greatest Trumpet Player." Louis thought, "That's the only man in my corner." In 1935 Glaser began his decades-long stint as Louis's manager and friend. Founder of the giant Associated Booking Corporation, Glaser was a volatile, honest, and tough-minded agent, devoted to Louis, and convinced that with proper grooming his reticent client could become a superstar. "Forget all the goddam critics, the musicians. Play for the public. Sing and play and smile!" he urged Louis. "When I first hired Louis at the Sunset, he was shy, quiet. I used to act like a football coach: 'Louis, sing and make faces and smile. Smile, goddammit! Give it to them! Don't be afraid!' " (Hentoff-Shapiro, *Hear Me Talkin' to Ya*.)

Before Louis could force his entry into the white market he had to shake loose the limited and archaic format of the Hot Five and Seven—down-home blues, gutbucket jam, and ragtime parade stomps that were to pass rapidly from the black public's favor by the end of the 1920s. The Hot Fives show Louis struggling to shake free the confines of New Orleans music and inferior cohorts. Sessions like *Potato Head Blues* (Smic 2/7) and *S.O.L. Blues* (Smic 2/6) showcasing Louis's bravura trumpet made

Louis Armstrong: Louis's manager trained him like a football coach. "Louis, sing and make faces and smile. *Smile* goddammit! Give it to them! Don't be afraid!" (Photograph courtesy of the Rutgers Institute of Jazz Studies.)

startling departures from the Oliver band of yesteryear. Louis was pushing his way to stardom, but aside from those brief rousing dates with Sidney Bechet, with whom he did not get along, Louis had yet to find an equal to goad and challenge him and did not until his historic encounter in 1927 with Earl Hines, the father of modern jazz piano.

ARMSTRONG AND HINES: A REVOLUTION IS BORN

Earl Hines's departures from ragtime and its offshoot, "stride," were radical and all-important. To make his right hand heard over Carroll Dickerson's big band at the Sunset Cafe, in an era before sound amplification, this classically trained pianist smashed out brassy ringing octaves with his right hand. Critics were soon to dub this "trumpet style" piano because Hines's right hand lines sounded like replicas of Louis. But Hines had been working on such a concept all along. When he first met Louis in a session he thought: "Here's a guy who's doing the same thing on trumpet that I'm doing on the piano." Hines's left hand was even more revolutionary than his horn-like right and marked the first clean break from ragtime syncopation. Suddenly, in mid-stride, Hines's left would leap into some unexplored realm, scuttling crablike into the treble, snarling into double-time, offtime, yet never losing the beat. At 22 Hines was the first jazz artist to meet head-on the problem that was to absorb future musicians, not all of them pianists—how to free jazz from the rhythmic restrictions of 4/4 dance music and still swing? And Hines outswung them all, seeming to always push the beat without getting ahead of it. His tireless muscular technique articulated each note with the precision of Horowitz, but a Horowitz who could swing. His fickle shifting of rhythmic gears proved the despair of early drummers and bassists. Hines's triumphs seem all the more remarkable because he appeared without antecedents. You can hear Oliver in Armstrong, and Armstrong in Roy Eldridge, but Hines was a genuine original.

The revolution of Louis and Earl is best understood by comparing their only recorded duet, the 1928 *Weatherbird* (Smic 3/1), with the 1924 duet of King Oliver and Jelly Roll Morton on much the same tune, Jelly's *King Porter Stomp* (*Louis Armstrong and King Oliver*, Milestone M-47017). You may have trouble believing these two records were made only four years apart, but then, many musicians in 1928 had trouble believing Louis and Earl on *Weatherbird*, which showed what marvels of invention were possible once these two giants were freed of inferior sidemen. Driving Louis into daring and incredible feats, Hines uncorks a three-minute history of jazz piano, pulsing from Jelly Roll and Fats Waller to intimations of Art Tatum to come, 1940s bebop, and a touch of free jazz of the 1960s.

With Hines, Louis marched boldly into the future. Nowhere was this better shown than in the epochal *West End Blues* (Smic 2/9), a stunning transformation of a traditional 12-bar blues that became jazz's *Birth of a Nation*, perhaps the most widely-imitated and often-played record in jazz history. Gunther Schuller spoke for most critics and musicians:

> When Louis Armstrong unleashed the spectacular cascading phrases of the introduction to *West End Blues*, he established the general stylistic direction of jazz for several decades to come. Beyond that, this performance made clear that jazz could never again revert to being solely an entertainment or folk music. (Schuller, *Early Jazz*.)

West End Blues contains Louis's most beautiful blues vocal, a wordless duet with the clarinet far removed from the garrulous horseplay that sold the Hot Fives in the ghetto. In a brief chorus sandwiched between Louis's vocal and the staggering climax, Hines thrusts one of his inimitable springboard solos that made him, along with Fats Waller, the dominant keyboard influence until the arrival of Hines's pupil, Teddy Wilson, in the mid-1930s.

LOUIS SUPERSTAR

In 1929 Hines took off as a bandleader while Louis fronted the great band of Luis Russell, a nonstop aggregation of all-star soloists that stomped other New York bands out of existence in "Battles of Music." This was to be by far the most exciting big band ever associated with Louis. Driven by the enormous boom of Pops Foster's bass, Louis outdid himself in timeless recordings of *St. Louis Blues* and *Mahogany Hall Stomp* (*The Genius of Louis Armstrong*, Vol. I, Columbia G 30416) with choruses based on deceptively simple blues "riffs" that all big bands and small combos were to use for decades to come. The triumph of the Count Basie Band in the 1930s was based on its ability to swing collectively in the Armstrong manner.

On the eve of the stock market crash of 1929, which launched the Great Depression, Louis hit upon the formula for Joe Glaser's longed-for commercial breakthrough with his recordings of two popular songs of the day: *I Can't Give You Anything But Love* (whose lyrics suited the depression mood) and Fats Waller's *Ain't Misbehavin'*. These hits from long-running Broadway shows made abrupt departures from the Hot Five's blues-and-jam format. Fronting big bands of no particular distinction, Louis stuck mainly to current popular hits, invariably starting in the low and middle range of the trumpet, sometimes with a cup mute, followed by his coarse-grained vocal, and climaxed with thrilling bravura explorations in the high register. Sentimental ballads like *Sweethearts on Parade* (Smic 3/2) were mixed with comic novelties like *Lonesome Road* and in-group "reefer" (marijuana) tunes like *Song of the Vipers* (Time-Life *Giants of Jazz*). The new format sold millions of records making Louis the first to complete the unusual trek from jazzman to superstar.

His nickname, "Satchmo' "—shortened from "Satchelmouth"—and his ecstatic grin were nearly as familiar to Depression America as the faces of Babe Ruth and the Marx Brothers. In 1932 he headlined the London Palladium and partied with the Prince of Wales. His reception on the Continent, especially in Paris, was frenzied. Thanks to Joe Glaser's ceaseless drum beating he landed lucrative cameo roles in Hollywood films, where as always, his trumpet took a back seat to singing and mugging.

By 1947, when big bands had become an untenable luxury only Ellington and a few others could afford, Louis formed his sextet of All-Stars that included former cohorts Earl Hines and Jack Teagarden. They returned to material from the Hot Five days, coinciding with a dixieland revival among the white middle class that demanded and got endless replays of *When the Saints Go Marching In*. Still, Louis's inspired trumpet and vocals in All-Star records like *That's For Me* (Time-Life *Giants of Jazz*) left no doubt that he was anything less than an eloquent improvisor. But

Earl Hines (left), Louis Armstrong, and Jack Teagarden: When the Big Band Era collapsed after World War II, Earl, Louis, and Jack disbanded their big bands to reunite as Louis Armstrong's All-Stars—and pose for this obvious publicity shot. (Photograph courtesy of the Rutgers Institute of Jazz Studies.)

the untamed adventures of youth now gave way to well-trod roads leading to the bank. To the despair of purist critics, Louis's nightclub and concert sets became as predictable as the tide, from the opening bars of *Indiana* to the showboat finish of his best-selling *Hello Dolly.* This was to be the image of Louis fixed in the public mind until his death in 1971.

Quite another image is cherished by critics and serious jazz lovers, particularly in Britain and Europe, who venerate the early Armstrong as a giant on a par with Stravinsky and Picasso but decry the latter-day Louis for "selling out." They could not reconcile the genius of *West End Blues* with the *Hello Dolly* minstrel shamelessly cavorting for white squares. Louis answered these critics in his remarkably candid interview with Richard Meryman:

> I'll play for the old-time people—they got all the money. In 1929, I was just idling away all day and blasting at night. Just trying to please the musicians. And they the ones with the passes, ain't puttin' out nothin'. These cats would bring their sandwiches, sit there and catch four shows a day. And I used to come off the stage,

almost had to be carried to the dressing room from running up and down, just blowin' and blowin' . . . to please the musicians. I forgot about the audience and it didn't do me no good. See, I think when I commenced to put a little showmanship in with the music people appreciated me better. The minute you sing *Hello Dolly,* there's always some cats out there saying "yeaaaaaaaaaaah!" Like the oldtimer told me when I left New Orleans, "stay before the public, please the public." Well, I'm with *him.* In *Hello Dolly,* the movements and the jive with the audience clapping, aw, it's all in fun. The people expect all that from me—comin' out all chesty, makin' faces. . . . I do that song *Hello Dolly* the same way every night because that's the way the people like it.

Musicians and critics who attacked Louis for pleasing the public tended to forget that his 1930s records of pop tunes still amaze us half a century later. One can imagine his disbelieving "aw, man," had he been told that these seventy-five-cent discs aimed at a mass market during the depression would still be in demand today. His versions of *Stardust, All of Me, Lazy River, Lord You Made the Night Too Long,* and dozens of other seasonal hits set the definitive standard for the next generation of jazz musicians and inspired countless youths regardless of color to pursue a jazz career. His glittering commercial success was ever a source of pride to blacks and a spur to musicians whose opportunities he expanded by tapping a vast new audience for American black music.

Early, Louis sensed our continuing national preference for vocal over instrumental music, and it was through his singing that his impact on the culture was most immediate. "Without Armstrong," wrote Richard Hadlock, "the story of jazz singing, up to and including Ray Charles, might have been quite different. His 'jive' vocals led directly to the styles of Cab Calloway, Louis Prima, the Boswell Sisters, the Mills Brothers, and his ballad singing deeply affected . . . Bing Crosby, Ethel Waters, Mildred Bailey, Lee Wiley and Billie Holiday" (Hadlock, *Jazz Masters of the Twenties.*) Holiday, hailed today as the premier jazz singer of all time, told how she wore out Louis's records as a child. Ethel Waters recorded a note-for-note imitation of his vocal on *I Can't Give You Anything But Love.* Flying in the face of current notions of pop singing, Louis's vocals, like Chaplin's comedy, worked on many levels to enrapture a total audience. People who had never heard authentic jazz were tickled by a voice they found funny and grotesque; canons of taste had blinded them to its rough-but-tender beauty that musicians found fully as inventive as his trumpet. With pop ballads like *Sweethearts on Parade* (Smic 3/2) and *I Gotta Right to Sing the Blues* (Smic 3/3), Louis went as far as he could with his intuitive merger of jazz and blues with the cream of white popular tunes and broadway show music. This was his permanent legacy, and it was left to his heirs—Roy Eldridge, Dizzy Gillespie, Lester Young, Charlie Christian, Charlie Parker,

John Coltrane—to build extensions of their father's house. From the early 1930s until his death forty years later, Louis made it clear that he had "paid his dues" to musicians and critics and lavished upon the public that made him rich the clowning and high-note virtuosity they paid for.

With the rise of the black consciousness movement, which first took root in the jazz community, Louis came under hostile attack from young modernists for being an Uncle Tom. Affronted by his goggle-eyed prancing for white folks and his antique racial asides, despised as the natural byproducts of his "old-time slave music," young black militants may have been unaware that Louis made his breakthrough during the worst of the depression. It was a time when blacks were "last hired and first fired," when a jazzman was socially synonymous with a pimp, and when whites, as well as "respectable" upwardly mobile blacks, were still decades away from accepting Miles Davis as a musician, rather than a tap-dancer, clown, minstrel man, or coon shouter. Most of Louis's angry black critics of the 1960s were yet unborn in 1931 when Louis introduced himself on a New Orleans radio show because the announcer refused to introduce "that nigger man." "It was the first time," Louis said, "that a Negro ever *spoke* on the radio down there."

His deep resentment of racial injustice was veiled by a grinning public mask, for he learned early that a black entertainer can't make waves. "It's all show business," he told Meryman in 1966, "I don't want to do nothin' that would ask people to . . . be depressed and thinking about marching and civil rights. We all have our moments for them problems."

Louis's "moment" came in 1957 when President Eisenhower refused to take action against Arkansas's Governor Faubus's anti-school-integration campaign in Little Rock. With an anger unprecedented in his long career, and at a time when public rebukes of the deified war-hero president were unheard of, Louis told an astonished press, "The president has no guts! The way they are treating my people in the South, the government can go to hell!" Seven years later, these out-of-character bursts of social outrage surfaced anew when he told newsmen after watching the 1965 Selma march on television: "They would beat Jesus if he was black and marched."

Charges that Louis was an Uncle Tom did not take into account what he had achieved at a time that seemed as remote to young urban blacks as the Civil War. Against the terrible odds of poverty and prejudice Louis emerged from the ghetto and a minstrel tradition to carve out an international empire. Unlike Nat "King" Cole and other front-rank jazz players, Louis did this to no lasting impairment of his talent. For all his catering to public taste—since the entertainer of his era knew no alternative to the obscurity and neglect that befell most of his breed—Louis was rarely anything less than a supreme musician, as was proved by many of his last records like *You Go To My Head* with Oscar Peterson, recorded when Louis was nearly sixty. The wonder of it is that his gifts were fully on a par with his rewards, an almost nonexistent blessing in the annals of American arts.

Earl "Fatha" Hines Revisited

Earl "Fatha" Hines, no less than Armstrong, was schooled in Joe Glaser's concept of pleasing the public, but Hines's dogged pursuit of the Bitch Goddess for over half a century met with middling success, at least in his own country. Hines still follows Louis's lead by singing and joking but does these indifferently. Fearful the public will not respond to a piano career cut loose from the trappings of old showbiz, Hines continues to play it safe, surrounding himself with bandsmen and vocalists, often inferior ones, rather than strike off on his own like Oscar Peterson. Through some miracle, his slavish devotion to a commercial format has done nothing to diminish his keyboard inventiveness that seems to multiply with every decade.

After his split with Armstrong in 1929, Hines embarked on a band-leading career with nightly broadcasts from the Grand Terrace Ballroom, a mob-owned club in Chicago. Although this hard-driving band featured solid arrangements and fine soloists sparked by the leader's high-voltage piano, it never cashed its chips during the Swing Era that made household names of Shaw and the Dorseys. Hounded by bad breaks and timing, he lost his best sidemen to more prestigious leaders like Ellington. In 1940 the Hines jinx was briefly broken by the two biggest record hits of his career: *Boogie-Woogie on the St. Louis Blues*, and *Jelly Jelly*, the sexually explicit urban blues that made an overnight star of his singing discovery, Billy Eckstine, who inspired, for better or worse, a legion of suave, lugubrious imitators. Meanwhile, Hines continued to record solos of his own compositions, like *Rosetta*, which made him the idol of younger pianists Teddy Wilson, Billy Kyle, and Nat Cole.

In the early 1940s Hines began a surprising new phase with a reorganized band that became a cradle of bebop or modern jazz. In hiring young revolutionaries like Charlie Parker, Dizzy Gillespie, and another singing discovery, Sarah Vaughan—the first woman vocalist to adapt bebop to a popular ballad style—Hines showed a capacity for change rare among his contemporaries like Armstrong who viewed this new music with fear and resentment. Louis even recorded an altered version of *The*

Whiffenpoof Song demeaning "Dizzy and all the cats at Birdland with their flatted fifths" as "poor little lambs who have lost their way." Being a "modernist" all along, Hines had little trouble relating to this strange new music, but with typical Hines luck this trailblazing bebop band never recorded due to an industry-wide recording ban by the musicians union in 1942 and 1943.

Pursuing a national trend, Hines junked his big band for good in 1947 to spend four years in a reunion with Armstrong and his All-Stars. Following this he found little market in the U.S. for his unclassifiable gifts in a doctrinaire era that split the jazz world into two warring factions— "modern" and "dixieland." Hines chose the latter in 1955 when he settled in the San Francisco area for a five-year run at Club Hangover with a six-piece combo, playing *Dixieland One-Step* and *High Society* on a 77 note spinet, careful to avoid modern chords that would clash with this older format, which he finally abandoned when the dixieland revival had run its course.

A robust athlete who looks far younger than his 77 years, Hines today shuttles between Europe, Asia, South America, and Japan in pursuit of the Armstrong-like fame that ever eluded him. Fronting lackluster combos, his programs are short on his timeless piano and long on crowd-pleasing gimmicks, interminable drum solos, and tasteless vocals. Yet when Hines decides to solo he shows the imagination and technique that never slacken, like some Bartók or Stravinsky turned on to jazz, daring more, swinging more than he did in the 1920s. Hines proves himself one of the few current pianists capable of sustaining an entire program without the customary crutch of bass and drums required by so many one-handed descendants of bebop wizard Bud Powell. With extended solo time on small jazz labels (Chiaroscuro, Master Jazz, Halcyon, Flying Dutchman), Hines emerges as a consistently rewarding soloist, never coasting, never falling back on meaningless runs, unpredictable save for his rocklike endurance, perpetual springboard beat, and recurrent ability to surprise.

Hines's solo engagements are rare in this country. In England and Europe his concerts attract sold-out crowds in leading concert halls and are reviewed in major journals, often by first-string classical critics like the London *Times'* Max Harrison (who also functions as a jazz critic). In sad contrast, recent solo concerts in his native San Francisco area barely filled 600-seat auditoriums and were not reviewed by a single metropolitan daily paper. Such experiences hardly encourage Hines to embark on the solo career that is rightfully his and ours. He continues to be hopelessly locked into a 1920s compulsion to "please the public" and lure the mass audience that has ever eluded him. (Earl Hines died in April 1983 just as this chapter was completed.)

Fats Waller: "Folks Loved to Hear Him Sing."

Hines and his friend Fats Waller were the twin founts from which all future pianists would drink, whether some young "modernists" know it or not. Waller boozed and partied to an early death in 1943 before he could fully reap the commercial rewards that began to fall within the jazzman's grasp after World War II. Still, his appeal among whites starting in the mid-1930s rivaled Armstrong's for much the same reasons. Both took identical roads to reconcile the demands of their art with those of the marketplace.

The wayward son of the minister of Harlem's Abbysinian Baptist Church, Thomas Waller showed an early talent for organ, piano, and the composing of joyous melodies that were to pour from his pen by the hundreds. Like Hines he was grounded in the classics, taking a special delight in Bach under the guidance of legitimate teachers. Dropping out of school at fourteen, he became an accomplished bluesman and theater organist, mastering the skills of accompanying silent movies. At seventeen he drew notice from the godfather of Harlem stride pianists-composers, James P. Johnson, who told his wife: "I know I can teach this boy." "From then on," said May Wright Johnson, "Fats would bang on our piano 'til sometimes three, four in the morning. I would say to him, 'Now go on home, or haven't you got a home?' But he'd come every day and my husband would teach. Of course, the organ doesn't give you a left hand, and that's what James P. had to teach him." (Hentoff-Shapiro, *Hear Me Talkin' to Ya.*)

Johnson was the patriarch of the ticklers who strove to "cut" each other in Harlem's jungle of cabarets and piano clubs, a fierce combative tribe that included Eubie Blake, Willie "The Lion" Smith, Abba Labba, Jack the Bear, Stephen "the Beetle" Henderson, Luckey Roberts, and the young disciple, Duke Ellington. No tickler would dare enter a club to assert his prowess until he had mastered Johnson's test piece, *Carolina Shout* (Smic 2/4), usually learned by slowing down a piano roll. Young Fats had the advantage of learning it from the master himself. A neglected genius yet to be given his due, Johnson wrote popular black Broadway revues with evergreen hits: *If I Could Be With You One Hour Tonight*, *Running Wild*, *Old Fashioned Love*, and the runaway dance craze, *Charleston*, that became synonymous with F. Scott Fitzgerald's "Jazz Age" of the Roaring Twenties. He also composed ambitious but rarely performed symphonic works and tone poems and remained in steady demand in record-

James P. Johnson: Fats Waller's teacher, the
godfather of Harlem "stride" pianists is still a
leading contender for the dubious honor of
America's most neglected musical genius.
(Photograph from the Richard Hadlock
Collection.)

ing studios as a one-man-band behind Bessie Smith and Ethel Waters.
After a series of crippling strokes from which he recovered again and
again with little loss of his pianistic powers, James P. Johnson died in
1955, shrouded in obscurity but leaving a treasure of recordings and piano rolls that proved him the "stride" tickler without equal until the flow-
ering of his pupil, Fats Waller.

The alliance of Johnson and Waller was suggestive of Haydn and
Mozart. Fats was no innovator, adding little to what James P. had done but
taking the elder's style and raising it to new heights of artistry and public
acceptance. As Robert Craft said of Mozart, "If he had never lived, the
history of music may have been no different, but it would have been im-
measurably poorer."

Fats's "take charge" personality overflowed into piano and organ
romps bursting with uncontained joy, delicacy, and that melding of disci-

pline and abandon so peculiar to jazz. None who came before, and few who came after could equal his walloping left or the sneaky behind-the-beat laciness of his meticulous right. At any tempo his beat was swinging and contagious. No one could top his ability to charge up a small combo.

If Fats's reputation had rested on his keyboard work alone he might have shared the fate of James P. Johnson as a "musician's musician," but Fats had other gifts denied his quiet, reserved teacher—a zest for showmanship fully the equal of Armstrong's, a droll bust-out humor, and a bumptious way of burlesquing trite pop tunes. As with Louis, it was Fats's singing and clowning that wooed and won the public. His millions of fans found his piano merely a frolicsome backdrop for his comedy. In the mid-1930s he cut the first of over 300 records for Victor and Bluebird that endeared him to the nation as a poke-fun singer. Aptly titled "Fats Waller and his Rhythm," his gleeful sextet resounded on juke boxes and radio with *I'm Gonna Sit Right Down and Write Myself a Letter*, and *Flat Foot Floogie*, whose foolish lyrics became sitting ducks for outrageous lampoons punctuated with raffish cries of "Aaaaaaaaah mercy!" and "One nevah knows, *do* one?" His repute as a singer was matched by his success as a composer of nearly 500 songs, many of which remain standards: *Ain't Misbehavin'*, *Honeysuckle Rose, Keepin' Out of Mischief Now*, and *Jitterbug Waltz*. Recent research firms up the belief that he also wrote a number of hits sold outright to other songwriters for a pittance: *On the Sunny Side of the Street* and *I Can't Give You Anything But Love*. His piano and organ compositions—*Viper's Drag, African Ripples, Handful of Keys*—comprised his finest work but never approached the sale of boisterous novelties like *Your Feets Too Big* or *The Joint is Jumpin'*. These parodies displayed his sure instinct for combining popular appeal with solid musicianship. Like Armstrong, his singing was firmly rooted in jazz, but unlike Louis, his playing, and that of his sidemen, never strayed beyond the bounds of taste. Nearly all of his records include generous dollops of superb piano along with the buffoonery, spurring his combo to outswing themselves. *You're Not the Only Oyster in the Stew* (Time-Life *Giants of Jazz, Waller*) is a model of how to swing at a slow tempo; the breakneck *Oh, Susanna!* has never been matched for pure, rollicking stride or *Our Love was Meant to Be* for unabashed lyric beauty. Dizzy Gillespie said, "Fats did what I've always been trying to do; he played good music while himself and his audience were having fun."

Beneath the mask of carefree abandon, Fats was plagued by musical frustrations that never troubled Gillespie. His reedman Gene Sedric said:

> Fats was sometimes very unhappy about his music. He was appreciated for his showmanship ability, but very few of Waller's fans knew how much more he could

play than what he usually did on records. He didn't try to prove anything with his singing. It was a matter of fun with him. But I deeply believe that, in later years, his novelty singing and his showmanship overshadowed his playing. Yet he wanted to do great things on organ and piano—which he could do. There were many times when we played engagements during which he felt like himself and wanted to play great. But when he played as musically as he could, many people in the audience would think he was lying down and they'd yell, "Come on, Fats!" He'd take a swig of gin or something and say resignedly, "Aw right, here 'tis." (Hentoff-Shapiro, *Hear Me Talkin' to Ya.*)

Fats's son Maurice was even more revealing about his father's failure to reconcile artistic with commercial demands:

He had a terrific personality that overlorded his true greatness at the piano. I used to sit listening to him play at home until four in the morning sometimes. That's when he wasn't entertaining, just playing. He spent a lot of times composing things that were never published . . . they weren't commercial. (Maurice Waller, *Fats Waller.*)

When Waller's son answered the inevitable question, "Are you any relation to Fats Waller?" the invariable response was, "Oh, I just *loved* to hear him *sing!*" It is as though Leonardo da Vinci were remembered only as a cartoonist of toothless old crones.

Duke Ellington:
Our Greatest Composer

We look to the future for the American composer, not, indeed, to the Horatio Parkers and Edward MacDowells of the present, who are taking over a foreign act ready-made and are imitating it . . . but to someone as yet unknown . . . who will sing the songs of his own nation, his own time and his own character. (London *Times*, 1913.)

Of the three seminal jazz artists to gain mass acclaim before World War II, Duke Ellington is the most difficult to explain. His veiled, princely psyche, more complex than Armstrong's or Waller's, was given to philosophical turns and levels of sophistication uncommon for jazz musicians of his time. Duke's canny coming to terms with commercial, racial, and internal pressures that collapsed less hardy peers from Fletcher Henderson to Charlie Parker has long been a source of fascination—and annoyance—to critic-spectators of the maddening clash between the Duke as artist and the Duke as crowd-pleasing showman.

Edward Kennedy Ellington was born in 1899 to an educated, well-to-do Washington, D.C. family that enveloped him in the unstinting love and

Duke Ellington: "If it were not for my orchestra, how could I hear my music?"
(Photograph courtesy of the Rutgers Institute of Jazz Studies.)

security worthy of an ideal Freudian upbringing. Marked as a special child, he was started on piano at seven and soon cultivated the poise, flair for leadership, and ducal charm that earned him his title. Smitten with ragtime, the teenaged Ellington gave up a painting career to gig around Washington as band pianist at parties and dances. "I was getting so big," he told his Boswell, the British critic Stanley Dance, "that I had to study some music to protect my reputation. I had elementary lessons at school, and I used to slow down James P. Johnson piano rolls and copy them note for note. Now Doc Perry taught me about reading and I took harmony lessons from Henry Grant." (Dance, *The World of Duke Ellington*.)

Duke's move to New York brought him into after-hours contact with Harlem's piano kings, James P. Johnson and Willie "The Lion" Smith, whose two-fisted styles left a lifelong mark on Ellington both as pianist and composer. Fronting a six-piece band at Broadway's Kentucky Club, a popular hangout for musicians and showpeople, Ellington launched his half-century career as bandleader in the mid-1920s with scarcely a glimmer of the glories to follow within a matter of months. His first records sound pitifully dated beside the concurrent Henderson and Morton; compare Henderson's 1926 *Stampede* (Smic 3/6) to Ellington's *Animal Crackers* recorded the same year. But "Duke Ellington and his Washingtonians" bore seeds of greatness that soon germinated to push orchestral jazz beyond its strict function as dance music and into the hothouse of abstract art. Much of the credit for the origins of what critics were soon to

78

call "the Ellington effect" belongs to "growl" trumpeter Bubber Miley, whose toilet-plunger mute evoked plaintive sobbings and terror-ridden screams. His ageless solos with the early Ellington Band stun the listener with all the force of Armstrong leaping out of the earth-bound Henderson band; they pointed in the direction Duke was to follow all his life.

Late in 1927, a year after Ellington waxed such cornball novelties as *Animal Crackers*, the band made an incredible leap forward with a series of blues that cast Miley in the role of co-composer and the dominant solo voice: *The Black and Tan Fantasy, Creole Love Call, The Mooche*, and the band's theme for many years, *East St. Louis Toodle-oo* (Smic 6/4, 6/5). For more than four decades these ominous mood pieces formed the keystone of Ellington's ever-growing repertoire, nourishing a forest of offshoots. With each new version the scoring was enriched, and Ellington's piano developed from its lame ragtime parlour style in the early 1920s into an essential part of the band, providing orchestral fills, backing soloists either as a "stride" accompaniment or in lush, romantic modes that set Duke apart as a distinctive piano voice. But his proud succession of trumpeters were instructed never to stray from the paths carved by Bubber Miley, dead at 29, one of jazz's endless victims of the Prohibition high life.

The Ellington-Miley "jungle style" evolved from necessity at Harlem's Cotton Club where the band began a five-year tenure in 1927 that had germinal effects on Duke's music. An expensive mob-owned club offering lavishly costumed productions with large casts, the Cotton Club catered to white-tie and ermined slummers in naive quest of primitive tribal rites provided by the clever management in the guise of coffee-colored chorines in palm-leaf scanties, avidly pursued by nearly naked African chiefs to the lewd shrieks of Ellington's wa-wa brass and wailing reeds. Ellington had to write background scores for these constantly-changing floor shows, pushing him into composing abstract tone poems and impressionist mood pieces, unlike other black bandleaders of that time who performed almost exclusively for dancers. Duke caught the eye of shrewd business agent Irving Mills who arranged for a regular radio broadcast from the Cotton Club that spread Duke's fame beyond the confines of Harlem and the jazz subculture.

With mounting success, Ellington swelled his band to full Henderson proportions with an unmatched wealth of distinctive soloists. Commanding the devotion and loyalty of his long-term crew, he imposed his benign will on this symbiotic group that turned rehearsals and performances into spontaneous arranging workshops. The ill-fated Miley was succeeded by Cootie Williams who mastered the "plunger's" art under the guidance of Joseph "Tricky Sam" Nanton, a sorcerer who used the plumber's friend to turn the trombone into a human voice crying in anguish, laughing obscenely, or growling in anger. The grand tradition of

New Orleans clarinet virtuosity lived on in Barney Bigard, whose liquid, bluesy reed fluttered like a crazy flag above the stomping ensemble charged by the big-toned whump of Wellman Braud's bass. Johnny Hodges sang through his alto sax with a silky authority unchallenged until the advent of Charlie Parker. Hawkins disciple Harry Carney was the first to coax jazz from the cumbersome baritone sax and served as anchorman of the reed section for almost fifty years. Decades-long tenures in the Ellington band were not uncommon and account in large part for the steady evolution of the "Ellington effect" and the proficiency of difficult ensemble passages. Such constancy of personnel made a further testament to the leader's unmatched charisma and managerial aplomb in a business where performers were as touchy as opera divas and prone to change shop with breathtaking dispatch.

Writing with the individual timbres and styles of his stellar soloists in mind, Ellington created an inimitable body of music. He broke all the rules of music schools and harmony books, writing only what sounded good to him, neither knowing nor caring that music academies said it couldn't be done. In 1927 he scored the wordless vocal of Adelaide Hall as a coequal jazz soloist in *Creole Love Call*. He was the first to write true concerti for individual band members. He composed chamber jazz for odd combinations: bass clarinet, muted trombone, tenor sax, and baritone sax in the high register. André Previn said: "Stan Kenton stands before a hundred reeds and brass, makes a dramatic gesture, and every studio arranger in the audience knows just how it's done; Duke Ellington lifts his little finger, three horns make a sound—and nobody knows *what* it is." Straining at the three-minute limit imposed by the standard in the record industry, he became the first authentic jazz composer to write and record extended works, starting in 1931 with *Creole Rhapsody* (Smic 6/6). His briefer compositions numbered over two thousand. Ellington's gift for massing unique orchestral sounds, plus his boundless irridescent charm, elegance of carriage, speech and dress, and unruffled dignity, were the admiration of all musicians from Armstrong to Coltrane. Dizzy Gillespie said, "I break out in gooseflesh every time Duke comes into a place."

DUKE'S MIXTURE: THE ELLINGTON FUSION

Big band jazz of New York
Ragtime
Harlem "stride" piano
Broadway and Follies show music
Popular songs of the day
New Orleans jam
New Orleans clarinet tradition—Barney Bigard
Kansas City tenor sax tradition—Ben Webster

Bubber Miley's "jungle style"
The blues in endless variations
Impressionist European harmony—Debussy, Ravel, Delius
Latin influence—Juan Tizol, *Caravan, The Flaming Sword*
Black gospel music—*Come Sunday*
Modern string bass—Jimmy Blanton
Mood and "jungle" pieces as backgrounds for dance productions
Original ballads—*Sophisticated Lady, Solitude, Mood Indigo*
First use of human voice as an instrument in jazz—*Creole Love Call*
First extended jazz compositions—*Creole Rhapsody, Reminiscing in Tempo*
First authentic jazz concerti—*Clarinet Lament, Concerto for Cootie*
"Ellington units"—chamber jazz
Portraits of black artists—Florence Mills, Willie "The Lion" Smith
Avant-garde bebop—*Cottontail*
Billy Strayhorn's composing-arranging
Impressionist tone poems—*Perfume Suite, Tone Parallel to Harlem*
"Train" pieces—*Daybreak Express, Happy-Go-Lucky Local*
Sacred Concerts

His uncanny way of coming up with the right word at the right time was legendary. When his tenor sax star Ben Webster told him, "Governor— you've got to pay me more money! You're workin' me to *death!*" Ellington replied softly, "But Ben—I can't afford to pay you what you're worth—*nobody* can." (Time-Life *Giants of Jazz*, Album notes.)

Ellington's reputation as a hit tune writer was launched in 1930 with the haunting blues-tinged *Mood Indigo*, followed by *Sophisticated Lady, Solitude, In a Sentimental Mood, It Don't Mean a Thing if It Ain't Got that Swing, I Let a Song Go Out of My Heart, Satin Doll, Caravan* and *Perdido* (both written with his trombonist, Juan Tizol), and dozens more that survive today in the repertoire of all musicians and vocalists, pop as well as jazz.

In 1933 his aggressive manager organized the first of many band tours to England and the Continent where Ellington was stunned to find himself lionized by fanatical record collectors, classical music critics, composers, famous intellectuals, and royalty who did not dance to his music but listened, convincing him of its durability and worth. This first encounter with British and French devotees prompted him to compose more ambitious and extended works.

When the Ellington band seemed to have reached its peak in the late 1930s, three additions thrust it to even greater heights—that have yet to be scaled in the history of big band jazz. In 1938 Billy Strayhorn joined as staff arranger-composer and Ellington alter ego. Submerging himself in the Ellington idiom, the shy, diminutive Strayhorn made an incalculable contribution to the Ellington book. From the time he pooled his talent with Ellington's until his death thirty years later, few scores in which Strayhorn did not have a hand found their way into the band's library. *Take the A Train*, which succeeded *East St. Louis Toodle-oo* as the band's theme song, was entirely his doing. Few songwriters ever matched the melodic invention of *Passion Flower, Day Dream, Chelsea Bridge,* or *Lush Life*, whose exquisite melody was perfectly matched by Strayhorn's own lyrics. Guitarist Mundell Lowe said *Lush Life* is one of the few songs he knows that requires no improvisation because the line as written cannot be improved. Strayhorn's ballads are not as well known as Ellington's, possibly because they are rather difficult to sing.

The bursting-at-the-seams tenor sax of Ben Webster, battle-tested in marathon Kansas City cutting sessions, was employed in 1939 to augment the long-tenured reed section. Whether on up-tempo stomps like *Cotton-tail*, dirty blues like *Sepia Panorama*, dreamy ballads like *All Too Soon*, or

Billy Strayhorn and Duke Ellington: This musical symbiosis, rare in any art form, endured from 1939—when Strayhorn joined the band as composer, arranger, and Ellington's alter-ego—until Strayhorn's death in 1967. (Photograph from the Ralph J. Gleason Collection.)

Ben Webster: Tenor sax veteran of countless
Kansas City cutting contests, Ben joined the
Ellington reeds in 1939 to fire up Duke's
"Golden Era" band lusting for a new voice.
(Photograph from the Richard Hadlock
Collection.)

the moody introspection of *Blue Serge* (Smic 7/3), Ben fired up a band
lusting for a new voice. Since no book was written for Ben he had to "find
my own note," imparting an indefinable dissonant wail to the reeds that
sent critics back to the thesaurus for new adjectives of celebration.

The most revolutionary change came with the addition of Jimmy
Blanton, the first "modern" bassist to use the instrument melodically as
well as rhythmically. Plucking or bowing with violinlike agility, Blanton
imparted a new drive to the band and upset all previous notions of bass
playing, heretofore rooted in the whump-whump concept carried over
from the tuba. "Blanton was the first bass player I heard who had this
carryover from note to note," said his disciple Ray Brown, "and those
notes just *rang*! I used to play along with his records with Ellington when I
got home from high school, and he made a large impact on me." (Chevron
School Broadcast, "Music Makers.") Ray Brown was not alone; during his
two brief years with Ellington before his death from tuberculosis at the age
of 21, the shy unassuming Blanton convinced all future bassists from Oscar Pettiford to Mingus and Richard Davis that there was no other way to
play this once-clumsy instrument. The dramatic difference between Blan-

ton and all bassists who came before him can be plotted by hearing his work on *Ko-Ko* (Smic 7/2), *Harlem Air Shaft* (Smic 6/7), and *Blue Serge* (Smic 7/3) and comparing it with the bass on Ellington's earlier records like *Creole Rhapsody* (Smic 6/6), with Count Basie's bassist on *Taxi War Dance* (Smic 5/8), or with Fletcher Henderson's *Wrappin' It Up* (Smic 3/7).

The triumvirate of Strayhorn, Webster, and Blanton signaled the golden age of Ellington—1940 to 1942. Of the many Victor recordings from this period, few are anything less than consummate masterpieces, and none give the listener anything more than an approximation of what this miracle of a band sounded like in person. Meanwhile, individual soloists with the band—Johnny Hodges, Rex Stewart, Barney Bigard, Cootie Williams—fronted their own recording sessions of "Ellington units," cadres of seven or eight band members, usually with Duke on piano, who left a legacy of distinctive chamber jazz.

The war years of the 1940s cost Ellington many of his key men, and he began to lean on Strayhorn when the going got rough in an era that wiped out most of the big bands. Wholesale changes in 1950 brought in a crew of modernists—trumpeter Clark Terry and drummer Louis Bellson. Aside from brief flashes of glory the band rarely caught the inspirational fire of the youthful 1920s and the mature 1940s. As the band grew more dispirited, Ellington's piano, once fashionably dismissed as technically limited, took on added luster and magnificence to become the dominant voice in the ensemble, suggesting that his more obvious gifts as composer-arranger had long overshadowed his keyboard prowess. "Nobody realizes how much piano Duke can play," said Johnny Hodges. His twilight years became a triumph of honorary degrees, White House invitations, and sacred concerts in American cathedrals. When he was denied the Pulitzer prize at the age of 66, prompting indignant resignations from that Committee, he responded with his customary put-on suavity: "Fate is being kind to me; Fate does not want me to become too famous, too young." His death in 1974 was mourned in headlines, not consigned to the back-page oblivion usual for jazz obituaries in the American press.

In more subtle and unsettling ways than Armstrong or Waller, Ellington's obsession for mass adulation colored the public performances of his declining years. Carried to quirkish extremes as though to spite critics, his compulsive pandering to a total audience was long the despair of purists, especially abroad where devotees had little knowledge of the racial, economic, or cultural pressures that shaped the music they embraced with messianic fervor, largely through the social vacuum of the phonograph. His first London concert of 1933, an outrage to most of the 4,500 fans and critics who had committed his records to memory, followed a pattern Ellington was to repeat throughout his career. British critic Derek Jewell reported: "When Ellington heard some people laughing during the 'growl' solos of 'Tricky Sam' Nanton and Cootie Williams, and perceived a certain restlessness when the band played slower numbers, he switched to items from his vaudeville routines." This shocked the faithful who came from all over Europe to bathe in the evocative mysteries of *Black and Tan Fantasy* and *The Mooche*. To Duke's boundless amusement, Irish critic Spike Hughes issued bulletins to the audience warning them not to laugh at "Tricky Sam's" plunger trombone, "which is not humor but a great work of art," and enjoined spectators not to applaud solos but to wait until the end of a number, just as they would at any concert recital. (Fifty years later, jazz audiences still ignore Hughes's injunction.) In the 1960s Jewell wrote: "Ellington's European concerts consisted entirely of old favorites, although Duke later claimed that this was because audiences demanded the numbers and wouldn't let the band get on to newer stuff like the *Liberian Suite*." (Jewell, *Duke*.)

As Ellington's career progressed his public facade grew ever more whimsical. Concert and night club appearances grew almost as predictable as Armstrong's, with dreary repeats of limp routines: Harry Carney holding the interminable note on *Sophisticated Lady*; Tenor saxist Paul Gonsalves cranked up in the vain hope of recapturing the frenzy of his 27 blues choruses of *Crescendo in Blue* that electrified the 1956 Newport Jazz Festival; marathon drum solos of dubious taste, and Duke's perennial bid for a piece of the rock'n'roll action: *One More Time* bellowed by the most degraded singer Duke could find. Prime soloists like Cootie Williams and Lawrence Brown were limited to one brief solo per show, and strangest of all, Duke coached his men to repeat note-for-note the solos they had created on records, as though he felt the public wanted to hear nothing they had not heard before. To dissuade Ellington from the jaded programming critics had come to expect, Monterey Jazz Festival founder Jimmy Lyons commissioned him to compose a special suite for the 1960 Festival. Knowing well that if Duke was asked not to program threadbare routines he would be certain to include them out of perversity, Lyons hit upon the devious ploy of billing the concert "Ellington Carte Blanche," with frequent reminders to the maestro that the evening was his to do as he wished. At a rehearsal the night before the debut of his new work, *Suite Thursday*, Ellington spent most of an hour on a tricky eight-bar passage for tenor sax and two muted trombones. As he told a successful bandleader who advised him to cut his weekly payroll of $4,500 when the grosses failed to cover it, "The band you run has got to please the audience. The band I run has got to please *me*. If it were not for my band, how could I hear my music?" But when "Ellington Carte Blanche" was offered to 7200 fans, aside from the marvelous *Suite Thursday* the program was identical to what all had heard before, down to the detestable finale of *One More Time*. When a brash critic admonished him publicly for repeating such clichés Ellington, in a rare display of temper, waved his arm toward his orchestra and shouted: "Look! What you see on that stage are fifteen men making a living!" These paradoxes were an eternal part of the Ellington mystique.

Ellington seemed to hunger for the massive audience his nation always denied him. Despite his prestige abroad he never rivaled Benny Goodman, Tommy Dorsey, Glenn Miller, Artie Shaw, Stan Kenton, or Dave Brubeck in their heyday. His records sold well though never in the league with Shaw's *Begin the Beguine,* Miller's *In the Mood,* or Brubeck's *Take Five,* let alone the Jefferson Airplane's *White Rabbit.* He had cause to be cynical of what critics advised him to play. Brutal attacks on his 1935 experimental four-part *Reminiscing in Tempo* left ugly scars; "I only wrote it for them!" was his wounded cry on reading the scornful reviews from Britain and Europe. His most ambitious extended work, *Black, Brown and Beige,* was poorly received when premiered at Carnegie Hall in 1943, and it took 35 years for a recording of the fifty-minute work to be issued in its entirety (Fantasy-Prestige). Ironically, his best music was played in the early 1940s to acres of dancers crowding a few listeners huddled near the bandstand. In his final years, when no one danced and everyone listened, his concert performances could verge on embarrassment. Like some cold sober John Barrymore, Ellington lived out his days in a perverse parody of his enormous talent with dogged reruns of popular hits and flippant baubles like *Pretty and the Wolf.* Once-charged-up bandsmen sat night after night like bored mandarins, victims of Byron's "awful yawn which sleep cannot abate." Their leader always lusted after that monster record hit, the all-time bestseller he felt was his due. Audiences in the United States were never large enough. In every major foreign city he would hold court backstage for the great and near-great, but in his own country he never lured the round-the-block crowds that the Kingston Trio or Tijuana Brass did. Toward the end he sensed the public might not hold still for his best work, like the orchestral suites and Sacred Concerts into which he poured his final energies.

Yet for all his crochets, quirks, and put-ons, Ellington could still astound, even to the last. Though his bands grew indifferent and time-serving in later years, he remained a prolific, often inspired composer and his piano an ever-increasing source of wonder. This magic, or the hope of it, kept us coming back to Ellington to the end.

"Jazz Is Too Good for Americans."
(Dizzy Gillespie, *Esquire.*)

Few black artists who came of age in the 1920s were as lucky as Armstrong, Ellington, and Waller. Most could count themselves fortunate to command a cult following, mainly in England and Europe where the cults

Duke Ellington: (Photograph from the Ralph J. Gleason Collection.)

Duke Ellington: Critics and purist fans had long been befuddled and annoyed by the often maddening conflict between Ellington the artist and Ellington the crowd-pleasing showman (see photo on page 87). (Photograph by Grover Sales.)

were larger and where relative freedom from racial tension and the readiness to embrace jazz as serious art music has swelled the ranks of expatriate jazzmen since the 1930s. Ellington cornetist Rex Stewart spoke of the "restorative effect" of European tours: "You have to be a Negro to understand why. You can go anywhere, talk to anybody. You've eaten hot dogs all your life and are suddenly offered caviar. You can't believe it." (Hentoff-Shapiro, *Hear Me Talkin' to Ya.*) Sidney Bechet could not support himself in music and ran a tailor shop in Harlem in the late 1930s before he spent his last blissful years in France where, wrote Leonard Feather, "he transcended jazz fame to become a national vaudeville figure and . . . personality in the Maurice Chevalier class." In Paris you can find Rue Bechet intersecting Rue Armstrong. The first jazz book of consequence was written by a Belgian, Robert Goffin, the second by a Frenchman, Hugues Panassié. The first exhaustive discography was the work of another

Frenchman, Charles Delaunay. Britain has spawned many superior jazz journals and scholars—Max Harrison, Leonard Feather, Charles Fox, Stanley Dance. An Italian firm issued every record Bix Beiderbecke made, including multiple takes, in fourteen volumes. Companies in Australia, Argentina, New Zealand, France, Britain, and Germany reissued massive sets of Ellington, Bechet, Armstrong, and Henderson.

White musicians as well as black began to follow the expatriate route: tenor saxists Dexter Gordon and Stan Getz, trumpeter Bill Coleman, and the father of modern bebop drumming, Kenny Clarke, who warned Charlie Parker during a Parisian tour: "Bird, you're slowly and surely committing suicide in America. Come over here and *live*. Here you will be treated as an artist—the French understand these things." (Russell, *Bird Lives!*)

When Parker returned to New York in 1951 the police barred him from playing in Birdland, the club named for him, due to a drug violation. Billie Holiday, the cult jazz/comic Lord Buckley, and many others suffered the same loss of livelihood when police withheld their "cabaret card" work permit in the jazz capital of the world. Veteran clarinetist Albert Nicholas, widely admired for his flawless technique and sumptuous tone, worked in a New York subway because his style was at variance with current fashions. Few audiences are as parochial as American jazz fans, or more ruthless in dismissing as "old-time cats" the heroes of the past. Some older musicians like Earl Hines hung tough by playing dixieland, making careful concessions to white tastes and living up to what they thought white audiences expected. Author Richard Wright told how his parents beat him to make him aware of the disguises needed for survival in the white world.

The White Jazzman as Dropout

It may seem odd that white jazzmen of the 1920s and early 1930s found even fewer opportunities to make a living from this music than their black counterparts. Black bandleader George Morrison told Gunther Schuller, "When I first started out my career in 1911, if a white boy picked up an instrument it was a disgrace to his family. They'd disown him. They wanted nothing but the colored man to play for them." (Schuller, *Early Jazz*.) Except for militantly middle-class blacks (like Fats Waller's father) bent on aping whites, playing jazz was a step up, a legal escape from drudgery and its humiliations. Black artists were rooted in their culture, but the white jazzman was in open rebellion and learned to live with— and maybe glory in—the role of outcast. The sudden explosion of jazz during World War I seduced archetypal white dropouts—second-generation German, Jewish, Italian, and Irish teenagers from Illinois, Texas, Missouri, and Iowa on their way to becoming second basemen, doctors, bartenders, racketeers, and accountants until whipped around by the sound of jazz.

Despite the deep aversion of respectable whites to "nigger music," jazz began to infect genteel families like the Goodmans, the Dorseys, and the remarkable Teagardens of Texas. Helen Teagarden, a ragtime piano teacher, schooled her four children, including the great trombonist-singer Jack, to become professional jazz musicians. The Teagardens openly consorted with blacks in Harlem clubs, jam sessions, and recording studios in the 1920s, a time when interracial encounters other than clandestine sexual couplings were unheard of outside the jazz community. Ellington trumpeter Louis Metcalf admired these early whites

> who fought to prove the value of jazz. It was known as "jig" (black) music, and those men like Jack Teagarden, Benny Goodman, and the Dorseys had to fight it all the way. They didn't care nothing about color or that jazz had a bad stamp to it. Why, Bix would come uptown to Harlem to blow with us, eat with us, sleep with us. (Hentoff-Shapiro, *Hear Me Talkin' to Ya.*)

The Teagardens of Texas/1933: From left to right are trumpeter Charles, trombonist Jack, pianist Norma, mother Helen, and drummer Cub. Ragtime pianist Helen Teagarden raised all her children as jazz musicians. (Photograph courtesy of Norma Teagarden.)

The Teagardens of Texas/1953: Norma, Jack, Cub, Charles, and Helen. Ragtime pianist Helen Teagarden raised all her children as jazz musicians. (Photograph courtesy of Norma Teagarden.)

When Jewish clarinetist Milton "Mezz" Mezzrow, the prototype of Norman Mailer's "white Negro," was jailed for selling marijuana, he entered his race as "Negro" on the police blotter, preferring the jailhouse company of "my people" over that of white squares and racists. White trumpeter and Armstrong copyist Jack Purvis "wanted to play with colored bands so bad," said bassist Pops Foster, "that he stayed out in the sun for hours getting tanned, and then he'd black his face." (Foster, *Autobiography of Pops Foster*.) When Armstrong played in Chicago's Sunset Cafe in the 1920s, club manager Joe Glaser "let all the white kids in free—Benny Goodman, Muggsy Spanier, Tommy Dorsey, Gene Krupa—hell, they were kids and never had any money." (Hentoff-Shapiro, *Hear Me Talkin' to Ya*.)

The religious zeal of these white acolytes involved taking a vow of poverty, never dreaming they could make a living, let alone get rich, from "playing hot." Black sidemen with Henderson, Ellington, and Don Redman, for all their daily bouts on the road with racism, brutality, terrible

food, crummy hotels, and jim-crow sheriffs, did enjoy the luxury of playing uninhibited jazz night after night on the job. The white musician resigned himself to better paid but musically strangling tenures with
"sweet" hotel society orchestras, vaudeville outfits, and what Benny
Goodman despised as "funny-hat bands." Leaders like Ben Pollack and
Red Nichols, who gave Goodman and Teagarden a chance to stretch out,
were rare. The best a white jazzman could hope for until the mid-1930s
was a chair in the huge well-paid aggregation of Paul Whiteman, world
celebrated as "The King of Jazz," where the third cornet of Bix Beiderbecke was allowed a few brief outbursts per show to enliven pompous
concert arrangements of *Sweet Sue* and *Dardenella*. Bix's most promising
disciple, Jimmy McPartland, drudged in Art Kassel's commercial dance
band during Prohibition for a healthy $140 a week, "but a clause in my
contract said we would play so much jazz. I wouldn't take the job otherwise." (Hentoff-Shapiro, *Hear Me Talkin' to Ya.*) This clannish white jazz
clique could only let go in unpaid after-hours jam sessions in Harlem in
the days when whites could still safely go there or on rare record dates
connived by entrepreneur-critic John Hammond or guitarist Eddie Condon. Condon was an unstoppable missionary with a salty Irish wit who
organized interracial record dates throughout the worst of the depression
in the face of mulish opposition from segregation-minded record executives. The market crash of '29 that ruined the record market, combined
with the public taste for the "sweet" or "mickey mouse" bands of Guy
Lombardo and Meyer Davis, convinced white jazzmen they would never
make a living from the music they loved. All this changed overnight
in 1935, less than two decades after the Original Dixieland Jazz Band
launched the "Jazz Age."

The "Jazz Age"
of the Roaring Twenties

Though the 1917 recordings of the Original Dixieland Jazz Band (ODJB)
strike us as laughably dated today, their importance to black players as
well as whites would be hard to exaggerate. These first records of jazz
music of any sort started an international jazz-dance mania during World
War I that surpassed the ragtime fever of 1900. The ODJB's first release
was the first million-seller in phonograph history, and their influence on
the coming generation of white players like Beiderbecke was incalculable.
Even though the ODJB had more in common with vaudeville than with
authentic black New Orleans jazz, they composed a large body of excellent marching band tunes and blues that weathered well to form staples of
dixieland combos to this day: *Original Dixieland One-Step, Sensation Rag,
Bluein' the Blues, Lazy Daddy, Livery Stable Blues*, with its raucous barn-

The Original Dixieland Jazz Band/c. 1917: They cut the first jazz records, which launched the "jazz age" of the Roaring Twenties. Notice that the "front-line" dixieland instruments of cornet, clarinet, and trombone came out of the marching bands. (Photograph from the Richard Hadlock Collection.)

yard brayings, and *Clarinet Marmalade*, a jazz adaptation of a marching band showpiece for the piccolo.

This dizzying success of the ODJB was the start of another recurring phenomenon in American music, including rock 'n' roll: Each successive wave of Afro-American music, from the "Jazz Age" through the Rock era, made its first impact on white middle-class youths by way of white imitations of authentic black music. (According to legend, before the Victor Talking Machine Company gambled on the ODJB they offered black New Orleans trumpeter Freddie Keppard the chance to make the first jazz records, but Keppard refused because he "didn't want people stealing my stuff off records.")

Another recurrent pattern throughout the twentieth century is that white middle-class youth always adopted black music as their anthem of revolt against the culture of the elders, beginning with ragtime's assault upon rigid Victorian moral-sexual codes. Catalyzed by the sudden changes unloosed by World War I, the "Jazz Age" signaled one of the most dramatic breaks with social convention in all history. You have only to compare the dress and hairstyles of women before and after the war to grasp these changes that scandalized pulpit and press. Such changes were worldwide as was deftly chronicled in the BBC television series *Upstairs, Downstairs*. "Flaming Youth" was the name the media hung on the rebellious young, openly defying the law of Prohibition and the sexual taboos of their parents. Addicted to jazz dancing of a frankly provocative nature—the Charleston, Black Bottom, and Bunny Hug—"Flaming Youth"

93

was also known as the "Lost Generation" of a country swept into war on a tidal wave of hysterical jingoism, only to be washed ashore after the Armistice of 1918 on a desolate beach of disillusionment. It was the age of debunking as post-war youths discovered that the "War to make the world safe for Democracy" was a horrible nationalist bloodletting to make the world safe for profits. "Everything they told us about the war," said the Lost Generation, "was a lie. Everything they told us about sex, God, flag, home and Mother, was a lie." If this sounds familiar to those who came of age in the fifties and sixties, it is not because "History Repeats Itself" as the cliché goes; the anti-war movement, radical movement, women's movement, sexual freedom and birth control movement, and the black movement were well underway before and during the 1920s until interrupted by the depression and the rise of Hitler, which forced more pressing concerns on the tribe. This historical continuum was further interrupted by World War II, followed immediately by the cold war and McCarthyism, only to break out anew with a vengeance in the mid-1950s.

Life in Prohibition America had become so stifling that famous artists and writers like Gertrude Stein, Ernest Hemingway, Ezra Pound, and T. S. Eliot fled to England and the sidewalk cafes of Paris. The misfits of Winesburg, Ohio and Sauk Center followed the lead of Europe half a century earlier by fleeing to the bohemias of Greenwich Village and Chicago, refuges for writers, painters, poets, town atheists, homosexuals, "free souls," radicals, socialists, anarchists, and the disciples of Freud, Marx, Thorstein Veblen, Stravinsky, Picasso, Havelock Ellis, Isadora Duncan, Margaret Sanger, Sherwood Anderson, D. H. Lawrence, and Bertrand Russell. These outcasts found joyous voice when Sinclair Lewis (*Babbitt, Main Street*), H. L. Mencken, and George Jean Nathan opened fire, in the avidly-read *American Mercury*, on the mean, hypocritical, money-grubbing, and sexually thwarted American hinterland they had left behind forever.

The Chicagoans: Founders of the White Jazz Religion

The American Mercury became the bible of dissident college youths, the "Young Intellectuals," and that strange new tribe of white musicians who adopted black jazz as a religion. Clarinetist Milton "Mezz" Mezzrow wrote in his autobiography, *Really the Blues*:

> We (the jazz musicians) read the *American Mercury* from cover to cover, especially the section 'Americana' where all the blue-noses, bigots, and two-faced killjoys in this land-of-the-free got a going over they never forgot. . . . It looked to us that H. L. Mencken was-yelling the same message in his magazine that we were trying to get across in our music; his words were practically lyrics to our hot jazz.

Francis "Muggsy" Spanier: Irish "Kid Muggsy" was never the same after hearing Louis Armstrong with King Oliver in Chicago's south side ghetto in the 1920s. (Photograph from the Ralph J. Gleason Collection.)

Mezz was a highly visible, though not especially gifted, member of this alliance of young white jazz acolytes centered in Chicago in the twenties: clarinetist Frank Teschemacher, the ringleader fated for early death; trumpeters Muggsy Spanier and Jimmy McPartland; clarinetist Pee Wee Russell, a recruit from St. Louis; pianists Joe Sullivan and Jess Stacy; tenor saxist Bud Freeman; drummers Gene Krupa and Dave Tough, the house intellectual. Benny Goodman was a remote and serious outsider to this hard-drinking bunch, but a Chicagoan nonetheless. The Chicagoans were ringmastered by two fast-talking entrepreneur-musicians, Eddie Condon, a four-string guitarist and raconteur who "could sell hell to a bishop" and Red McKenzie, a racing jockey turned singer. This live-for-the moment crew broke into jazz with the ODJB before graduating to a more authentic white combo, the New Orleans Rhythm Kings. "But when we heard King Oliver with Louis Armstrong," said Bud Freeman, "we never listened to the Rhythm Kings again." The Chicagoans were further smitten with two white innovators who left a permanent stamp on jazz: Bix Beiderbecke and Jack Teagarden.

Bix Beiderbecke:
Jazz's First Tragic Hero

Since his death at 28 in 1931, Bix Beiderbecke has loomed as the tragic hero of the Jazz Age; if he had played the typewriter instead of the cornet he would have sounded like F. Scott Fitzgerald. With each decade, the Bix mystique has multiplied to inspire a rash of legerdemain, conjecture, bad novels, and worse movies (*Young Man with a Horn*), and one useful book,

Mixed group on CBS television: Chicagoans Eddie Condon (guitar), Joe Sullivan (piano), Pee Wee Russell (clarinet), and Max Kaminsky (trumpet) took up black music in the 1920s with religious fervor. This 1950s photograph shows them with Zutty Singleton (drums), Billy Taylor (bass), and Benny Morton (trombone). Once more, the classic dixieland/marching band line-up prevails. (Photograph from the Ralph J. Gleason Collection.)

Bix: Man & Legend, by Sudhalter and Evans with Dean-Myatt, which chronicled his brief life almost day by day. Bix's breathtaking cornet flights were enhanced by a whiplash attack, harmonic ideas far in advance of his contemporaries, and a ravishing tone that beggars description. Hoagy Carmichael pictured the tone as "someone shooting silver bullets at a crystal bell." Eddie Condon said, "Bix sounded like a girl saying, 'yes.' " Every note that issued from his horn sent musicians into a trance of open-mouthed wonder that has hardly abated to this day; you will still see bumper stickers proclaiming, "Bix Lives!" The subject of endless romantic hoopla, Bix, it was said, drank himself into an early grave out of musical frustration, a victim of the eternal clash between the artistic temperament and the crass commercial demands of show business. He was doomed to play with inferior musicians, often members of the large Paul Whiteman band, which many jazz historians have accused of stifling Bix's natural genius. These attacks don't hold up since some of Bix's finest solos were recorded with Whiteman: *Sweet Sue, From Monday On, Lonely Melody, Mississippi Mud, Dardenella,* and *China Boy.* And when Bix led the brass section, kicked along by Steve Brown's bass, the four-acre Whiteman Band could drive and swing, as in *From Monday On.* Aside from the romantic mystique, Bix left a permanent legacy of far-reaching proportions.

Before Bix American popular music divided itself into "sweet" and "hot." Hot players like the Chicagoans regarded sweet players in fashionable society bands with lofty contempt; sweet players looked down on hot musicians as "fakers who can't read and have no legitimate tone." Bix proved it possible to play sweet and hot at the same time, becoming the first to play slow romantic ballads with genuine jazz feeling, something all jazz musicians have done since he pointed the way in 1927 with *Singin' the Blues* (Smic 3/5) under the leadership of his associate, saxophonist Frankie Trumbauer. *Singin' the Blues* had a germinal influence on an entire generation of jazz players, black as well as white. Lester Young wore out several copies of the record, copying the solos note for note. Lester was particularly taken with Trumbauer's "way of telling a little story" and his light airy sound that seems a pale reed version of Bix's cornet. The Henderson Band of 1932 recorded a facsimile of *Singin' the Blues* with cornetist Rex Stewart doing his best to recreate Bix's solo (*The Complete Fletcher Henderson*: 1927–1936, Bluebird AXM2-5507). An even more exquisite example of Bix's merger of romantic lyricism and jazz is heard on Trumbauer's *I'm Comin' Virginia* (Time-Life *Giants of Jazz, Bix Beiderbecke*). On nearly all of his records Bix soars beyond an oom-chuck, nonswinging rhythm section that appears to get in the listener's way more than his. On those rare occasions when he had a good drummer to drive him, as with Gene Krupa on the novelty horseplay of *Barnacle Bill the Sailor* (Victor LPM 2323), the fire still sears after half a century.

Bix was also the first to blend jazz with harmonic and melodic concepts commonly found in Debussy, Ravel, and Stravinsky but rarely, if ever, heard in jazz. As the first "modernist" he paved the way for the more advanced players to follow: Lester Young, Teddy Wilson, and Benny Goodman, whose early alto sax solo on *Blue* (Time-Life *Giants of Jazz, Goodman*) was a transparent Bixian transplant. Through these players Bix made an indirect impact on modern jazz of the 1940s. Miles Davis told critic Gene Lees, "I didn't listen to Bix, but I heard a lot of Bobby Hackett and *he* heard a lot of Bix." Hackett's cornet, an unabashed imitation of Bix, graced the gelatinous ponderosity of Glenn Miller's hit record *String of Pearls*, vastly admired by Dizzy Gillespie and other bebop pioneers for its advanced harmonic intervals and celestial tone. Hoagy Carmichael, the supreme composer of timeless ballads, cited Bix as his major influence; many of his songs, especially *Stardust* and *Skylark*, were directly inspired by Bixian improvisations.

Bix never got over his early love of the Original Dixieland Jazz Band, using the dixieland format on his records of "Bix and his Gang." "In doing so," noted Richard B. Hadlock, "he established the basic principles for playing dixieland in a new way that have endured to this day . . . and helped to revitalize this dying art." (Hadlock, *Jazz Masters of the Twenties.*)

Finally there are the imperishable Bix piano suites, forwardlooking fusions of jazz with the impressionist harmonies of Debussy and Ravel and the work of American composers he admired, Edward MacDowell and Eastwood Lane. Bix could barely read music but "had ears that could hear paint dry" and improvised at the keyboard in much the same way as on the cornet. These spontaneous creations were transcribed to sheet music by Paul Whiteman's best arranger, Bill Challis, who gave Bix all the solo space in the band he could get away with and even scored long passages for the brass in Bix's style. One piano suite, *In a Mist*, has fascinated musicians of all persuasions since Bix recorded it in 1927; Red Norvo, with Benny Goodman on bass clarinet, waxed a version in the 1930s, as did Bunny Berigan; Clark Terry, with Ben Webster, cut a stunning edition of it in 1964; Ry Cooder, the versatile rock-eclectic guitarist and musical folklorist evoked the Trumbauer-Bix spirit with delightful versions of *In a Mist*, *Flashes*, and Bix's dixieland-type tune, *Davenport Blues*, in 1978. Jess Stacy and Ralph Sutton are among the many pianists who keep the Bix suites alive in their public and recorded repertoire.

A restless bohemian whose short life was consumed by twin passions for music and bootleg booze, Bix succumbed to pneumonia in 1931, idolized by musicians and utterly unknown to the public. After that the romantic legend of the "Young Man with a Horn" took hold.

Jack Teagarden:
King of the Blues Trombone

When Jack Teagarden made his big move from Texas to Manhattan in 1927 he set the jazz world on its ear. No one had ever heard the trombone played this way. Kid Ory's New Orleans "tailgate" style, carried over from the marching-band tuba, can be heard in all its good spirits and limitations on Louis Armstrong's *Hotter Than That* (Smic 2/8). At the other end of the trombone spectrum was Miff Mole, a much-admired white New York musician who employed a trumpetlike technique that raised jazz trombone to new levels of proficiency but with an absence of jazz feeling that bordered on the glacial. Teagarden combined the technical precision of Mole with a genuine feeling for the blues, the first white musician to do so. Teagarden headed straight for Harlem when he hit New York. "You could not keep Jack out of Harlem," said Fletcher Henderson's tenor sax star Coleman Hawkins. "He made every house-rent party . . . he must have never slept, playing horn night and day." (Riverside LP interview.) Jack also impressed Henderson's trombonist Jimmy Harrison who, as Hawkins testified, "never heard anyone play trombone like Jack before." (Harrison, whose later style became remarkably close to Teagarden's, died at 31 in 1931 before he could fulfill his unusual promise.)

Teagarden sang blues and ballads with the same lazy, unforced breath-of-Texas charm that infused his trombone. Like his associate Louis Armstrong, his horn playing was a noble replica of his voice. He developed a unique mute perfectly wed to his easy blues playing, a "glass and a half trombone," manipulating a drinking glass over the end of the slide with the bell removed to produce an urgent, smokey tone unlike anything in jazz. Prime examples of this style can be heard on the 1929 *Tailspin Blues* and the magnificent 1947 *St. James Infirmary* that also features Teagarden's blues singing at its most affecting. Both are available in the Time-Life *Giants of Jazz* Teagarden package which readers are urged to get, since the complete omission of Teagarden from the *Smithsonian Collection* was its most serious oversight. The Time-Life package also contains excellent examples of Teagarden's widely-imitated ballad trombone and vocals, *I Gotta Right to Sing the Blues* and *Stars Fell on Alabama*. His bravura solo on *Lover* is a most unusual display of technical prowess rarely used for its own sake. Teagarden is one musician of whom it can be truly said that he never made a record that was dull or lacking in taste.

Few have described the Teagarden manner as well as the late critic Otis Ferguson in the *New Republic*:

> In both tonal and rhythmic attack there is that constant hint of conquest over an imposed resistance which is peculiar to jazz and therefore undefinable in other terms. Something like the difference between driving a spike cleanly into a solid oak block and the hollow victory of sinking it in lathe and plaster.

Teagarden and the Chicago jazz disciples took to each other at once, enjoying a working alliance and kinship that endured from the late 1920s until Teagarden's death in 1964. The 1929 blues *Knockin' a Jug* teamed Teagarden and Louis Armstrong in one of the earliest interracial recording sessions. With the end of the Big Band era Louis, Jack, and Earl Hines all disbanded their orchestras and reunited in 1947 as the Louis Armstrong All-Stars. The Jack and Louis vocal-instrumental duets are among the most joyously matched in all of jazz.

Jack Teagarden and his trumpeter brother Charles, along with the Dorsey Brothers, Tommy and Jimmy, Glenn Miller, and the rowdy Chicagoans who survived the rigors of Prohibition, all became more or less famous, perhaps to their astonishment, when the Benny Goodman Band launched the Swing Era almost overnight in the fall of 1935.

"Swing Is Here!"
The Big Band Era, 1935–1946

Following ragtime in 1900 and jazz in 1917, "Swing" was the third and thus far the largest wave of Afro-American music to flood the national mainstream. With sudden and hysterical joy millions of white youths embraced swing in a frenzy of "jitterbugging," a black-inspired dance whose wild Dionysian flings loomed in alarming contrast to the sedate waltzes and fox trots of the elders, in the same way that the Charleston and Black Bottom scandalized parents in the Roaring Twenties. Swing afforded an emotional and physical release heretofore the exclusive property of blacks. The ominous split between youth and age that began with "Flaming Youth" in the Twenties now widened to an unbridgeable gap as young America severed the ties of dance, music, and canons of comportment and taste they once might have shared with their elders. Foretelling the Rock Revolution of the 1950s, mobs of rapt teenage truants, ancestors of Beatles groupies, swarmed after a host of white bandleaders who followed in the wake of Goodman: Artie Shaw, Glenn Miller, Gene Krupa, Harry James, Jimmy Dorsey, and his brother Tommy, whose bony balladeer Frank Sinatra was never to be outdone, even by Presley and the Rolling Stones, as a Svengali capable of unleashing the pent-up sexual hysteria of adolescent maidens.

Swing gave birth to a new phenomenon with far-reaching consequences: A huge record market beamed exclusively at teenagers sprang up overnight. Despite the warning imprinted on record labels—"This record is not licensed for radio broadcast"—early prototypes of the disc jockey flooded the airways with Goodman's *And the Angels Sing*, Tommy Dorsey's *Marie*, Glenn Miller's *Chattanooga Choo-Choo*, and Artie Shaw's *Begin the Beguine*. Goodman's "Camel Caravan" was the first weekly sponsored program of authentic jazz on the airways; in 1938 he broke a long-standing taboo with a concert in Carnegie Hall that foretold of jazz concerts and festivals to follow. Suddenly swing was big business as an avid teenage market made instant millionaire-superstars of Artie Shaw and Harry James, who intermarried with top Hollywood stars providing endless copy for gossip columns and movie fan magazines. Big money was making swing respectable. A number of once-scuffling white jazzmen who survived the depression on what Eddie Condon called "a transparent hamburger diet" now enjoyed the prestige and income of the Marx Brothers and Clark Gable.

But white America in the 1930s was still decades away from a readiness to embrace the black musician as culture hero. White imitative bandleaders consistently topped Ellington, Basie, Lunceford, and Henderson in record sales, airplay, and *down beat* reader's polls. Though black musicians did not figure as large in the swing craze, they made definite gains from this sudden mass enthusiasm for a style they had pioneered in a less commercial form. This failure to grant black artists their fair cut of the swing market lent much fuel to the recurrent charge of young black jazz musicians of the 1940s and their immediate heirs in the black consciousness upheavals of the 1960s that "the white man stole our music and made millions off it." This anger found reinforcement in the 1950s when Elvis Presley, Bill Haley, Jerry Lee Lewis, and other white spinoffs of black rhythm 'n' blues far outsold the black originals. (When Presley died in 1977 there was no acknowledgement during the month-long front-page hoopla or the public accolades from President Carter and Frank Sinatra that the entire Presley apparatus—his guitar and vocal stylings, his songs, his stance, and his gamey pelvic grinds—was borrowed outright from T-Bone Walker, Bo Diddley, and other charismatic black bluesmen whose acts Presley had repeatedly caught in Harlem's Apollo Theater, or that his enormous record hit *Hound Dawg* was a flagrant copy of the original by "Big Mama" Willie Mae Thornton.)

The inevitable backlash against the appropriation of black music by a white-controlled industry and press was what shaped the writing of revisionist scholars of the 1960s led by LeRoi Jones (Amiri Baraka), a black playwright who forced his way into the field of jazz criticism, long dominated by whites, determined to purge history of key white figures like Benny Goodman and his grey eminence John Hammond. The recognition of the permanent musical-social impact of these men has been further obscured by an intellectual and educational establishment often blind to the importance of nonverbal languages, like music, in shaping our social landscape.

Architects of
the Swing Era

The prime mover behind the success of the Swing Era (but better known to the youth of today as the father of the folksinger of the same name), John Hammond was listed in Feather's *Encyclopedia of Jazz* as a highborn critic-entrepreneur who "used his advantages to effect so much musical, racial, and social good that a complete tribute to the work he has done would take a full book." This book has since been written, *John Hammond on Record*, by Hammond and Irving Townsend.

Count Basie, John Hammond, and Joe Williams: Jazz messiah and Yale drop-out John Hammond (center) is flanked by one of his many discoveries Count Basie (left) and by Basie Band blues singer Joe Williams. (Photograph courtesy of the Rutgers Institute of Jazz Studies.)

Scion of the rich and socially prominent Vanderbilt-Sloan aristocracy, Hammond dropped out of Yale in 1931 because it bored him. He poured his boundless enthusiasm and energy, hardly abated today at the age of seventy-six, into two passions shared by few of his rank and station at the time: an all-consuming love of Afro-American music, and a seething fury over the systematic social injustice suffered by the creators of this incomparable art. At 21 Hammond began his lifelong dedication to advancing the cause of jazz, the fortunes of its unsung geniuses, and to fighting racial inequities on every level of American life.

Unlike many silver-spoon radicals, Hammond's idealism had practical results. His immense family wealth and social position were backed by a sound business sense and an inside working knowledge of show business and the record industry. Patrician self-assurance coupled with a persuasive boyish charm that beguiled guitar pickers and coupon clippers alike helped him get his way. His contentious writing on jazz filled the pages of leading newspapers, magazines, and trade journals in England as well as in the U.S. He covered the racial *cause célèbre* of the early 1930s, the Scottsboro Boys trial, for *The Nation* and *The New Republic*. Hammond's devotion to Bernard Shaw's first rule for critics—"pure joy at the good, pure rage at the bad"—left no doubt where he stood; there were no gray areas between the "wonderful playing of Lester Young" and the "complete mediocrity" of Young's more famous imitators.

His seemingly endless fount of money, time, and energy was funneled into the careers of countless musicians both great and obscure who he found jobs for, put through school, got out of jail and hock, hospitalized, dried out, recorded, buried, loaned money to with no hope of repayment; of writers he found publishers for; magazines he underwrote; racial and activist groups he subsidized and guided; historic concerts and benefits he produced. The recording sessions he organized and supervised include a who's who of jazz, blues, gospel, and even rock. His discoveries and protegés included Count Basie, Billie Holiday, Teddy Wilson, Lester Young, the boogie-woogie pianists whose revival he sparked almost single-handedly, Charlie Christian, Big Joe Turner, Aretha Franklin, George Benson, Bob Dylan, and Bruce Springsteen. A stock joke among critics was that whenever Hammond was asked if he knew such-and-such a record his invariable reply was, "I was personally in the studio at the time."

Hammond began his career as recording supervisor and talent scout for Columbia Records in 1932, the year he organized a session that foretold the Swing Era three years away. In the midst of the depression the 22-year-old fanatic badgered reluctant Columbia heads into recording his enduring love, the Fletcher Henderson Band. Like many of Hammond's early sessions, these sides were aimed for simultaneous or even exclusive release in England where the sale of purist jazz was brisker. With these impromptu versions of *Honeysuckle Rose* and *King Porter Stomp* (called "head" arrangements because they existed more in the musicians' minds than on paper), Henderson brought to perfection a long-aborning style of big band swing that, in Benny Goodman's hands, would soon revolutionize the dancing and listening habits of white America.

The Henderson formula, used throughout the Swing Era with slight variation by hundreds of bands, black and white, called for a compliment of:

brass	3 trumpets
	2 trombones (later 3)
reeds	3–4 saxes doubling on clarinet
rhythm	piano
	rhythm guitar (acoustic)
	string bass
	drums

The function of this unit was to swing collectively at any tempo with that peculiar blend of relaxation and tension that stamped the playing of Louis Armstrong. Given a skillful arranger like Henderson and the inspired soloists who filled his band, this formula produced irresistible dance music

Fletcher Henderson Band: Goodman launched the Swing Era of the 1930s using the identical instrumentation—and often the arrangements—of black big bands. (Photograph from the Frank Driggs Collection.)

for Depression America yearning for escape. Smoothly blended reeds answered the riffing brass in a cry-and-response pattern born in the black sanctified church. Leaving ample room for his soloists, Henderson contrived deceptively simple brass and reed backgrounds to bring out the best in Coleman Hawkins, Joe Smith, Red Allen, and J. C. Higginbotham. His foundation was the rhythm section whose pulsing, heartbeat drummers Walter Johnson and Big Sidney Catlett believed "drums should be felt and not heard." Catlett once boasted he could swing an entire band of fifteen with nothing but a wire brush and a telephone book. The Henderson style that carried over into the Swing Era was summed up in the 1934 *Wrappin' it Up* (Smic 3/7), which makes a fascinating comparison to Goodman's version of Henderson's identical arrangement (RCA Victor LP 1239). You have only to compare these two records, among many others, to recognize Henderson as a prime architect of the Big Band Era.

Henderson did not "invent" big band swing but was a focal point for an alliance of black arrangers and bandleaders with interchanging personnel: Don Redman, a former child prodigy whose advanced arrangements like *Stampede* (Smic 3/6) fired up the early Henderson band (an unsung hero of jazz, Redman led the excellent McKinney's Cotton Pickers band before forming his own orchestra, idolized by the musicians and ignored by the public); Horace Henderson, a skilled arranger and far better band pianist than his older brother Fletcher; John Nesbitt of McKin-

Benny Goodman Orchestra: Goodman launched the Swing Era of the 1930s using the identical instrumentation—and often the arrangements—of black big bands. In the Goodman band were Jess Stacy on piano and Gene Krupa, the band's great drummer-showman. (Photograph from the Frank Driggs Collection.)

ney's Cotton Pickers; and versatile Benny Carter, a resplendent alto saxist with fertile ideas and a gorgeous tone, a better than average trumpeter, and an unparalleled arranger whose scoring for sax sections served as a model throughout the Big Band Era. Carter's consummate skill in arranging for four reeds can be heard on Lionel Hampton's recording of Carter's *When Lights Are Low* (Smic 5/6), a summit meeting of Carter's alto with the tenors of Coleman Hawkins, Ben Webster, and Chu Berry.

While this New York-based confederation had been slowly evolving a style later popularized by Goodman, dozens of jumping Southwest "territorial" bands centered in round-the-clock Kansas City were working along even freer lines, unfettered by the commercial restraints and managerial interference that plagued Eastern bands: Andy Kirk and his Twelve Clouds of Joy featuring the superb piano and arrangements of Mary Lou Williams; Harlan Leonard; Walter Page's Blue Devils; and Bennie Moten, whose "stride" pianist Bill Basie was to exalt big band swing to its highest peak. Their distance from major recording capitals kept these Kansas City-Texas-Oklahoma outfits under-recorded while the Henderson-Redman-Carter confederation was amply represented on wax.

Though the Henderson band struck Hammond as the finest exponent of dance music he sensed was on the verge of inflaming the public, Henderson was to play an unsung but crucial role in Swing's breakthrough into the white culture. The most obvious reason why Goodman was destined to carry Henderson's standard into battle was that Goodman was white in an era not ready to embrace black artists on the order of Ray Charles, Stevie Wonder, James Brown, and Jimi Hendrix. The notion of a black bandleader with a commercially sponsored radio show was unthinkable in the 1930s, certainly in the South. (As late as the 1950s, TV network plans to produce the Nat "King" Cole Show were killed for fear of offending Southern advertisers.) But Goodman had advantages other than his socially acceptable color to equip him to launch the Swing Era, prompting thousands to take up the clarinet and, as we will see, the drums.

Benny Goodman: "King of Swing"

The eighth of eleven children born to a poor Russian-Jewish family in Chicago, Goodman became a child virtuoso on the clarinet through the self-discipline and mania for perfection that marked his career as bandleader. His prodigious classical technique melded with a feeling for the authentic blues style and woody New Orleans tone of Jimmy Noone, a fixture since 1918 in black Chicago clubs that Goodman haunted while still in short pants. He also came under the spell of white clarinetist Frank Teschemacher, a "hot" player who lacked Goodman's fluid proficiency but whose explosive take-offs and strangled cries inspired all of Chicago's white jazz tribe. Like all "modernists," Goodman was Bix-influenced; when he donated his record collection to Harvard's Widener Library in 1940, many well-worn Bix records were found.

Goodman's first recorded solos with the Ben Pollack band in 1926 (Time-Life *Giants of Jazz, Goodman*) reveal a fully turned-out 17-year-old master of Teschemacher's agitated hard-edged style. His tone, which he could vary at will, ranged from Mozartian purity to dirty smears. At twenty he was in constant demand in top hotel bands and pick-up sessions with others destined for prominence in the Swing Era to come: Jack Teagarden, Bunny Berigan, Joe Sullivan, Bud Freeman, Gene Krupa, Joe Venuti. Goodman survived the stock market crash better than most white Chicagoans as a three-hundred-dollar-a-week sideman in radio orchestras, pit bands of Broadway musicals, and expensive New York nightclubs. The nightclubs required violin sections in the house band, a typical albatross of that era, as was the constant harrassment by club managers about what to play and how long and how fast to play it. With Hammond's help Goodman put together the first of his big bands in 1934, aiming for broad audience appeal with current hit tunes and creamy dance arrangements, while the messianic Hammond urged Goodman toward a more Henderson-like sound, pressing upon him a number of swinging sidemen like drummer Gene Krupa. Hammond persuaded Goodman to hire Fletcher Henderson as staff arranger. A victim of erratic work habits, an easy-going temperament at odds with the demands on a bandleader, and an auto accident that left him permanently impaired, Henderson had broken up his band for lack of engagements and was happy for the chance to write dozens of charts that formed the core of Goodman's library. Henderson's arranging skills seemed to multiply as his bandleading powers declined. Were it not for his foolproof scores of Goodman's earliest hits—*King Porter Stomp, Sometimes I'm Happy, Blues Skies* (Time-Life *Giants of Jazz, Goodman*)—the Goodman band might have made no more than the modest splash of the Dorsey Brothers Orchestra or Glen Gray and the Casa Loma Orchestra, instead of the tidal wave only months away. As one musician remarked, "All you have to do is play the notes as Fletcher wrote them and it would be impossible *not* to swing."

When his band grew into a national institution that faced growing demands for records, air time, and movie work, Goodman spelled the ailing Henderson by hiring a stable of the finest black arrangers of the day: Mary Lou Williams, Chappie Willett, Jimmy Mundy, Benny Carter, Horace Henderson, and Chick Webb's versatile saxist Edgar Sampson, who composed and arranged some of Goodman's biggest hits: *Stompin' at the Savoy, Lullabye in Rhythm*, and *Don't Be That Way*, all standards to this day.

Goodman's first break was the National Biscuit Company's *Let's Dance*, a three-hour Saturday-night coast-to-coast radio show, contrasting his burgeoning brand of swing with Xavier Cugat's pop-latin band and Kel Murray's "sweet" society orchestra. Goodman was heard last, too late for many New Yorkers, but just in time for the West Coast, three hours earlier. This was to prove crucial to Goodman's breakthrough, first occurring in California.

A landmark contract with RCA Victor, the most prestigious label of the day, stipulated Goodman would get royalties on record sales, an unusual benefit for jazz artists, long the victims of multiple swindles that were the rule of thumb in the record industry. Hammond found a valuable ally in another Goodman enthusiast, young Willard Alexander of the giant MCA booking agency. Alexander, who became a leading entrepreneur of the Swing Era, arranged a national ballroom tour starting at New York's fancy Roosevelt Grill, balliwick of Guy Lombardo and his Royal Canadians, the geriatric's delight. Accustomed to Lombardo's toy-piano tin-kling and whimpering reeds, the hotel manager was aghast at Goodman's wall-to-wall volume and gave the band notice on opening night. This nightmare pursued Goodman across the country. Goodman's alto saxist Hymie Shertzer told Mort Goode,

> In Denver no one came. A few people were dancing and the owner came running up and said, "Hey, man, these arrangements are too long. You got to cut them to no more than a minute," and right across the lake was another ballroom that was jammed every night, Kay Kyser. He used to play hokum numbers, and all the guys wore these crazy hats. They were drawing the crowds, and we were really, really ready to fold up. (Liner Notes, *Benny Goodman Vol. I*, RCA-AXM2-5505.)

Then in Sweet's Ballroom in Oakland and the Palomar ballroom in Los Angeles something clicked. These dance halls were mobbed by young jitterbugs who heard the band on *Let's Dance*. After restraining the band all summer to fend off the inevitable "Too loud!" screams of ballroom managers, Goodman pulled out all the stops, calling for his "killer-diller" numbers. "When Bunny Berigan stood up and blew *King Porter Stomp*," said Goodman, "the place exploded." The Swing Era was underway.

Given the demands of the entertainment world and the public taste for flashy conductors, Goodman seems an unlikely candidate for the mass adulation that followed. Utterly devoid of theatrical presence, his vague and sheepish manner suggested a reform rabbi presiding over his first *bar mitzvah*. No one regarded this elusive bandmaster in rimless specs as a sex symbol or showbiz personality. It would be tempting, though not en-tirely true, to say that Goodman made it solely on the strength of his clari-net playing and the drive of a handpicked crew that rehearsed Hender-son's fail-safe charts to a fare-thee-well under the baleful eye of a martinet nicknamed "The Ray" by cohorts who claimed Goodman's laser beam stare could turn erring sidemen to stone. His impatience with anything less than perfection paid off with a sound that sent young America into ecstasies of airborn dance. When the band played five shows daily at Time Square's Paramount Theater, police had to quell the can't-sit-down kids, stoned out of their minds on music and nothing else, who leaped from their seats to jitterbug in the aisles to the tune of front-page headlines.

At first Goodman's crafty commercial sense dictated the generous programming of insipid current hits sung by lithesome sirens whose sex-ual allure loomed in inverse ratio to their vocal gifts. Once his popularity was assured Goodman briefly defied convention by hiring the definitely non-svelte but subtly swinging Mildred Bailey, followed in 1941 by Peggy Lee, a tasteful singer whose version of *Why Don't You Do Right?* an ob-scure depression-era blues recorded by Lil Green, made an overnight star of Goodman's new find. The Big Band Era's elevation of comely but mediocre singers over their more gifted accompanists was a practice that sooner or later tainted most name bandleaders except Count Basie, whose vocalists rarely fell below the level of his great soloists. (This convention was caught on film with unintentional irony in Martin Scorcese's *New York, New York*.) Goodman was careful to pick crowd-pleasing soloists: fiery Bunny Berigan was replaced by Harry James and Ziggy Elman, whose daring technical exploits set audiences screaming. The premier showman of the band was the demonic drummer Gene Krupa, no less responsible for the Swing craze than his boss whom he constantly up-staged with a tom-tom beat that set the Goodman band apart from re-cently dethroned dance kings, Hal Kemp, and the Casa Loma Orchestra. Krupa was as exciting to watch as to hear, given to wild lank-haired flail-ings, primitive grunts, and boxer's sweat, a movie stereotype of the jazz musician at work. Subtlety was not Krupa's long suit, and it's doubtful if Goodman would have made such an impact with the less theatrical but more tasteful Dave Tough, who replaced Krupa when he left Goodman to form his own band. For better or worse, Krupa made the drum solo a permanent fixture in both big band and small combo jazz and inspired thousands to take up the instrument. For all its showboating and heavy-footed boom, Krupa's tribal beat formed the hypnotic pulse that radically changed the way white America danced, listened, and responded to music.

Goodman's triumph opened the door for hundreds of white bands based on the Henderson-Carter-Redman format: Glenn Miller, a compe-tent trombonist and strict taskmaster, scored a phenomenal success in 1939 with the processed ooze of *Moonlight Serenade, Moonlight Cocktail*, and bleached treatments of black big band blues, *Tuxedo Junction* and *In the Mood*. Brief lapses into authentic jazz like cornetist Bobby Hackett's breathless Bixian interlude in the juke box hit *String of Pearls* gave way to Miller's precision crafting of a well-oiled engine to enrapture the widest possible audience. Following Miller's wartime disappearance on a lost air-craft, his machine resisted dismemberment, purring on into infinity under the stewardship of former sidemen who kept the legend aflame for aging nostalgiacs.

Tommy Dorsey, the flawless trombone virtuoso, was widely admired for his seamless legato phrasing by such diverse talents as Charlie Parker and Frank Sinatra, who catapulted to stardom as Dorsey's vocalist. While he employed top solo talent like Bunny Berigan, Bud Freeman, pianist Joe Bushkin, and black arranger Sy Oliver, Dorsey aimed for a more commer-cial market than Goodman; many of his record hits, like those of his equally gifted brother Jimmy, qualified as pop. But when Tommy Dorsey decided to cut loose with occasional up-tempo blues like *Well Git It!* the band caught fire.

Clarinetist Artie Shaw, whose high register technique and advanced harmonic style impressed many black players including Ellington's Barney Bigard, outsold Goodman in 1939 with *Begin the Beguine*, a middle-of-the-road dance sensation that made an overnight celebrity of a complex Jewish intellectual ill-prepared to handle sudden notoriety. At the height of his fame Shaw quit the music business with a much-publicized jeremiad against the "rat race." Shaw returned with new bands that were far more adventuresome though less successful than the *Begin the Beguine* crew. His 1944 to 1945 outfit featured the premier black trumpeter Roy Eldridge as a regular band member along-side inspired young bebop musicians, pianist Dodo Marmarosa and guitarist Barney Kessell. This aggregation cut some of the most unusual and enduring records in Swing Era history and left no doubt that Shaw was a superb clarinetist. The band's chamber group, the Gramercy Five, was especially rewarding (*Artie Shaw Featuring Roy Eldridge*, RCA Vintage LPV-582). Shaw's excellent autobiography—not ghost written—*The Trouble With Cinderella*, is a bitter, reflective, and well-written indictment of the American success syndrome.

Woody Herman, another clarinetist-leader and an engagingly black-tinged vocalist, sold a million copies of his jump blues, *Woodchopper's Ball*. For over forty years Herman's chameleonlike knack for regrouping his "herds" to feature pacesetting young soloists and arrangers abreast of current styles—swing, bebop, "cool," and 1970s electronic jazz-rock—made him unique and revered among bandleaders.

A cooperative band fronted by Bob Crosby, Bing's brother, never sold in the league with Miller and Shaw but enjoyed steady success with a wealth of fine soloists playing quasi-dixieland arrangements adapted for a big band that came closer to authentic blues and gospel than any white orchestra of the period. Bassist Bob Haggart's arrangements of *I'm Praying Humble* and *Dogtown Blues* (*The Best of Bob Crosby*, MCA2-4083) were modeled after the country gospel voicings of Mitchell's Christian Singers, a rural South Carolina quartet of black workingmen whose diamond-in-the-rough harmonies and religious fervor stayed untouched by any hint of urban sophistication. Haggart's artful translations of grass roots black music imparted a distinctive sound to the Crosby band that gave thousands of whites their first tentative taste of sanctified church music.

But no white band of the 1930s matched Goodman's ability to produce consistently exciting music in the face of grueling commercial pressures or to make records that bear repeated hearing after five decades. Revisionist jazz writers of the 1960s, bent on obliterating Goodman as a "nonperson" in jazz history, conveniently forgot that as instrumentalist and bandleader few commanded more respect among his peers regardless of color, nor was this respect evoked by Goodman's personal popularity, an attribute he lacked to a legendary degree. Goodman may share responsibility for the sudden decline of the clarinet after the 1930s because many musicians felt he had taken the instrument as far as it could go. In a poll of 120 leading musicians conducted by Leonard Feather in 1956, fifteen years after Goodman's career had peaked, he was still named the top clarinetist by more than half the voters, including Miles Davis, Lester Young, Oscar Peterson, Woody Herman, Tommy Dorsey, Dizzy Gillespie, Nat Cole, Count Basie, Duke Ellington, and most of his key soloists.

Goodman's prestige among musicians increased when he formed the Benny Goodman Trio with Krupa and the impeccable black pianist Teddy Wilson. The Goodman Trio, and a year later the Goodman Quartet with vibraphonist Lionel Hampton, was a landmark in American social history and a musical innovation of large consequence. Black and white musicians had recorded together since the 1920s, but until Goodman took Teddy Wilson on the road in 1936, no mixed group had ever performed on a public stage. The courage required for this challenge would be hard to exaggerate, particularly in the South. A few years before Goodman brought his integrated group to Dixie, Earl Hines and his entire band were made to walk in the street off the sidewalk in Fort Lauderdale. "Going South was an invasion for us," said Hines. "In 1931 you could call us the first Freedom Riders." (Dance, *The World of Earl Hines.*) While on tour, Ellington avoided the daily humiliations of Jim Crow hotels and diners by chartering a private pullman car that slept and dined his entire band.

By 1935 Hammond was convinced the time had come to storm racial barriers and thrust the Goodman Trio on its reluctant leader. Hammond found his 23 year-old protegé, Teddy Wilson, specially equipped as the opening wedge, assisted by Goodman's enormous public image. A disciple of Earl Hines and a child of intellectual college teacher parents, Wilson brought to the keyboard a personal and musical dignity that proved Hammond right. Counter to the stereotype of the mugging minstrel man, Wilson's studious approach suggested Horowitz rather than Fats Waller—but a Horowitz who could swing. His quiet gentility, firm classical touch, understated beat, and tasteful harmonic shifts won him the immediate acclaim of musicians and the public alike. He quickly replaced Hines and Waller as the prime influence on pianists until the ascendancy of Bud Powell's Parker-like innovations of the mid-1940s. Dozens of records under Wilson's name established another Hammond find, Billie Holiday, as the most admired if not the most rewarded jazz singer of all time. Backed by the cream of the Calloway, Basie, Ellington, and Goodman bands, the Wilson-Holiday sides burst with a freshness and spontaneity that seem to increase with age. (Many of these essential records are available: *Billie Holiday: The Golden Years*, Columbia 3CL 21, 3CL 40; also the Wilson, Holiday, and Lester Young packages in Time-Life's *Giants of Jazz* series.)

Benny Goodman (left) and Teddy Wilson/1935: When the
"impeccable Mr. Wilson" joined the Benny Goodman Trio in 1935,
it marked the first time a racially mixed group had appeared in
public in the United States. The Goodman Trio also introduced
Teddy Wilson as the prime piano influence of the period. In the
1930s, Wilson's close-cropped "natural" was a radical departure
from the customary "conk" (straightened hair) worn by black
jazzmen and entertainers. (Photograph from the Richard Hadlock
Collection.)

The Goodman Trio and Quartet gave mass audiences their first taste
of chamber jazz, proving that this music, long denounced in pulpit and
press as cheap, low-class vulgarity, need not be loud or lacking in subtlety
and solid musicianship. The graceful interplay on *After You've Gone* and
the serene romantic inventions of *Body and Soul* (Smic 4/3) captivated
millions who had never heard authentic jazz of consequence. In 1938

Goodman joined the Budapest String Quartet to record the Mozart Clarinet Quintet, and the same year, the Goodman Band made the debut of jazz in Carnegie Hall. The "live" recordings of this triumphant concert, issued many years later (Columbia CL 814/6), became one of the bestselling jazz albums of all time. At the same time, Goodman commissioned Bela Bartók to compose *Contrasts For Violin, Clarinet, and Piano*, a lively Hungarian folk piece he recorded with violinist Josef Szigeti and Bartók at the piano. Goodman's interest in classical music had been whetted by Hammond, who played viola in amateur string quartets. Their adhesive relationship took on a familial bond in 1941 when Goodman married Hammond's sister Alice.

The Trio's success prompted Goodman to make it a foursome in 1936 with black virtuoso Lionel Hampton, who first introduced the vibraharp as a major jazz instrument. Rivaling Krupa in joy-of-performance, stage magnetism, and the penchant for sweating through a tuxedo, Hampton combined technical wizardry with a propulsive drive and lyric inventiveness that mounted in chorus after chorus. His exploits on fast numbers, whether on vibes, drums, or piano, which he played mallet-style with two fingers, bordered on the incredible. Like Wilson, he fronted his own all-star pickup recording sessions (*When Lights Are Low*, Smic 5/6) that take their place with the Wilson-Holiday sides, and the Goodman Sextet to follow, as definitive small combo swing, briefly despoiled by Hampton's quaint attempts at singing, the one gift the gods denied him. The black half of the Goodman Quartet were among the first famous jazzmen who did not "conk," or straighten, their hair, a rigid convention among black entertainers of that day. Wilson's and Hampton's closecropped "naturals" were adopted by increasing numbers of musical-social rebels in the 1940s, before the Afro hairdo flowered in the "black is beautiful" 1960s. Most of these black trends governing modes of dress and attitude first took root in the jazz community, where Wilson and Hampton emerged to become role models for the coming generation.

Wilson's and Hampton's appearance with Goodman was considered so risky that they were treated as an adjunct to an all-white band, a "special attraction," and not members of the band proper. Goodman's step emboldened other white leaders like Charlie Barnet to push integration further by hiring blacks to sit in otherwise all-white brass and reed sections. The renegade son of a wealthy family that vainly urged him into corporate law, Barnet built a superior Basie-flavored band that housed black musicians Trummy Young, Oscar Pettiford, and young Lena Horne, in her first big break. Gene Krupa hired Roy Eldridge and even featured the black trumpeter in public vocal duets with comely, white Anita O'Day, an unheard-of violation of the ancestral taboo. Artie Shaw also hired Eldridge as well as Billie Holiday, who claimed she was made to wear light makeup so as not to look too dark on stage. In 1939 Goodman featured the seminal guitarist Charlie Christian as a regular band member. Following World War II, when small combos replaced the big bands, integrated groups cut both ways when even such militant blacks as Miles Davis, Charlie Mingus, and Archie Shepp hired white sidemen during the most turbulent years of the black consciousness movement when "crow-jim," a backlash form of prejudice, was rampant throughout the jazz world. Like the white jazzmen of the 1920s, many of their black counterparts in the 1960s held a musician's ability more important than his color.

The Spread of
Black Music
in the Swing Era

COUNT BASIE AND LESTER YOUNG

Goodman's success unlocked the cellar for a host of underground black artists who shaped the future of Afro-American music. Though their immediate financial returns were puny compared to white swing superstars, black artists were "movin' on up" from the days when Count Basie headed a nine-piece band at Kansas City's Reno Club seven days a week from nine P.M. to six A.M., meeting a weekly payroll of eighteen dollars per man. Basie went unrecorded for four lean years after 1932 when he piled into a dilapidated bus with the Bennie Moten Band for the long drive from Kansas City to Victor's studios in Camden, New Jersey to cut ten sides in a single day. "We didn't have any money," said Moten reedman Eddie Barefield.

> On the way to Camden we found us a rabbit and four loaves of bread, and we cooked the rabbit right on a pool table. That kept us from starving, and then we went on to make the records. After that we just turned around and made it back to Kansas City. We hung around there for a while not doing much of anything. (Russell, *Jazz Style in Kansas City and the Southwest.*)

After Moten's death Basie took over the band at the Reno Club, which had a late hours broadcast by a small local station. It was picked up one night in Chicago by John Hammond on his short-wave car radio, a rarity in the 1930s. Hardly bothering to pack, Hammond pointed his car toward Kansas City. "My first night at the Reno Club in May 1936 still stands out as the most exciting musical experience I can remember." Hammond enticed Goodman's manager Willard Alexander to Kansas City, and they brought the Basie band to New York. Before Hammond could talk balky

Brunswick Records into signing Basie, the competitive low-priced Decca label lured the naive bandleader into a disastrous contract that tied him up for three years and paid him a flat $750 for 24 full band sides without a cent of royalties. "It was typical," wrote Hammond in *down beat*, "of some of the under-scale deals which record companies imposed on unsophisticated Negro and 'country' artists." (The story of Hammond and Basie is recounted in Ross Russell's definitive *Jazz Style in Kansas City and the Southwest*.)

The records Basie made under these shocking conditions from 1937 to 1938 took on the historical importance of the Armstrong Hot Fives. Generations of jazz players committed them to memory and could play the solos note for note. Worn copies of *Doggin' Around* (Smic 5/7), *Taxi War Dance* (Smic 5/8), and the band's much-imitated jump-blues theme, *One O'Clock Jump*, formed an essential part of the itinerant jazzman's luggage. Basie's first records set his band apart from all others, rivaled only by Ellington whom Basie had bested in a "Battle of the Bands" in Kansas City. "His ensembles," wrote Hammond, "had all the virtues of a small combo, with complete relaxation plus the drive and dynamics of a disciplined large orchestra." The rhythm section seemed to float on air, an inspiration to dancers and musicians alike. Once a devotee of Fats Waller, Basie schooled his wondrously matched trio of guitar, bass, and drums to take over the traditional timekeeping role of Waller's "striding" left hand, freeing Basie to explore new avenues of no-wasted-motion piano "comping"—filling in with judicious placement of staccato notes, a deceptively simple device that made the most of discreet silences and generated tremendous swing. Blending the firm big-toned beat of bassist Walter Page and the shimmering cymbal-like guitar chords of Freddie Greene, drummer Jo Jones shunned Gene Krupa's leaden bass drum thumps and tom-tom dramatics to cook up an insinuating sizzle with wire brushes and high-hat cymbal that exploited tonal resources most drummers overlooked. This "All-American rhythm section" remained the model for big band and small combo swing, with Jo Jones a patriarch among modernists Kenny Clarke and Max Roach, who revolutionized jazz drumming in the bebop era to follow.

Weaned on the freedom of Kansas City clubs whose owners only wanted to keep the dancers happy, Basie played more unadulterated jazz with fewer commercial trends than any name bandleader of the Swing Era but Ellington. Current pop tunes like *Blame it On My Last Affair* swung as joyously as Kansas City stomps like *Moten Swing*. Counter to an almost inviolable convention, Basie hired singers for their vocal prowess rather than good looks. Plump, affable Helen Humes handled standard ballads like *My Heart Belongs to Daddy* with a tasteful feeling rare among big band vocalists. The legendary bluesman Jimmy Rushing, "Mr. Five-by-five," swelled the largest of halls with his unmiked cries of *I'm Gonna Move to the Outskirts of Town*, which introduced authentic Kansas City blues singing to white audiences and foretold the coming popularity of Louis Jordan, Ray Charles, and James Brown.

Only Ellington and the early Henderson band could boast such a roster of great soloists: trumpeters Buck Clayton and Harry Edison, trombonists Dicky Wells and Vic Dickenson, saxists Herschal Evans and Buddy Tate, all backed by the world's greatest rhythm section and the leader's incomparable piano when he was moved to solo. But the band's crowning jewel and most distinctive solo voice was tenor saxophonist Lester Young.

Unlike Armstrong, Miles Davis, or Coltrane, Young's first recordings in 1936 reveal a fully-formed artist of 27 with a revolutionary style to challenge long-reigning tenor king, Coleman Hawkins, whose robust improvi-

Lester Young: The crowning jewel of the Basie Band invented, not only a new way of playing the tenor sax, but also a new way of playing jazz. (Photograph from the Ralph J. Gleason Collection.)

sations first brought the instrument to maturity. In his pre-Basie days Lester's light, throaty, almost vibratoless tone puzzled and upset veterans in the Henderson band where he replaced the mighty Hawk for a dispirited half year. In a rare interview with Francois Postif, the laconic, secretive tenorman told how Henderson's wife

> took me down to the basement and played Coleman Hawkins on one of those old windup record players and she'd say, "Lester, can't you play like this?" Every morning that bitch would wake me up at nine o'clock to teach me to play like Coleman Hawkins . . . it wasn't for me. I can't make that. So I went to Fletcher and asked him, "Would you give me a nice recommendation? I'm going back to Kansas City."

When Lester joined Basie, the other featured tenorman, Herschal Evans, taunted, "Why don't you play alto, man? You got an alto *tone*." Young tapped his head: "There things goin' on up there, man—some of you guys are all belly." (Hentoff-Shapiro, *Hear Me Talkin' to Ya.*) Billie Holiday, who inspired Lester to unscaled heights of lyric beauty on their record dates with Teddy Wilson, reassured her sensitive cohort and friend, " 'Don't listen to people who tell you to play like Hawk—you have a *beautiful* tone, and some day everybody will be copying *you*!' And it came to *be*!" (Hentoff, *The Jazz Life.*)

As Billie predicted, Lester became the role model for a new generation of jazz players who came of age in large urban centers before and during World War II and were more musically sophisticated than their forebears. Charlie Parker, in his turn the godhead for all future jazz musicians, first mastered the alto sax by haunting Kansas City clubs where Lester took on all comers and by memorizing Lester's solos off records. Bebop tenorman Dexter Gordon said:

> "For the musicians of the generation before mine, Coleman Hawkins was the one and only model. Lester changed all that. Everybody of my generation listened to Lester and almost no one else. We bought all his records and when he appeared anywhere in our area we all turned out and stood in front of the bandstand to listen and figure out what he was doing and how he was doing it." (Russell, *Jazz Style in Kansas City and the Southwest.*)

Like Armstrong, Lester's influence was all-embracing and touched Miles Davis, John Lewis, Lee Konitz, Gerry Mulligan, Stan Getz, and other adherents of the "cool" school that dominated jazz in the early 1950s. Standing immobile, seeming almost asleep, Lester was the essence of "cool" relaxation. The cigarette that smoldered lazily between his fingers never impeded the flow of notes spun out like endless strings of macaroni, long loping lines that flew over the barriers of notated bars to form wondrous strands of melody rich in fresh intervals and unexpected turns, swinging with a sly subtlety that lay beyond even Hawkins's powers. Lester's infrequent excursions on the clarinet were no less remarkable, producing a tone of such wistful loveliness that Benny Goodman was moved to make him a present of his instrument.

"Prez" to his peers, a contraction of president, Lester was the original hipster with his crushed pork-pie hat, boneless shuffle, and lean cryptic argot—"I got eyes" for approval, and "no eyes" for dissent—aped by aspiring jazzmen and their white hangers-on, those ancestors of 1950s beatniks. It would be hard to imagine one less suited for the dull regimen of army life than this poetic and privatized bohemian. Drafted during World War II, he was confined in a Georgia stockade nearly eighteen months for smoking pot and distilling homemade liquor and emerged from the army shattered by encounters with racism and brutality. His manner and playing became vague and disengaged. There were still moments of his former brilliance on record dates with Nat Cole and concerts with Norman Granz's *Jazz at the Philharmonic* that featured Lester until his death of acute alcoholism in 1959, but the fire of youth had been smothered. Lester's playing in his final years, like Holiday's singing, was stripped down, like an out-of-shape champion trying to go the distance with style but no stamina. But Lester Young had long since left his imperishable mark, for he had invented not just a new way of playing tenor sax but a new way of playing jazz.

THE BOOGIE-WOOGIE REVIVAL

Count Basie's and Lester Young's emergence from the obscurity of Kansas City clubs was quickly followed by the boogie-woogie craze, another branch of underground black music that suddenly penetrated the white culture in the late 1930s. Once more, John Hammond played the catalytic role in rescuing this compelling form of piano blues from oblivion, thrusting it into national prominence.

Boogie-woogie piano flourished throughout the depression in urban ghettos, particularly in Chicago, as a folk entertainment in dives, after-hours clubs, and the popular "house-rent parties," impromptu round-the-clock bashes in private flats that charged twenty-five cents admission for a goodly supply of pigs knuckles, beer, bathtub gin, dancing, and blues singing. The piano was always the center of these free-wheeling socials that gave birth to a distinctive keyboard blues variously known as "the fives," the "dirty dozens," and the name that stuck, "boogie-woogie," (boogie being slang for Negro). This piano style combined classic blues with infinite variations on "walking" or repetitive bass figures that stressed the percussive qualities of the instrument and made it ideal as dance music of a frankly sexual nature. In his much-copied 1928 recording, *Pinetop's Boogie-Woogie,* Pinetop Smith spiced his barrelhouse blues with spoken asides:

> *Gal, you with the red dress on,*
> *when I tell you to git it,*
> *I want you to shake that thing!*

Boogie-woogie pianists, often doubling as singers, found their way into recording studios whose product was aimed exclusively at ghetto blacks, listed in the catalogues as "race" records. Besides Pinetop Smith, who did not live to see Tommy Dorsey's orchestral transcription of his *Boogie-Woogie* sell a million records, this colorful tribe included Cripple Clarence Lofton, Speckled Red, Little Brother Montgomery, Romeo Nelson, Montana Taylor, Jabbo Williams, Jimmy Yancey—one of the most expressive blues players at slow tempos—and a threesome that introduced boogie-woogie to white audiences and imitators: Pete Johnson of Kansas City, Chicago's Albert Ammons (father to the famous tenor saxist Gene) whose bass figures seem to have been fired off by cannon, and Meade "Lux" Lewis who raised this style to its highest point with *Honky Tonk Train Blues* (Smic 4/2). This impressionist train ride, with its total rhythmic independence of the left and right hands and its sheer physical demands, proved the despair of countless imitators. First recorded in Chicago in 1929 for the Paramount "race" label, it was much prized as a rarity in the 1930s by a new phenomenon, the white "hot collectors." These were a fanatical clan that combed Salvation Army depots, pawn shops, and ghetto tenements in avid pursuit of out-of-print Armstrongs and Bessie Smiths, always hoping for a bonanza unknown to fellow collectors in those days before jazz records were codified by research specialists like the French Charles Delaunay (*Hot Discography*) and when musicians and bands recorded under a bewildering variety of pseudonyms to avoid contractual obligations. One of the largest "hot" collections had been amassed by John Hammond who came across a rare copy of *Honky Tonk Train Blues* and immediately left for Chicago to find its creator. He discovered Meade "Lux" Lewis washing cars in a garage and brought him back to New York, together with Albert Ammons and the Kansas City team of pianist Pete Johnson and blues shouter Big Joe Turner whom Hammond found working in a remote K.C. dive. For the first time authentic boogie-woogie was now on major record labels. Thanks to Hammond, Ammons, Lewis, and Johnson made guest appearances on Benny Goodman's weekly radio show. Hammond helped organize an historic series of Carnegie Hall concerts in 1938 and 1939, "From Spirituals to Swing" (Vanguard 47/48), to showcase his new discoveries along with Basie, Lester Young, Mitchell's Christian Singers, the Golden Gate Quartet, Sidney Bechet, and

Big Bill Broonzy in a summit meeting of country blues, gospel, "stride," swing, and boogie-woogie.

With Barney Josephson, Hammond opened the first interracial nightclub in America, Cafe Society Downtown in the Village featuring his boogie-woogie discoveries. A typical lineup at Cafe Society Downtown in 1941 would include: Billie Holiday, Art Tatum, Meade "Lux" Lewis and Albert Ammons in four-hand duets, Pete Johnson and Big Joe Turner, an all-star house band led by Teddy Wilson, and a new type of radical social satirist, Zero Mostel. There were no intermissions and, for musicians and improvident young jazz fans, no cover or minimum.

Cleo Brown, a classically-trained pianist with an authentic feel for this elusive style, made a modest hit with her Decca recording of *Pinetop's Boogie-Woogie*. In keeping with the familiar pattern, white imitations of boogie-woogie far outsold the originals. Tommy Dorsey's *Boogie-Woogie* hit was followed by another juke box favorite, Will Bradley's *Beat Me Daddy, Eight to the Bar*, and *Down the Road Apiece* with pianist Freddie Slack playing stiffly "correct" versions of this funky party music. Bob Crosby's band headlined pianist Bob Zurke in pale carbons of *Honky Tonk Train Blues* and another Meade "Lux" classic, *Yancey Special*. The best of white big band boogie was Goodman's *Roll 'em*, superbly arranged by Mary Lou Williams; ironically, it was never one of Goodman's major hits.

Boogie-woogie slid into an inevitable decline through overexposure but so completely infiltrated the white culture that it was again revived in the 1960s when rock stars began to re-mine the mother lode of the blues. Echoes of Pinetop Smith cropped up in rock groups like Steppenwolf, Commander Cody, and British bluesman John Mayall who tried his piano hand with *Boogie Albert*, a possible bow to Albert Ammons and a re-minder of Mark Twain's saying that "the difference between the right word and the almost right word is the difference between lightning and the lightning bug."

Transition to "Bebop" or Modern Jazz

While hundreds of amateurs and college youths were vainly struggling with *Honky Tonk Train Blues*, a new generation of black artists scorned boogie-woogie as "old time music" and turned to modernists Teddy Wilson, Lester Young, and guitarist Charlie Christian who mirrored the growing urban sophistication of pre-World War II Harlem, Detroit, Chicago, Pittsburgh, and Los Angeles. These young rebels about to mount a full-scale musical and social revolution modeled themselves after a different breed of musician. Where older trumpeters followed Louis Armstrong, young Dizzy Gillespie patterned his style after Roy Eldridge's advanced

Django Reinhardt: The Belgian gypsy guitar
wizard became the first, and to this day the most
important, non-American influence in jazz. His
phenomenal technique seems all the more
incredible considering that the last two fingers of
his mangled left hand were rendered nearly
useless by a fire in his gypsy caravan.
(Photograph from the Richard Hadlock
Collection.)

harmonic language and fiery outbursts in the upper register taken at
frightening tempos (Smic 5/4, 5/5).

An overseas phenomenon that started to attract notice among young
musicians was guitarist Django Reinhardt, an illiterate Belgian gypsy living in Paris, the first foreign musician to make a large impact on American
jazz musicians and fans. Django's unique fusion of gypsy music and jazz,
his warm throbbing tone, and his inspired fast runs endeared him to all
musicians and made him the center of a cult following that included novelist James Jones. It was rumored that when the Nazis occupied Paris a
high-ranking officer on the German general staff asked a French officer
during the armistice negotiations where he could find Django Reinhardt.
Django's dazzling technical feats were all the more startling since the last

two fingers of his left hand were rendered nearly useless by a fire in his gypsy caravan. Today, any well-stocked shop carries dozens of his records, either solo, sitting in with members of the Ellington band, or as a member of the Quintet of the Hot Club of France with violinist Stephane Grappelly, who is still active today.

Art Tatum, a nearly-blind pianist from Toledo, emerged from the twin traditions of Hines and Waller as a clear forerunner of modern jazz, a major influence on bebop innovator Charlie Parker, and a continuing source of frustration to every piano player from the time he cut his first record in 1932. One cannot write about Tatum without dealing in superlatives. The consensus among critics and musicians, classical included, is that Tatum was the greatest pianist jazz has produced or is likely to produce, the standard by which all others are doomed to be judged. Oscar Peterson, the Canadian who carries on the Tatum tradition today, said: "When I was a teenager, I was feeling very smug about my prowess at the piano, very sure of myself, when my father laid my first Art Tatum records on me. I slid into a funk and didn't touch the piano for three months—I felt it was useless to practice." Earl Hines called Tatum "the greatest there ever

Art Tatum, Erroll Garner, and Count Basie: Nearly all jazz pianists feel that Art Tatum was the greatest pianist jazz ever produced—or is likely to produce. His awestruck fans included George Gershwin, Oscar Levant, and Vladimir Horowitz. (Photograph from the Ralph J. Gleason Collection.)

was. He was doing things on the piano that were frankly impossible, and he made them look so easy, with no sweat at all. He was so far ahead of his time that the public had no idea what he was doing."

Had Tatum lived beyond the fifties he might have played in major concert halls instead of "toilets" and dives as a "musician's musician," that evasive way of describing a towering talent badly rewarded by his society. Unlike Waller, James P. Johnson, and Bud Powell, Tatum did not compose in the formal sense but took thousands of popular songs like *Too Marvelous For Words* (Smic 5/2) and *Willow Weep For Me* (Smic 5/1) as the foundation for awesome displays of harmonic and rhythmic invention crafted with an effortless technique that surpasses human understanding. He combined Gieseking's delicacy of touch and Horowitz's precise attack with Waller's romping stride and Hines's "trumpet-style" inventions. It was rumored that he had two styles: one, a pat display of technical show-pieces like *Humoresque* for white audiences and two, the all-stops-out fantasias reserved for blacks in after-hours Harlem clubs where he played for hours free of charge. This legend was born out with the recent release of *God Is in the House* (Onyx ORI-205), "live" recordings of Tatum's after-hours flights in 1940 and 1941 that offer unmistakable portents of the Charlie Parker to come. Like Lester Young, Tatum today sells far more records than during his lifetime, which ended in 1956 at age 46.

Although Lester Young tended to supplant Coleman Hawkins in the affection of young saxophonists, the Hawk remained a constant source of inspiration to the coming generation of beboppers who memorized his epochal 1939 solo on *Body and Soul* (Smic 4/4) which even enjoyed wide currency among the public. An unclassifiable modernist, Hawkins stood nearly alone among the major figures of the 1920s in viewing the bebop rebellion with an open and sympathetic mind; he fronted the earliest be-bop recording sessions in 1944 with pioneers half his age—Gillespie, Oscar Pettiford, and Max Roach. When a young "modern" saxist complained to Cannonball Adderley during a Hawkins performance that "Coleman Hawkins makes me nervous," Cannonball replied: "Why, man—Coleman Hawkins is *supposed* to make you nervous! He's been making saxophone players nervous for forty years!"

Another elder statesman worshipped by young beboppers was Ellington, especially in his golden era of the early 1940s. We have seen how his bassist, Jimmy Blanton, pointed the way for all bassists to follow, but the Ellington influence as composer was equally potent. The 1940 *Cottontail* (Time-Life *Giants of Jazz, Ellington*) contains an arranged chorus for five reeds that sounds like bebop five years hence. Compare *Cottontail* to Parker's *Moose the Mooche* of 1947 (*The Very Best of Bird* Warners WB 3198), both based on *I Got Rhythm*. Then hear *Supersax*, a quintet of

Coleman Hawkins (right) with Gerry Mulligan: Hawkins, "the inventor of the tenor sax," made saxophone players nervous for forty years. He remained a constant source of encouragement to gifted players half his age, like baritone saxist Gerry Mulligan. "Gerry's got the spirit," Hawk said. (Photograph from the Ralph J. Gleason Collection.)

white saxophonists that scored Parker's improvisations on *Moose the Mooche* in five-part harmony (*Supersax Plays Bird*, Capitol ST-11177). The startling resemblance between *Supersax* and Ellington's saxes on *Cottontail* is far from coincidental. Leonard Feather's "Blindfold Tests" for *down beat* left no doubt that modern jazzmen, including Miles Davis and Sonny Rollins, idolized Ellington.

CHARLIE CHRISTIAN
AND THE DAWN OF BEBOP

An unrecorded veteran of Oklahoma-Missouri "territorial" bands, Charlie Christian was discovered in an Oklahoma City club by John Hammond acting on an urgent plea from Mary Lou Williams to catch "the greatest electric guitar I've ever heard." Hammond agreed at once and phoned a most reluctant Benny Goodman: "I've found your new guitar player!" In September 1939 Christian joined Goodman as a featured soloist in the band and in the newly-organized Goodman Sextet. His impact on young musicians was as instantaneous and complete as Jimmy Blanton's.

Christian was not the first to play an electrically amplified guitar; Floyd Smith with Andy Kirk and Basie's Eddie Durham both preceded him. But Christian was the first to show how the new technology could be applied to this previously all but inaudible instrument, in a big band or small combo, to elevate it from a rhythmic to a solo voice on an equal footing with the trumpet and saxophone. In his liner notes to *Solo Flight, The Genius of Charlie Christian* (Columbia G 30779), Gene Lees explains that

> an amplified guitar is in many ways as different an instrument from an unamplified guitar as a piano from a harpsichord . . . the amplifier just doesn't make the notes louder—it makes them longer . . . making it possible to play sustained legato lines as on a clarinet or a violin. It was this difference that Christian understood and explored. In the process he revolutionized jazz guitar.

In Christian's hands the guitar could play audible unison lines with other front-line instruments and stand beside them as a solo voice capable of playing hornlike improvisations. For Christian the amplifier was no gimmick or end in itself but a tool to put him on an equal footing with soloists he admired, like Lester Young. What impressed young players even more than Christian's electronic sound was his incredible flow of original ideas. That such advanced concepts were expressed on an instrument once relegated to a supportive role in the rhythm section made Christian all the more exciting and opened new vistas for all jazz guitarists.

Christian stunned the jazz community as the focus of the new Benny Goodman Sextet in 1939, which framed an ideal setting for the popular bandleader's latest find in an olympian series of recordings that brought the art of small group swing to its peak (*Breakfast Feud* and *I Found a New Baby,* Smic 6/3, 6/2). With Ellington's sad but resigned blessing—"It's too great an opportunity for you to miss,"—trumpeter Cootie Williams left to join Christian in the Goodman Sextet, prompting white bandleader Raymond Scott to write an Ellington-like dirge, *When Cootie Left the Duke.*

Ailing Fletcher Henderson was replaced on piano by Basie; the Basie-style rhythm section at one time included his incomparable drummer Jo Jones, whose work on the final rideout of *I Found a New Baby* is a marvel of quietly subtle swing. Lionel Hampton's irrepressible vibes and the urgent Hawkins-inspired tenor of Georgie Auld goaded Goodman into the finest playing of his career. The ensembles on fast blues like *Wholly Cats, Benny's Bugle,* and *Breakfast Feud* were worthy of the Budapest String Quartet; slow ballads like *On the Alamo* and *Rose Room* glow with a beauty undimmed by time. But the undisputed star of the Goodman Sextet was Christian, whose long single-string lines wrote the book for all guitarists to come: Barney Kessel, Herb Ellis, Joe Pass, Tal Farlow, Wes Montgomery, Larry Coryell, Pat Metheny, Charlie Byrd, Roy Buchanan, Pat Martino, Cal Collins, Eddie Duran, George Barnes, Emily Remler, Bucky Pizzarelli, and Mary Osborne.

Even more important than Christian's impact on other guitarists was his lasting influence on the music at large and on the young revolutionaries he jammed with after-hours in Harlem where they could explore beyond the by-now trite conventions of big band jazz: Charlie Parker, Dizzy Gillespie, Thelonious Monk, and Kenny Clarke. These founding fathers of the modern jazz movement embraced Christian as an early *sympatico*. Monk recalled to this writer: "Charlie used to come uptown to Harlem to sit in with me every night after he finished with Goodman." This passion for jamming with the avant-garde took an early toll on the tubercular Christian who literally played himself into the grave by his twenty-third year, a few months after Pearl Harbor.

By the outbreak of World War II, Swing had reached an artistic stalemate. Ellington and Basie had carried big band swing to frontiers never to be extended, and the Goodman Sextet did the same for small combo swing. While Charlie Christian and his fellow rebels at Minton's Playhouse in Harlem were sowing the seeds of a far-reaching revolt, Archie Bunker went off to war whistling "the tunes Glenn Miller played, songs that made the Hit Parade," and came home to confront strange and upsetting changes in jazz and the "uppity" attitude of young blacks who made them. Like Roosevelt's New Deal, the Big Band Swing Era became a casualty of World War II, leaving behind a permanent legacy: The Big Band Era spread black music throughout the white culture and marked the beginning of racial integration in the United States. By the end of the war it was common to find black and white musicians playing together in public before racially mixed audiences. And when millions of young white Americans were wearing out Ellington and Basie records, asking Teddy Wilson and Lionel Hampton for their autograph, and tacking Billy Eckstine's picture to their bedroom wall, it was no longer possible to sell them the myth of white superiority that had long proved a comfort to their elders.

"Bebop!"
Jazz Joins
the Avant Garde

Bop is a word which throws up its hands in clownish self-deprecation before all the complexity of sound and rhythm and self-assertive passion which it pretends to name; a mask-word for the charged ambiguities of the new sound, hiding the serious face of art. (Ralph Ellison, *Esquire* 1959.)

From the time of Lester Young and Charlie Parker onwards, jazz musicians began to demand talent of their listeners. This is the distinctive feature of an art form that is no longer popular. (André Hodeir, *Réalités* 1973.)

For years they were telling me, "play commercial, be commercial." I say play your own way. You play what *you* want, and let the public pick up on what *you* are doing—even if it does take them fifteen, twenty years. (Thelonious Monk, 1959.)

Bebop, the frivolous and misleading tag slapped on the emerging modern jazz movement of the mid-1940s, was a revolution of lasting significance on many fronts: musical, psychological, economic, and racial. It was also the first genuine avant-garde movement in jazz. We have seen how the new technology speeded jazz through stylistic changes within a few decades that were spread out over several centuries in classical music. In a few brief years, bebop recapitulated in nearly every aspect the European avant-garde of the nineteenth and early twentieth centuries.

Because the media has tossed "avant-garde" about with flippant inaccuracy, a brief redefinition may help to illuminate the little-understood role of bebop as a watershed not only in jazz but also in the society at large. The most readable survey of the avant-garde movement is Dwight Macdonald's *Masscult & Midcult*, the first in his collection of essays *Against the American Grain*. (Da Capo Press.)

The European avant-garde movement began and spread in the nineteenth century as a revolt of serious painters, composers, novelists, and poets against what they despised as the backward taste and vulgar sensibilities of the newly-risen class of patron-consumer, the middle class or bourgeoisie. Before the Industrial Revolution in eighteenth century England and the French Revolution of 1789 thrust the middle class onto center stage in history, the patrons of "high art" (as distinct from "folk art") were limited to the Church and the aristocracy. This elite class was distinguished from the rest of society by the ability to read, along with the more obvious privileges of money, land-owning, and power. With the sudden spread of literacy among the rising middle class, coinciding with the development of quick printing, a new marketplace sprang up for "penny dreadfuls," low-priced trashy novels dripping with gore, mayhem, and cloying sentiment. The English novel-buying public much preferred the gooey moralizing of Samuel Richardson's *Pamela* to the unbuttoned satirical realism of Henry Fielding's classic *Tom Jones*, just as book buyers were later to celebrate the historical romances of Sir Walter Scott over the genius of William Blake.

This gap between the vision of dedicated artists and public taste widened as the nineteenth century progressed. This is not to say that relations between artists and patrons during the Old Regime were unruffled bliss; Michelangelo's stormy to-do's with Pope Clement VII, who commissioned him to paint the Sistine Chapel, are well known, as is the conflict between J. S. Bach and church wardens who found his Sunday cantatas noisy and distracting. Still, one could sense that Bach "wrote his time" just as Michelangelo "painted his time;" artists before the French Revolution stayed somewhat in harmony with the princely and priestly consumers of their work. All this changed by the early nineteenth century. Haydn and Clementi began to augment their income by selling their compositions in the marketplace. Beethoven (1770–1827) became the first composer of rank to depend on the sale of sheet music manuscripts and concert performances for much of his income, his final energies to be poured into a series of ground-breaking string quartets violently rejected by public and critics alike. Well before the end of the nineteenth century Beethoven's late quartets were universally acclaimed as the foundation of modern string quartet literature and a towering achievement in Western culture. When the French novelist Stendahl (1783–1842) was scorned by critics for *The Red and the Black*, he replied with devastating accuracy, "But this is not for you. It's for a later age." Vincent Van Gogh (1853–1890) sold two paintings during his lifetime; today crowds stand in line for hours to see an exhibition of his priceless works.

When this gap between the artist and the middle-class consumer widened to an unbreachable chasm, serious artists in every field withdrew from active competition in the marketplace and decided to create for themselves. This gave rise to what the French called the *avant-garde*, composed of artists and a sympathetic cult that formed an elite not based on birth, money, or social position but on taste and sensibility. Unlike the old aristocracy, "anyone could join who cared about such things," wrote Dwight Macdonald (*Against the American Grain*), who saw the avant-garde as responsible for "most of the major creations of the last seventy years (1960)"—the painting of Matisse, Cezanne, Van Gogh, Picasso; the poetry of Rimbaud, Yeats, Baudelaire, Eliot, and Pound; the novels of James Joyce; the compositions of Stravinsky and Bartók; the architecture of Frank Lloyd Wright and Gaudi.

The European avant-garde followed a pattern that applies to the be-bop movement with striking fidelity:

1.   The avant-garde rejected the artistic conservatism of the old order and withdrew from competition in the marketplace to forge their art along radical new lines of their own choice in direct rebellion against the stuffy conventions of the middle-class public, established critics, and the Academy (university), which had long supported a backward form of pretentious art, *kitsch* for the elite.

2.   Avant-garde artists rejected in its entirety the middle-class lifestyle, philosophy, customs, modes of dress and demeanor, and attitudes toward money and sex and launched a total assault on bourgeois notions of acceptable art. This revolt prompted the migrations of artists to bohemian communities in Montmartre and, later, Greenwich Village to escape the trappings of conventional bourgeois life.

3.   Avant-garde painting, sculpture, poetry, novels, and music split the culture into two passionately warring armies, arousing the hysterical opposition of establishment critics and professors while generating the equally heated support of a hyperactive cult of *cognoscenti*—those "in the know" or as the jazz world says, "hip."

4.   Gradually, often over many decades, the avant-garde infiltrated and became accepted by, in this order, the critics, the Academy, and the public. When this occurred, the old avant-garde became the New Establishment. Stravinsky, Picasso, and Joyce, once the targets of unbridled attack by academics, are now taught in all universities. Picasso reproductions adorn countless living rooms and executive suites, while Stravinsky's *Le Sacre du Printemps*, which unleashed a full-scale riot at its Parisian debut in 1913, is now as conventional symphonic fare as Ravel's *Bolero*.

5.   The success of the old avant-garde gave rise to what the French call *"l'avantgarde pompier"* or the phony avant-garde, spurious work passing itself off as genuine avant-garde, preying upon the vulnerability of upwardly mobile enthusiasts unsure of their own taste and desperately afraid of being caught culturally short like the detested bourgeoisie of yesteryear that denounced Stravinsky, Picasso—and Charlie Parker—as anarchists and fakes. This mordant fear makes possible the totally black canvas hanging in New York's Museum of Modern Art and the plastic-wrapped motorcyle in the Chicago Art Museum, inspiring that special nonlanguage of art criticism wickedly lampooned in Tom Wolfe's *The Painted Word*: "The serene, yet dynamic plasticity of its existential givens. . . ." This phony avant-garde spawned such spectacles as John

Cage's "concert" for twelve radios, each tuned at random to a different station. As we will see, in the 1960s and beyond the jazz world nourished its share of counterparts to Cage's cacaphonic "Concert for Twelve Radios."

Aside from its racial overtones, which of course were of utmost importance, the bebop movement followed this pattern to the letter.

The founders of bebop, all of them veterans of big bands during the Swing Era, developed their new music in revolt against the rigid musical-commercial demands of big band jazz which had reached an artistic impasse by the early 1940s, Ellington excepted. Adventuresome young bandsmen like Parker and Gillespie grew bored with the same arrangements night after night, the stereotyped riffing brass and reed sections, the lack of adequate solo space to give them the much-needed chance to stretch out and test new ideas. Militant young players had long been annoyed with the commercial straightjacket of big band swing: nonplaying leaders and trite arrangements of pop hits sung by toothsome young ingenues hired for sexual allure rather than vocal ability.*

By the early 1940s, gifted sidemen in black big bands were repeating what white jazzmen tied down to "Mickey Mouse" hotel bands in the 1920s had muttered: "Man, there's *got* to be something better than this!" They found "something better" in unpaid Harlem jam sessions after they finished their regular band jobs. Minton's Playhouse and Monroe's Uptown House became unofficial rehearsal halls for Dizzy Gillespie, Thelonious Monk, Charlie Parker, Kenny Clarke, Tadd Dameron, and Charlie Christian, glorying in extended solo time, trading ideas and "new chords" found in exercise books, unfettered by the restrictions of big bands. These pioneers experimented with harmonies, chord progressions, and rhythms generally new to jazz. Their radical transformations had practical as well as creative functions; the new "changes" and unexpected rhythmic accents scared unwanted traditional players off the stand at cutting contests. When someone called for "Rhythm"—Gershwin's *I Got Rhythm* as outlined in the first chorus of the Don Byas version (Smic 7/4)—and heard instead Bird's and Dizzy's startling transformation, *Shaw Nuff* (Smic 7/6),

---

*A classic joke among jazz musicians goes:
A jazzman died and went to heaven, where the group leader was hipping him to the action:
"One groovy thing about this place, man, is we have jam sessions every night, and you can sit in with anybody that ever lived."
"You mean, I could sit in with *Bix*?"
"Every night."
"I could sit in with *Bird*?"
"Nine o'clock tonight, man."
"I could be a member of Duke's band? Actually?"
"Any night you want—there's only one catch."
"What's the catch?"
"Well, the Boss has got this thing going with this chick who likes to sing . . ."

played in unison at a punishing tempo, old-time swing players would pack up their horns and stomp out, growling about "Chinese music" and "wrong changes" played by "weird actin' cats who don't know their horns."

Those black musicians who created bebop felt—mistakenly as it turned out—they were concocting a style so involved and demanding that, for once, "the white man couldn't rip it off and get rich off it." The bebop movement aired the long-standing resentment of the commercial structure of the entertainment industry owned and dominated by whites—the mass media, music trade press, record companies, dance halls, booking agencies, nightclubs, and radio stations. Throughout the 1920s and 1930s jazz artists had bitterly seen white imitations of black music far outsell the originals, while Glenn Miller, Tommy Dorsey, and Artie Shaw were media-whooped at the expense of Basie and Ellington. Bebop was a natural byproduct of this smoldering resentment against white copycats getting rich off black music.

True to the pattern of the European avant-garde, bebop aroused a frenzied opposition bordering on lunacy and split the jazz world down the middle. In the Swing Era, when someone said, "I'm a jazz fan," everyone knew what was meant. With the advent of bebop this was no longer true; it was either "I dig Dizzy and Parker" or "I can't stand those guys and their sick music. It's not even jazz. You can't dance to it." And the beboppers replied, "*You* can't dance to it." Today one still finds thousands who grew up during the Big Band Era whose interest in jazz stopped with Benny Goodman and who have yet to make the unfamiliar trek to the land of modern jazz. In the same way, the world of classical music was split by Stravinsky and Schoenberg who upset the devotees of Brahms and Chopin. With few exceptions, notably Coleman Hawkins, Benny Carter, Mary Lou Williams, and Red Norvo, older musicians shared Armstrong's outspoken contempt for bebop. Tommy Dorsey said bebop "set music back twenty years." Nearly all of the jazz critics save Leonard Feather, Ross Russell, and Barry Ulanov—in those days an exclusively white breed—denounced bebop as an aberration and a short-lived fad. John Hammond called it "a collection of nauseating clichés."

White audiences weaned on big band swing were shocked and disoriented by the strange behavior of the beboppers, on stage and off. These young rebels rejected outright the minstrel tradition of joke-telling, tap dancing clowns. Aside from the atypical put-ons of Dizzy Gillespie, beboppers went to extreme lengths to spurn the conventions of "old showbiz;" they did not announce tunes and acknowledged audience applause, if at all, with a curt nod. Harbingers of a new black awareness, they demanded recognition as artists rather than as entertainers. Their cool aloofness signaled, "Either you accept our music as a statement that speaks for itself,

THE BEBOP MUSICIANS

The Forerunners	Teddy Wilson, piano
	Lester Young, tenor sax
	Charlie Christian, guitar
	Clyde Hart, piano
	Art Tatum, piano
	Nat "King" Cole, piano
The Pioneers	Charlie Parker, alto sax
	Dizzy Gillespie, trumpet
	Thelonious Monk, pianist-composer
	Tadd Dameron, composer-arranger
	Kenny Clarke, drums
	Max Roach, drums
	Bud Powell, piano
Early Disciples	Miles Davis, trumpet
	John Lewis, pianist-composer
	Milt Jackson, vibraphone
	Ray Brown, bass
	Fats Navarro, trumpet
	J. J. Johnson, trombonist-composer
	Sonny Stitt, alto and tenor sax
	Dexter Gordon, tenor sax
	Charlie Mingus, bassist-composer
	Oscar Pettiford, bass
	Art Blakey, drums
	Roy Haynes, drums
	Boyd Raeburn, bandleader
	Don Byas, tenor sax
	Al Haig, piano
	Dodo Marmarosa, piano
	Barney Kessel, guitar
	George Wallington, piano
	Gerry Mulligan, baritone sax
	Red Rodney, trumpet
	Stan Levey, drums
	Shelly Manne, drums
	Zoot Sims, tenor sax
	Stan Getz, tenor sax
	George Shearing, pianist-leader
	Stan Kenton, bandleader
	Lennie Tristano, pianist-composer
The Older "Converts"	Woody Herman, clarinetist-leader
	Lionel Hampton, vibraphonist-leader
	Mary Lou Williams, pianist-composer
	Red Norvo, vibraphonist-leader
	Artie Shaw, clarinetist-leader
	Coleman Hawkins, tenor saxist-leader
	Billy Strayhorn & Duke Ellington
	Budd Johnson, reeds
	Benny Carter, reeds, trumpet, arranger, bandleader

without all that Uncle Tom shuck-and-jive, or forget it." When Dizzy and Bird brought the first bebop combo to the West Coast in 1945, their reception was so disastrous that the owner of the Hollywood club told the band after two nights, "You guys have got to sing, or dance, or do *something*!" Beboppers adopted a mode of dress far removed from Cab Calloway's flamboyant zoot suit or Ellington's white-tie elegance. A severe, quiet pinstripe would be topped off by a beret and horn-rimmed glasses, a sly send-up of the uptight white world, a studied pose at variance with the traditional garb of the black entertainer-minstrel. Some beboppers refused to straighten or "conk" their hair in defiance of a rigid convention of black show business. Charlie Parker's close-cropped "natural" made an early proclamation that "black is beautiful."

The bebop uprising foretold the coming rejection of Christianity as the "white man's religion." Black jazzmen converted to Mohammadanism, studied the Koran, and took Muslim names: Alto saxist Edmund Gregory became Sahib Shihab, reedman Williams Evans became Yusef Lateef, pianist Fritz Jones became Ahmad Jamal, and in 1947, long before Cassius Clay became Muhammad Ali, Argonne Thornton took the name

Charlie Parker: In the 1940s, Bird's close-cropped "natural" made an early proclamation that "black is beautiful." (Photograph from the Ralph J. Gleason Collection.)

Dodo Marmarosa: In the 1940s, some white
devotees of bebop, like pianist Dodo
Marmarosa, became so adept at the new music
that they were accepted by the black pioneers.
Charlie Parker paid Marmarosa the supreme
compliment when he told Leonard Feather:
"Man, Dodo Marmarosa's a bitch!" (Photograph
courtesy of Prestige-Fantasy Records.)

of Sadik Hakim in clear anticipation of the Black Muslim movement soon
to sweep the nation's ghettos. With bebop the black mask fell away or was
altered to suit the new black Americans' image of themselves, not what
the whites thought that image should be. Beboppers and their white followers, those archetypal hipsters pictured in Norman Mailer's *The White
Negro*, formed a secretive clan sealed off from the "square" mainstream,
speaking an exotic private slang, dedicated to a difficult new music that
required disciplines foreign to the Swing Era. The white beboppers, antecedents of fifties beatniks and sixties hippies, gloried in the role of social
outcasts, in open rebellion against their middle-class origins.

    With their insistence on seeming "cool," on being in control, many
beboppers dropped the "uncool" drug alcohol in favor of marijuana, a

casual euphoric common to the jazz subculture since the 1920s. Many sought escape through the ultimate "cool" drug, heroin, which took a fearful toll of bebop musicians and the black communities in the 1940s and 1950s. Though the special appeal of heroin in the bebop world was a complex phenomenon that resists oversimplification, some reasons are obvious—the destructive role model of Charlie Parker widely known as an addict from the age of fifteen until his death at thirty-four. Some claim the mafia distributors pushed the drug with added zeal among jazz musicians because they had money to spend and were easy to locate in jazz clubs. Even more than pot smoking, "shooting up" became an act of willful defiance of the law and the middle class, enhancing the drug's rebellious appeal. Heroin seemed to hold a special attraction for white beboppers, due in large part to their determined pose to be "in" and "extra cool" to gain acceptance among their black cohorts. Defensive jazz writers have pointed with truth to the medical profession as, statistically, the largest users of hard drugs, but this is avoiding the issue. Heroin casualties among jazzmen reached epidemic proportions in the 1940s, though many, like Gerry Mulligan, survived to kick the habit and some, like John Lewis, Dizzy Gillespie, and Clifford Brown, shunned the drug entirely. Marijuana and heroin use and allied forms of bizarre antisocial behavior were linked to bebop in the public mind, conditioned by a mass media whose morbid fascination with addiction outweighed any impulse to acquire and propagate the slightest understanding of bebop, musically or socially. *Life* told millions of readers that the "Kings of Bebop" were Slim Gaillard, a composer-singer of inane pseudo-bop ditties about hipsters dining on "avocado seed soup," and Harry "The Hipster" Gibson, a zonked-out stereotype trafficking in drug-related novelties like "Who Put the Benzedrine in Mrs. Murphy's Ovaltine?" Bebop jokes abounded then like Polish jokes do in the eighties, usually stressing the musician's addiction to drugs and outlandish behavior. The press found "good copy" in Dizzy Gillespie's beret, horn-rimmed specs, and goatee but stayed indifferent to the music he pioneered, how it departed from Swing, and why it signaled the arrival of a new urban black in revolt.

Besides the fount of misinformation gushing from a sensationalist press, there were other causes for the long delay of bebop's acceptance by the public. The musicians union, the AF of M, banned all members from recording instrumental music from the fall of 1942 to the end of 1944 so that the big bands of Earl Hines and Billy Eckstine that served as cradles of bebop during these crucial years went virtually unrecorded. (The union ban did have a healthy side effect; a flood of small record companies, some of them jazz oriented, arose to challenge the virtual monopoly of the Big Three—Victor, Columbia, and Decca.) The spread of the new music was further delayed because its potential audience was overseas during World War II, removed from exposure to the experiments of Parker and Gillespie. On their return home veterans faced the more pressing concerns of post-war education and employment during bebop's most fertile era of 1945 to 1949.

The rise of bebop coincided with the swift decline of big bands that had enjoyed an unprecedented boom during the entertainment-hungry war years. Inflation, costs of keeping a big band on the road, and a heavy wartime tax on public dancing were followed by the sudden television explosion that kept former dance band fans at home glued to the tube. By the mid-1940s the small vocal-oriented combos of Nat "King" Cole and Louis Jordan proved small groups could be as lucrative as big bands with far less overhead and managerial hassles. Although there were excellent bebop big bands—Hines, Eckstine, and, later, Woody Herman, Dizzy Gillespie, and Boyd Raeburn—their artistic triumphs were more than matched by their commercial flops. For the bebop experimenters the quintet emerged as the most useful format both musically and economically, inspiring them to ignite one of the most original creative explosions in musical history.

How to Listen to Bebop

The bebop quintet of Parker and Gillespie put into practice one of the first principles of the new music's rejection of big band jazz—the musical economy of no wasted motion. One brass, one reed, and three rhythm dispensed with the doubling, repetition, and window dressing inherent to the big band format. Early on bebop dropped the rhythm guitar, because it was partially duplicating the functions of the piano, and that made one less mouth to feed on the road. This miniature edition of the big band did not start with bebop; Count Basie used a similar line-up in his vastly influential recording session in 1936 under the name of "Jones-Smith, Inc." featuring Lester Young in the most arresting debut in jazz recording history. All the young musicians, like Parker, memorized these records that foretold the outline of the bebop quintet to come ten years later (Time-Life *Giants of Jazz, Young*).

No advanced musical education is needed to hear the harmonic and rhythmic differences between swing and bebop, though, as always, the more we know about any kind of music and how it's put together, the more we can revel in the genius of a Bach or a Charlie Parker. (Readers wanting more technical but quite readable analyses should consult Leonard Feather's *Inside Jazz* and Ross Russell's essay *Bebop* included in the anthology, *The Art of Jazz*.)

As we have found, all jazz musicians, swing and bebop alike, must improvise on the blues, on up-tempo versions of pops like *I Got Rhythm* and *Sweet Georgia Brown*, and on slow romantic ballads. These ballads are the easiest place to start an exploration of how bebop expanded the harmonic and rhythmic language of swing.

THE BEBOP BALLAD

Charlie Parker's two "takes" of Gershwin's *Embraceable You* (Smic 7/8, 7/9) should be compared to a "straight" version of the song as performed by any number of singers—Ella Fitzgerald and Billie Holiday—to hear how Bird fashioned an entirely new composition from the melody. Unlike Benny Goodman's opening solo on *Body and Soul* (Smic 4/3) or Coleman Hawkins's first chorus on the same tune (Smic 4/4), neither version of Bird's *Embraceable You* makes the slightest bow to the original tune, but he plunges in immediately with a fresh conception of his own. Notice that Bird's tempo, like many bebop ballads, is unusually slow compared to Swing Era treatments, too slow for ballroom dancing; yet even at very slow tempos Bird is playing quite rapidly, cramming into *Embraceable You* a wealth of invention that threatens to burst the seams of Gershwin's ballad. Bird's widely-copied lyric style was equally creative on *How Deep is the Ocean*, *Don't Blame Me*, and *My Old Flame*, all included in *The Very Best of Bird* (Warner Bros. 2 WB 3198), among other reissue packages not so extravagantly titled. His famous reworking of *Just Friends* on *Charlie Parker with Strings* (Verve MGV-8004) is another "easy-listening" route to ease into the bebop ballad.

A dramatic contrast between the swing and the bebop treatments of the same song can be heard by comparing Dizzy Gillespie's *I Can't Get Started* (Smic 7/5) with Bunny Berigan's version, which can still be heard on jukeboxes today (*Bunny Berigan and his Orch.* Victor LPM-2078). Berigan made this tune so much his own in 1937 that it took youthful brashness on Gillespie's part to attempt it in 1945. Aside from surface similarities—the same song improvised on the same instrument—the striking differences in these versions recorded a mere eight years apart sum up the change from swing to bebop. In his finest Armstrong manner, Berigan spills out thrilling cascades topped by a bravura climax worthy of Louis himself—it was in fact one of Louis's favorite records. The big band fronted by Berigan had two functions: to play dance arrangements at suitable tempos and to sustain long choirlike chords as a backdrop to showcase the leader's spectacular trumpet. Rejecting Berigan's broad-toned exuberance, Gillespie opens in a mood of quiet introspection much copied by younger trumpeters like Miles Davis. Dizzy's introduction is an original composition only marginally related to the song; suddenly this dissolves into his unadorned statement of the melody ("I've flown around the world in a plane") while the combo backs him with descending chromatic figures that open up new possibilities for Dizzy and the tune itself, far removed from Berigan's statement. Both of these versions sound as fresh and perfectly realized as the day they were recorded. One is no "better" than the other, any more than Mozart is "better" than Beethoven. Their profound differences reflect the differences in their respective eras and in their musical approach. Again, the listener should be reminded that Berigan's 1937 version was an instant hit while Gillespie's was ignored by the public, received little airplay, and was decried by most critics in 1945 as "Chinese music."

BEBOP BLUES

All jazz artists have been steeped in the blues. This is especially true of major figures like Armstrong and Parker, whose trailblazing improvisations on classic blues stunned their contemporaries by unearthing riches buried within this folk structure. Armstrong's *West End Blues* (Smic 2/9) made a dramatic departure from the rural simplicity of Robert Johnson's *Hellhound on My Trail* (Smic 1/3), pointing the direction jazz would take for years to come. Seventeen years after *West End Blues, Parker's Mood* (Smic 8/3) "modernized" the blues without adulterating either its essential folk qualities or its high emotional charge. Like Ellington and Lester Young, Bird made the blues the core of his repertoire: fast blues like *Bloomdido, Au Privave,* and *Bird's Blues* and medium tempo blues, *Now's the Time* and *Billie's Bounce,* are still studied and played today.

Any intent listener can immediately hear the harmonic difference between *West End Blues* and *Parker's Mood.* At a TV rehearsal, the blues singer Big Miller was accompanied by a versatile pianist who fed him old-time blues chords that, the pianist thought, would be in keeping with this singer's style. Suddenly in mid-song Big Miller slapped the piano top and hollered, "Modern changes! Modern changes!" What he wanted, and got, was the kind of "modern" blues piano John Lewis played behind Bird on *Parker's Mood.*

FAST BEBOP
AND "MODERN" TRANSFORMATIONS
OF POP TUNES

We started our introduction to the intricacies of bebop with slow ballads and slow blues because these are easier for beginners to assimilate than very fast tempos and unfamiliar tunes. This is true of all kinds of music. Fast bebop and bebop rhythm make more demands on the listener. When first introduced in the mid-1940s, bebop's furious tempos combined with "erratic" irregular beats to upset older musicians like Fats Waller, who chastised some youngsters in a jam session, "Stop all this boppin' and *a-stoppin'* and play the jive like the rest of us guys!" Fats' use of "a-stoppin' " was significant since it was bebop's *time* that threw him off. James Lincoln Collier, whose *The Making of Jazz* includes a lucid technical description of bebop (pps. 341–362), noted: "So profound did the bop revolution appear at the time that not one established swing player ever succeeded in playing bop. And it was mainly this shift in time that caused the trouble."

Bebop's departures from swing can be heard by comparing Count Basie's Kansas City Seven's *Lester Leaps In* (Smic 6/1) with the Gillespie Quintet's *Shaw Nuff* (Smic 7/6). Even after several decades of retrospection, when the advances of bebop have penetrated the jazz mainstream, it is hard to realize these two records were made only five years apart. *Shaw Nuff* was one of bebop's endless variations on *I Got Rhythm*. "What we did," said Gillespie, "was to use two or three substitute chords where Gershwin had used one." This was a common practice among the beboppers, who so radically altered the original song that they could call it by another name and avoid paying royalties to the publisher. Beboppers gravitated toward tunes based on more complex chord progressions than *I Got Rhythm*. Bird and Benny Harris took the beboppers "national anthem," *How High the Moon*, and fashioned it into *Ornithology*; Dizzy took a 1920s dance hit, *Whispering*, and changed it to *Groovin' High*; Tadd Dameron used Cole Porter's *What is This Thing Called Love?* as the basis for *Hot House*; the British convert to bebop, George Shearing, shaped his standard *Lullaby of Birdland* from the chord changes of *Love Me or Leave Me*; Thelonious Monk's *Evidence* (Smic 9/6) is a crafty transformation of *Just You, Just Me*.

Shaw Nuff, one of the earliest and most influential bebop records, cast the mold of the bebop quintet that survives today. Following a two-part harmony introduction by alto sax and trumpet that bears little relationship to the tune, Bird and Dizzy plunge into a swift-paced complex variation on *I Got Rhythm* played in unison as one instrument, like coupled stops on a Baroque organ. Notice how this variation contains sudden stops and unexpected turns, which is what Fats Waller lamented as "boppin' and a-stoppin'." After this unison passage, Bird, Dizzy, and pianist Al Haig solo in turn. Notice the difference between Al Haig and Count Basie on *Lester Leaps In*, both as soloist and accompanist. Haig does not play steady tempo or Basie's staccato riffs behind Bird and Dizzy but is "chord feeding"—placing carefully chosen chords in at precipitous and unpredictable moments. Notice that when Haig solos his right hand figures resemble Bird's alto sax runs in much the same way that Earl Hines's right hand paralleled Armstrong's trumpet in the 1920s. *Shaw Nuff* ends with a restatement of the opening unison theme followed by the two-part alto-trumpet fantasia. This pattern holds true for other bebop selections in the Smithsonian package: *Klactoveedsedsteen* (Smic 8/1), *Little Benny* (Smic 8/2), and Parker's masterpiece, *Ko-Ko* (Smic 7/7).

Ko-Ko (not to be confused with Ellington's *Ko-Ko*—Smic 7/2—an entirely different concept) is not easy listening and demands many careful hearings before the logic and structure of Bird's improvisations are made clear. This dazzling display galvanized all the young musicians in 1945 who could not believe that such articulated ideas could stream out of a horn with such incredible ease and speed. Before approaching *Ko-Ko* listeners should become familiar with *Cherokee*, the Ray Noble song Parker used as its foundation. (Many versions of *Cherokee* are available, the most famous being Basie's, *The Best of Count Basie*—Decca DXB-170—and Charlie Barnet's *The Big Bands*, by George T. Simon—Macmillan 48987.) Then go to 22-year-old Parker's *Cherokee*, a promising work-in-progress recorded at a jam session in 1942 (*Charlie Parker's First Recordings*, Onyx 221). On *The Charlie Parker Story* (Savoy MG 12079), the famous "take" of *Ko-Ko* is preceded by *Short Take #1* where Dizzy states the unaltered theme of *Cherokee* before Bird calls a halt. On the final take Bird and Dizzy, backed by Max Roach's sizzling cymbals, ping-pong back and forth in a fantasia that, again, bears no clear relationship to the original theme. Suddenly Bird swoops in for two staggering choruses, beginning his second one with a "quote" from *High Society*, a clarinet showpiece dating from the early marching band days of New Orleans. After Roach's drum interlude Bird and Dizzy recapitulate the opening fantasia, closing on an abrupt, unresolved figure of "buh-doodle-oo-eeeeeee-duh-be-bop," the sort of phrase Dizzy would sing to instruct a group, which may or may not be how bebop got its name. A few months later Bird was caught "live" in another glorious version of *Cherokee* (this time under its original title) in a jam session with the Nat "King" Cole Trio. Cole's piano "comping" and drive push Bird into screaming exultation, reminding us that jazz lost a glorious voice when Cole turned his sights to the greener meadows of ballad singing. This extraordinary session is available on *Yardbird in Lotus Land* (Phoenix Jazz LP 17), which also includes four "live" performances of the legendary Parker-Gillespie band at Billy Berg's in Hollywood in 1945, all recorded with remarkable clarity considering the circumstances and the time. They remain among the most exciting and authentic examples of bebop in full flower ever caught on disc.

Because Parker was perhaps the most brilliant improvisor in all of jazz it is easy to allow him to distract us from the bebop rhythm section that backed him and how it differed from its counterpart in Basie's *Lester Leaps In* (Smic 6/1) and the Goodman Sextet's *I Found a New Baby* (Smic

6/2). Bebop drumming became more complex and polyrhythmic; the floating relaxation of Basie's Jo Jones was succeeded by the agitated tension and unexpected "bomb-dropping" of Max Roach. Where swing drummers used the foot pedal on the bass drum to keep time, bebop drummers followed Jo Jones's lead in keeping time on the top cymbal but used the bass drums to "drop bombs," punctuating at will a soloist's phrase, urging the rhythm section along less predictable paths. Bebop drumming was in large part pioneered by Kenny Clarke, a veteran of big band swing whose unorthodox style so unnerved leaders that one paid him not to play. A striking contrast between the "swing" drumming of Dave Tough and the early bebop drumming of Kenny Clarke—both behind Charlie Christian—can be heard in *The Guitarists* (Time-Life *Giants of Jazz*), *Waitin' For Benny*, and *Charlie's Choice*.

The Founders of
Modern Jazz or Bebop

DIZZY GILLESPIE

Dizzy Gillespie is unique among beboppers. Unlike his cohorts who scorned the stage mannerisms of the past, Dizzy's antics and turned-on euphoria evoke memories of Fats Waller. Dizzy jokes and clowns on stage, but unlike Waller and Armstrong, his japes are racially barbed. At a dance date, Dizzy dropped a mute that was retrieved by a white youth; Dizzy fixed him with a foxy leer and gave thanks with "That's mighty white of you, boy!" This genial buffoonery, plus his roguish insignia of beret, goatee, and horn-rimmed glasses, captured the media's fancy, making him the symbol of bebop and its most publicized advocate. He was profiled by the *New Yorker* in a lengthy piece that made no mention of Charlie Parker.

Dizzy differed from the majority of bebop pioneer-outlaws in his refusal to seek refuge in self-pity, self-destruction, and their handmaiden, drug abuse, which wasted so many of his compatriots. Thanks to vast reserves of mental health, a secure sense of his own value, a remarkable lack of envy, and an irrepressible humor and gusto for living, Dizzy survives today as an elder statesman, still creating, refusing to coast on past contributions that are as manifold as they are little understood.

As a trumpeter, he directly inspired such diverse stylists as Miles Davis, Fats Navarro, Clifford Brown, Clark Terry, Freddie Hubbard, and Wynton Marsalis. It would be difficult to name any trumpeter of rank since the 1940s untouched by him. His big band of the mid-1940s was the first to fuse authentic Afro-Cuban music with jazz; the rhythm section of this spectacular but short-lived band was the nucleus of the Modern Jazz Quartet. He predated Stan Getz in introducing to the United States the bossa nova works of Brazilian jazz composers Antonio Carlos Jobim and Baden Powell. A thorough musician and theorist with a sound working knowledge of the piano, he composed a number of distinctive jazz standards, including many lyrical ballads at variance with his public image as a zany cut-up: *Con Alma, Woody 'n' You, A Night in Tunisia*. He gave a leg up to countless musicians, including trumpeters Lee Morgan and Jon Faddis whom he shared solo time with, a testament to a magnanimity rarely matched in jazz. His superb memoirs, *To Be or Not to . . . Bop*, are essential to an understanding of the bebop era and its legacy that Gillespie played so crucial a part in establishing.

BUD POWELL

None of the notoriety accorded Dizzy rubbed off on the premier bebop pianist, Bud Powell, idolized by musicians, utterly overlooked by the mass media, and consequently unknown to the public that may have found his volatile keyboard pyrotechnics "nervous" had they much chance to hear them. Adapting the piano to a bebop style, Powell exploited an amazing technique to execute Parker-like runs with his right hand, using his left to "feed chords" in irregular patterns. Widely admired by the best of the young pianists—Al Haig, George Wallington, Dodo Marmarosa—Powell was called the "Parker of the piano," a misleading title for someone as original and accomplished in every piano style from Art Tatum to Thelonious Monk. One persistent legend is that Tatum once accosted Powell in a club: "Man, you got a great right, but no left at all." Powell sat down and played an entire set with his right hand behind his back. His record of *It Could Happen to You* (Blue Note BLP 1504) could easily be taken for Tatum, showing a ballad side of Powell more accessible to his potential public than the frenzied inventions of *Un Poco Loco* (Blue Note BLP 1503), when he was teamed with the matchless latin-jazz percussion of Max Roach.

Powell records must be purchased with caution since they range from the magnificence of the early Blue Notes, Roosts, and Verves to the dulled edge of his later years, much like his schizophrenic, tragedy-ridden life. The lone Smithsonian inclusion, *Somebody Loves Me* (Smic 8/5), though a prime example of his inimitable bounce and Parker right hand, is hardly adequate representation of the versatile wizard who supplanted Teddy Wilson as the major keyboard influence. Unlike Tatum, Powell composed many unorthodox and infectious pieces: *Un Poco Loco, Glass Enclosures, Hallucinations, Tempus Fugue-it*. During one of his many confinements in psychiatric hospitals he told the resident psychologist, in

Bud Powell: The premier bebop pianist. In the 1940s he succeeded Teddy Wilson as the major keyboard influence. A revival of his amazing and versatile work is long overdue. (Photograph from the Richard Hadlock Collection.)

truth, that he had written over two hundred compositions; the doctor entered in the record that "the patient suffers from delusions of grandeur." (Gitler, *Jazz Masters of the Forties*.) After an erratic career interrupted by frequent nervous breakdowns, Bud Powell was beginning a new life in Paris, attracting the respectful audiences that were his due, when he died in 1966 at age 41. A full-scale revival of his work is yet to come.

THELONIOUS MONK

Of all the bebop pioneers, Thelonious Monk was the last to enjoy the recognition given Christian, Parker, Gillespie, and Bud Powell, all of them deeply influenced by this strange, elusive figure who created a unique body of music that struck many as outside the mainstream of bebop in the

Thelonious Monk: It took nearly twenty years for the jazz world to catch up with the unique language of the "Mojo-man of bop." (Photograph by Grover Sales.)

mid-1940s. While his peers were amply recorded on small jazz labels, were booked into prestigious clubs, and toured with Jazz at the Philharmonic, Monk worked in obscurity in New Jersey, an unemployable cult mystic whose public behavior was thought to be as unpredictable and forbidding as his piano and composing styles. Pigeonholed by the jazz press as "The Mad Monk, High Priest of Bop," he was written off as an eccentric noodler, a no-show on the job. As late as 1958 the owner of San Francisco's leading jazz club, the Black Hawk, told this writer:

> I heard about this Felonious guy—he's some kinda nut. He'll come in a club and stare at a wall. I mean, he's not like Erroll Garner or Oscar Peterson—he can't sit down and play you a regular show. Besides which, I hear he never gets out of New Jersey somewheres.

Leonard Feather, one of the few established jazz critics to champion bebop from its start, dismissed Monk in 1948 as a minor figure whose "place in the jazz scene . . . has been grossly distorted as a result of some high-powered publicity work . . . his lack of technique and continuity prevented him from accomplishing much as a pianist." (Feather, *Inside Jazz*.)

This "lack of technique" became the recurrent cliché, though there is much evidence that he played more conventional piano when he was coming up with the big bands. Billy Eckstine said, "I knew Monk when he played ten times as much as he does now. I think he has got a little weird in his music today, but I tell you, Monk could play." Mary Lou Williams cut closer to the bone:

> While Monk was in his teens he jammed every night in Kaycee, really used to blow on piano, employing a lot more technique than he does today. Monk plays the way he does now because he got fed up. . . . He felt musicians should play something new and started doing it. (Hentoff-Shapiro, *Hear Me Talkin' to Ya.*)

The oft-heard charge that "Monk can't play the piano," often made by musicians blind to everything but technique, is like the chestnut of yesteryear that Picasso didn't know how to paint "properly." The uninitiated were not aware that Picasso had already mastered traditional styles while still a child and had thrown them aside for "something new." It was the same with Monk. His music that falls so easily on our ears today, for all its stark departures from "conventional" bebop, was rooted in Ellington, Harlem "stride," and the blues. One night at the Black Hawk when his bassist failed to show for the opening set, Monk played "stride" with complete authority, something he did from time to time in a sardonic way to inject wit and surprise into his work, as in *Lulu's Back in Town* (Columbia CS 8984), *Tea for Two* (Columbia CS 8838), and his first recording of *Thelonious* (Blue Note BLP 1510). When Monk plays the blues he often strips them down to bare essentials as in *Bag's Groove* (Smic 10/1), the all-star session made notorious by Miles Davis's demand that Monk "lay out"—not play—behind his solo, prompting Monk to say, "Nothing new about that—Roy Eldridge had his piano lay out *years* ago." Like Ellington, an early idol, Monk used the blues as the basis for his distinct composing style as in *Mysterioso* (Smic 9/4), a piece of disarming simplicity that plunges the blues into an astringent bath—although describing Monk's music is like describing the color orange to a blind person. Monk uses ballads to explore a new realm of piano *sound*, unlocking harmonic possibilities hidden within the well-trod territories of *Liza, Sophisticated Lady, Honeysuckle Rose*, and the extraordinary *Darn That Dream*, all contained on *The Riverside Trios* (Milestone M-47052). His arresting treatment of Jerome Kern's *Smoke Gets in Your Eyes* (Smic 9/7) weaves a clever parody of Ravel's *Bolero* into the start of the second chorus. Monk displayed remarkable gifts for writing elusive slow ballads of haunting loveliness; unfortunately, none are included in the Smithsonian Collection. His best-known ballad, *'Round Midnight*, has been recorded by nearly every major jazz figure since he first wrote it in the early 1940s. Other lyric tunes that never achieved this popularity but are fully as captivating are *Ruby My Dear, Reflections, Crepuscule With Nellie*, and *Ask Me Now.*

Criss-Cross (Smic 9/5) and *Evidence* (Smic 9/6), a reworking of *Just You, Just Me*, are among the more austere of the original works dismissed as "weird" when they first surfaced. They present few difficulties to today's listeners who can recognize the hand of a genuine original following his own bent. His epic collaborations with John Coltrane at New York's Five Spot in the late 1950s (*Monk/Trane*, Milestone M-47011) belong in any basic jazz library, especially the amazing *Trinkle Tinkle* where Monk and Coltrane play the intricate theme as one voice. "Working with Monk," Coltrane told a *down beat* interviewer, "brought me close to a musical architect of the highest order. I learned from him in every way. I would talk to Monk about musical problems and he would sit at the piano and show me the answers by playing them."

Critics often ignore Monk's influence on other seminal figures. "I brought Bud Powell around when he first started," Monk told this author. "That's never been in print. *I'm* the only one he really digs." Powell's debt to Monk is evident on *Mediocre* and *'Round Midnight* (*Jazz Legacy of Bud Powell*, Verve VSP/VSPS 34) and when comparing the opening-closing theme of Monk's *Thelonious* (Blue Note BLP 1510) with the second to last chorus of Powell's *Conception* (*Masters of Modern Piano*, Verve VE 2-2514). Since *Conception* was written by George Shearing it may lend some credence to Monk's bitter aside that "Shearing stole so much jive from me." Monk's insistence that he had not been given his due dominated his conversation with me in 1959:

> Dizzy, he was playing like Roy Eldridge, he *changed* when he hear me. When he went with Lucky Millinder (1942) he got me hired on piano so's he could be around me. I told Miles (Davis), "You better stop playing like Diz, you want to get somewhere," but all you read today is how Miles followed Diz, Parker, Fats Navarro around like a puppy—everybody but me. (*Jazz: A Quarterly of American Music*, Issue 5, Winter 1960.)

In the late 1950s Monk began to enjoy the fame that long eluded him. Producer Orrin Keepnews issued volumes of Riverside albums that finally put to rest the persistent myth of Monk as a cultish plunker. Gunther Schuller and French critic André Hodeir wrote lengthy raves. The early Blue Notes and Prestiges were reissued; he won the *down beat* Critics Poll in 1958 and 1959 and even made the cover of *Time*. His once-forbidding pieces were recorded by Miles Davis, J. J. Johnson, the Modern Jazz Quartet, Sonny Rollins, and Cannonball Adderley. His stubborn pursuit of his private musical vision in the face of cruel neglect had at last paid off. After years of retirement beset by illness, Monk died in 1981. His obituaries at home and abroad and, most of all, his recorded work left no doubt that this once mysterious "Mojo Man of Bop" had earned a place with Armstrong, Parker, and Ellington in the pantheon of American music.

CHARLIE PARKER AND HIS AFTERMATH

The specter of Charlie Parker continues to haunt contemporary jazz. His pervasive influence during his brief, frenetic lifetime has increased with each year since his death in 1955. Newly found airchecks, jam sessions, and alternate takes provide fresh sources of wonder. A saxophone quintet called *Supersax* made a career of arranging and performing the recorded improvisations he tossed off in the 1940s. A last-minute substitute for an ailing member of *Supersax* described to Gene Lees the experience of reading and performing these orchestrated Parker solos: "Man, it was like changing your fan belt with the motor running." Alto saxist Lee Konitz told the *New Yorker's* Whitney Balliett: "I often tell my students to learn this or that Charlie Parker solo. He created our études, and to learn a Parker solo can change your life." British poet-critic Clive James places him "without hesitation among the two dozen most important twentieth-century artists in any medium." (*First Reactions*.)

Though he never suffered the massive neglect of the early Monk, Parker, throughout his most creative period, was recognized only among the in group of musicians and a very few writers. When a reporter asked drummer Art Blakey if Bird was a culture hero to black people he snapped, "They never heard of him." *down beat* poorly reviewed his early records, now acknowledged to be the most important in modern jazz, including his blues, *Now's the Time*, stolen outright a decade later by Chubby Checker as the international hit, *The Hucklebuck*. When a fellow musician admonished Bird for lacking the guts to kick heroin he replied, "Wait until everyone gets rich off your style, and you don't have any bread—and *then* lecture me about drugs." (Russell, *Bird Lives!*) When Parker died a few months short of his thirty-fifth year the coroner esti-

Charlie Parker: When Bird died at 34, the coroner estimated his age to be 55. (Photograph from the Ralph J. Gleason Collection.)

mated his age to be 55, a grim testament to a consuming high-octane life that prompted someone to call him the Dylan Thomas of jazz.

Long after his death Parker's influence cut fore and aft like a twin-bladed axe. Many musicians, regardless of instrument, were determined to play like him. Others who were as far apart as rhythm 'n' blues and "free jazz" players were just as determined *not* to sound like him. After Parker the feeling among musicians was where do we go from here?

The Crucial Split: Modern Jazz, R 'n' B and the New Orleans Revival

The advent of bebop split American music into a number of tributaries that shaped the current course of American music—rock and pop as well as jazz. While bebop disciples Miles Davis, Charlie Mingus, John Lewis, Bill Evans, and John Coltrane carried the message of Bird and Dizzy into exploratory areas now known as "modern jazz," a two-pronged reaction against bebop's complexities was underway: The New Orleans-Dixieland revival and rhythm 'n' blues. Both of these tangential movements were to have enormous effects.

NEW ORLEANS REVIVAL

Five years before the arrival of bebop, a New Orleans revival was afoot, fueled by the mounting resentment of purist white critics and fans against the heretical sophistication of Ellington, Tatum, Hawkins, Teddy Wilson, and similar modernists who they believed had tainted the purity of jazz by injecting European antibodies into what had been an incorruptible native folk art. Since history assures us that jazz from its earliest beginnings was a mixture of every cultural transplant to the New World, European as well as African, such notions seem quaint today. But these notions were cherished as articles of faith by keepers of the flame like French critic Hugues Panassié, who insisted that bebop was "degenerate noise" and a short-lived fad that lay wholly outside the "true" jazz tradition. This position found its fullest expression in *The Heart of Jazz*, by William L. Grossman and Jack W. Farrell:

> Much of Dizzy Gillespie's bop . . . is characterized by a nonsensicality of content, an end result Armstrong never intended but which came from an almost inevitable consequence of the departure . . . from traditional values and meanings. Ellington . . . might help find a way to perpetuate the eternal values in New Orleans jazz while expanding the idiom, but his musical imagination turns to the theatrical. He is, indeed a sort of jazz Wagner. He has the same sort of dramatic feelings about Negroes that Wagner had about Germans.

The New Orleans revival got off to a modest start in 1940 when collector Heywood Hale Broun issued recordings of veteran New Orleans blacks in quavering versions of blues and parade music of their youth around the turn of the century. The following year saw the beginning of white revival bands in San Francisco, when Lu Watters and the Yerba Buena Jazz Band copied the instrumentation, the tunes, and as far as they were able, the style of King Oliver's Creole Jazz Band recordings made twenty years earlier. By the time bebop was in full bloom dozens of white revival bands were thriving throughout the United States, Europe, Australia, New Zealand, and in England where a fever for "trad" (traditional) was rampant among the youth, including some of the founders-to-be of British rock.

The revival brought elderly blacks out of retirement—Bunk Johnson, George Lewis—and provided work for young whites—Turk Murphy, Lu Watters, and England's Chris Barber. It also forced modernists like Earl Hines, Jack Teagarden, and clarinetist Pee Wee Russell reluctantly into the

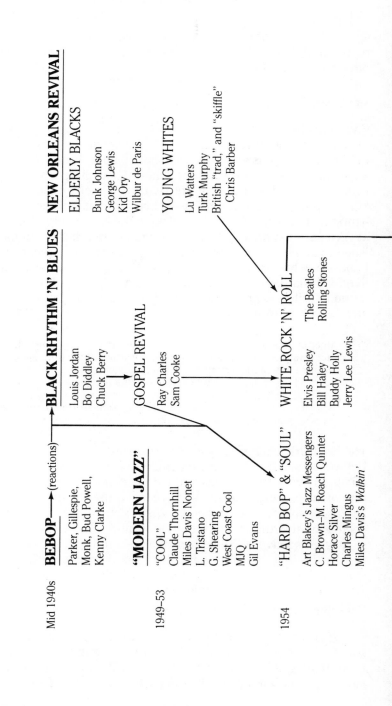

Mid 1940s

BEBOP───▶(reactions)   **BLACK RHYTHM 'N' BLUES**   **NEW ORLEANS REVIVAL**

Parker, Gillespie,   Louis Jordan   ELDERLY BLACKS
Monk, Bud Powell,   Bo Diddley
Kenny Clarke   Chuck Berry   Bunk Johnson
                                                                      George Lewis
                                                                      Kid Ory
                                                                      Wilbur de Paris

1949–53   **"MODERN JAZZ"**   GOSPEL REVIVAL   YOUNG WHITES

"COOL"   Ray Charles   Lu Watters
Claude Thornhill   Sam Cooke   Turk Murphy
Miles Davis Nonet   British "trad," and "skiffle"
L. Tristano   Chris Barber
G. Shearing
West Coast Cool
MJQ
Gil Evans

1954   **"HARD BOP" & "SOUL"**   WHITE ROCK 'N' ROLL

Art Blakey's Jazz Messengers   Elvis Presley   The Beatles
C. Brown–M. Roach Quintet   Bill Haley   Rolling Stones
Horace Silver   Buddy Holly
Charles Mingus   Jerry Lee Lewis
Miles Davis's *Walkin'*

Late 1950s **MODAL JAZZ**

Miles Davis Quintet with
  Bill Evans and Coltrane
George Russell

"THIRD STREAM"

Gunther Schuller
John Lewis
J. J. Johnson
Charlie Mingus

Late 1950s **"FREE JAZZ"** ———→ (reaction) ———→ **BOSSA NOVA**

Cecil Taylor   Stan Getz
Ornette Coleman   Jobim
Coltrane's *Ascencion*   Bonfa
Eric Dolphy

Late 1960s **"FUSION" OF JAZZ-ROCK**

Miles Davis's *Bitches Brew*

Lu Watters's Yerba Buena Jazz Band/c. 1943: The New Orleans revival got underway with white bands like Lu Watters's copying the instrumentation and style of the King Oliver Creole Jazz Band 20 years earlier. Trombonist Turk Murphy and second trumpeter Bob Scobey would eventually split to form their own revival bands. From left to right: Bill Dart, Wally Rose, Turk Murphy, Bob Scobey, Lu Watters, and Ellis Horne. The banjo and tuba are missing. (Photograph courtesy of the Rutgers Institute of Jazz Studies.)

dixieland camp during a doctrinaire era that split the jazz world into two warring factions. It is significant that, without a single exception, no young blacks could be found participating in the revival movement either as players or as listeners. They would as soon be seen chomping a watermelon on the front steps of city hall as partaking in what they scorned as "old-time slave, Uncle Tom, minstrel-man jive." Tempers ran high as lifelong friends and colleagues Hugues Panassié and Charles Delaunay stopped speaking because of bebop. Fistfights broke out in Parisian cabarets where Dizzy Gillespie performed, punctuated with cries of, "You dare to call this music!" The jazz press abounded with hate-ridden jeremiads about the "modernist degenerates of bebop" and the "moldy-fig reactionary revivalists," reminiscent of the doctrinal fury of sixteenth century Catholics and Protestants.

In retrospect, the revival produced foolish rhetoric but much also of lasting value, as did the ragtime revival three decades later; it rescued from obscurity a long-neglected style of collective improvisation and an imposing repertoire of excellent tunes. The best of these revival bands, Wilbur de Paris's New New Orleans Jazz (Atlantic 1219), exudes a vitality that bears repeated hearings today, but the same cannot be said for most revival players venerated to sainthood by their white idolators, some of whom launched a serious campaign to run Bunk Johnson for the presidency. What seems most remarkable about the revival movement is the emotional heat and religious fervor it unloosed—and why.

A rigid fundamentalist sect of white critic-collectors had grown comfortable with the soothing clichés of New Orleans-Dixieland and with the cautious geniality of the blacks who played it. There were exceptions, but, as a rule, black musicians before the bebop era tended to make themselves agreeable to the fan, as though they were beside themselves with delight that whites would actually appreciate their music. Though moved by generous impulses all too rare among whites of that time, many revivalists gave off an aura of patronage toward the "happy unspoiled darky," romanticized as the Noble Savage. The idealization of the Noble Savage recurs throughout history among intellectuals of sophisticated cultures verging on decadence: Horace in ancient Rome, Rousseau on the eve of the French Revolution, and our recent adoration of the Noble Red Man before his near annihilation and corruption by the onslaught of white civilization. The New Orleans revivalists adopted these notions with striking fidelity, viewing Bunk Johnson, Kid Ory, and George Lewis as reaffirmations of the "eternal values" of Morton and Oliver before the purity of jazz became polluted by jaded European influences. These revivalists were brought up short by the cool, studied arrogance of the beboppers, on stage and off, who made it clear, "We don't give a shit whether Mister Charley digs our music or not." This radical posture of a new generation of hip urban blacks proved as upsetting to white revival fans and critics as the shocking and unfamiliar sounds that signaled a revolutionary shift in black stance and attitude. When Armstrong hotly denounced bebop and its players to the press, Dizzy Gillespie replied, with all due reverence for Louis: "In these days, no cat need be a Tom."

RHYTHM 'N' BLUES (R 'n' B)

While the white reaction against bebop stoked the fires of the New Orleans revival, the black reaction spawned its own back-to-the-roots movement—rhythm 'n' blues (R 'n' B). Rejecting Parker's radical innovations with their heavy demands on listeners, R 'n' B harked back to simple elemental blues patterns propelled by an insistent danceable beat. Its appeal was immediate and gut-level, resting on a broader commercial base than either bebop or the rural blues of the 1920s and 1930s from which urbanized R 'n' B had sprung.

Following the classic age of women blues singers that culminated with Bessie Smith, Bluebird and Decca recorded a treasury of rural and city blues artists throughout the depression: Big Bill Broonzy, Peetie Wheatstraw (the Devil's Son-in-Law), LeRoy Carr, Scrapper Blackwell, Sleepy John Estes, Robert Johnson, Bumblebee Slim, Big Maceo, Kokomo Arnold, Lonnie Johnson, Leadbelly, Tampa Red, Harlem Hamfats, Georgia White, Blue Lu Barker, Rosetta Crawford, Lil Green, Rosetta Howard. As increasing numbers of blacks moved to large Northern cities, the blues began to reflect the growing urbanization. Some of the finest blues singers came to prominence with the big bands of the Southwest "territory": Jimmy Rushing, Jimmy Witherspoon, and Big Joe Turner whose *Shake, Rattle and Roll* became one of the big R 'n' B hits of the fifties. "We was gettin' plenty of airtime," recalled Turner, "when all those cats up in New York started hearin' us whammin' on these blues. We were doin' rock and roll before anybody ever heard of it."

The founding father of R 'n' B was a wailing blues alto saxist and singer out of the Chick Webb band, Louis Jordan. With his skillful jump combo, the Tympani Five, Jordan started in 1939 to cut a series of hit records throughout the bebop era, proving that a small unit could have mass appeal at a time when the big bands were on their way out. Jordan's repertoire included comedy-novelties like *Saturday Night Fish Fry, That Chick's Too Young to Fry,* and *You Run Your Mouth, and I'll Run My Business,* laced with an abundance of good-time blues: *I'm Gonna Move to the Outskirts of Town, Caldonia Boogie,* and *Buzz Me.*

The gulf that divided bebop from R 'n' B is apparent when comparing Parker's *Now's the Time* (*The Charlie Parker Story,* Savoy MG 12072) with Jordan's *Buzz Me* (*The Best of Louis Jordan,* MCA 2-4079). Both are 12-bar major blues; both feature alto sax solos; both are played at the same medium-jump tempo; and in their varying ways, both are superb examples of blues playing recorded the same year, 1945. Yet the differences are more apparent than the similarities, even to the untutored ear. *Buzz Me* is a straight-ahead jump blues and vocal, tailor-made to get the dancers up and moving—and to top record sales charts. *Now's the Time* shows how Parker enriched the blues with a new and complex harmonic-rhythmic language that made intellectual demands on its listener. Like *Buzz Me, Now's the Time* is body-based, inspiring dancer Honi Coles to create new steps, but its main appeal is not to the feet but to the head and heart.

Louis Jordan: The founding father of rhythm 'n' blues (shown in one of his more subdued moments) gave folks a show for their money. Bird just stood like a statue and blew (see photo on page 156). (Photograph from the Ralph J. Gleason Collection.)

In the "Twistin' Fifties," the blues theme of *Now's the Time* became the national anthem of millions of white teenagers under the name of *The Hucklebuck*, Chubby Checker's dance sensation (*Twist With Chubby Checker*, Parkway P 7001). To compare *Now's the Time* with *The Hucklebuck* is to liken Handel's *Messiah* to *Rudolph the Rednosed Reindeer*. The Checker hit is a children's version of the blues crafted for a twist-happy, rebellious youth who would have found *Now's the Time* as mystifying as Chinese opera had they much chance to hear it, which they did not. Few big-time disc jockeys, aside from Symphony Sid in Manhattan and Daddy-O Dailey in Chicago, aired the classic bebop records. With few exceptions the youth-market airways beamed an unvarying format of rhythm 'n' blues, "Top Forty," and later, rock 'n' roll.

Charlie Parker (Photograph courtesy of the
Rutgers Institute of Jazz Studies.)

How Rock 'n' Roll
Got Started

The children's revolt of the fifties was a phenomenon unique in history.
For the first time teenagers, and very young ones at that, swung an eco-
nomic-puchasing power virtually independent of the elders, creating their
own superstar heroes—the Beatles, Rolling Stones, Presley—their own
overnight millionaires trafficking in records, rock concerts, "happenings;"

their own magazines—*Mad Magazine* and, later, *Rolling Stone*—their own movies—*Beach Blanket Bingo, Love Me Tender*—and similar artifacts of pubescent rebellion.

Like the "Flaming Youth" of the twenties and the jitterbugs of the thirties, the children of the cold war seized upon white imitations of black music as their anthem of revolt. The growing fragmentation and divisiveness of American society reached epidemic proportions. This was no longer a culture of shared experiences between parents and children—the movies of Chaplin, Keaton, the Marx Brothers, Astaire and Rogers; the radio fare of Amos 'n' Andy and Jack Benny; the broadcasts of Joe Louis's fights; the fireside chats of President Roosevelt. In the fifties white middle-class youths launched a frontal assault on the elders who brought them the Bomb, Eisenhower, Joe McCarthy, bomb shelters, and an uptight sexual-moral code as embodied in the pallid emotionally-caged sounds of Pat Boone, Liberace, Dinah Shore, Eddie Fisher, Perry Como, and Lawrence Welk.

Spurning the genteel music of their elders and languishing in invincible ignorance of the entire jazz tradition from Scott Joplin through Charlie Parker, the children of the cold war twisted and boogied to a host of pied pipers who followed in the wake of Louis Jordan to ensnare legions of teenagers craving to shake ass: Chuck Berry, Bo Diddley, Fats Domino, Little Richard, Sam Cooke, and Ray Charles. The late critic Ralph J. Gleason, who made a point of keeping up with pop music trends, found that: "In 1952 and 1953 (record) salesmen began to report Southern white high school and college students were picking up on rhythm 'n' blues, primarily to dance to. A few alert disc jockeys observed this and switched to R 'n' B. They were deluged with greater audiences, both white and Negro, and more and more sponsors." (San Francisco *Chronicle*.)

As in the Jazz Age of the twenties and the Swing Era of the thirties, millions of white youths in the fifties got their first addictive shot of black music in the guise of cleverly packaged white facsimiles: Buddy Holly; Jerry Lee Lewis, who sold a carbon copy of Ray Charles's *Whud I Say?*; Elvis Presley, whose entire act was modeled on black R'n'B artists he had seen in Harlem theaters; and Bill Haley and the Comets, whose *Rock Around the Clock*, which gave the rock craze an initial push, was adapted from Trixie Smith's blues of the 1920s, *My Daddy Rocks Me With One Steady Roll*. Then came the Beatles with a version of Ray Charles's *Yeah, Yeah, Yeah!* and the Rolling Stones' *Love in Vain*, an electronic multitrack reworking of Robert Johnson's plaintive blues from the 1930s.

It was no accident that the triumph of black music among white youth coincided with the bus boycott in Montgomery and the emergence of Martin Luther King and Malcolm X. The Free Speech Movement on the tumultuous Berkeley campus made its headquarters in a record shop.

Black music supplied a common tongue for an underground alliance of ghetto blacks and middle-class white youths that exploded with the civil rights, anti-Vietnam, black, Indian, Chicano, women, and student uprisings of the sixties. This chaotic upheaval of the disaffiliated young elevated a host of trendy heroes: Mario Savio, Eldridge Cleaver, Rap Brown, Stokeley Carmichael, Jerry Rubin, Timothy Leary, Abbie Hoffman, Rennie Davis. But the youth-cult gods who survived the sixties as sanctified figures were not student activists, radical politicians, revolutionary theorists, or pop gurus but Bob Dylan, the Beatles, the Rolling Stones, Janis Joplin, and Jimi Hendrix.

When fifties' youth cut loose from the elders they did not "reject" Charlie Parker along with Pat Boone and Judy Garland because they never knew Parker or his music existed, except in pablum form like *The Hucklebuck*. True to that most American of maxims—Henry Ford's "History is bunk"—the children of the Bomb started from scratch to discover the blues secondhand through Elvis Presley, Buddy Holly, and the Beatles.

This alienation from the culture of the past was not limited to music but involved the root and branch of American life. A supermarket full of movies, novels, comic books, magazines, pop poetry, soft-core philosophy, theater, art, the occult, and instant nirvanas was media-crafted for a vast consumer audience frozen in perpetual adolescence. The comedy of Cheech & Chong, John Belushi, Steve Martin, and *Saturday Night Live* was beamed at a young audience bypassed by the rich mainstream of social satire of the fifties and sixties, which culminated in Lenny Bruce, who bears the same relationship to John Belushi that Charlie Parker bears to Chubby Checker. Hollywood hired bright twelve-year-olds at hefty fees to act as sounding boards for producers bent on luring young moviegoers who were known to rescreen their favorites ten times and more. By his own admission George Lucas made the *Star Wars Trilogy* with a 12-year-old audience in mind. An immense pop youth-cult warehouse was stocked with the novels of Tom Robbins, *Animal House, E. T., The Rocky Horror Show*, Andy Warhol flicks, *Raiders of the Lost Ark, Return of the Jedi*, Elton John, Led Zeppelin, Bette Midler, Carlos Casteneda, the Sex Pistols, *Tommy*, Rod McKuen, *Jesus Christ Superstar, Godspell*, and that embodiment of infantile regression, Brooke Shields, a child molester's fantasy exalted as sex goddess of the eighties.

Modern Jazz and
The Spread of Bebop

While the New Orleans revival and R 'n' B were enjoying their heyday, bebop gave birth to "modern jazz," a varied, constantly evolving art music. True to the pattern of the European avant-garde, the sounds of bebop slowly seeped into the mainstream of jazz to gain acceptance and eventual embracement by those who had once been quick to condemn it. By the early 1950s bebop, now called "modern jazz," was taken up by established musicians who commanded much larger followings than Bird and the short-lived bebop big bands of Earl Hines and Billy Eckstine that ran afoul of the union recording ban during the war.

Artie Shaw reorganized his band in the mid-1940s with trumpeter Roy Eldridge and young beboppers Dodo Marmarosa on piano and Barney Kessel on guitar (*Artie Shaw Featuring Roy Eldridge*, RCA Vintage LPV-582). Though not Shaw's most popular band, it was his best by far, with a splendid new version of his chamber group, the "Gramercy Five," that gave his fans their first tentative taste of bebop. Shaw's clarinet inventions were the finest of his career and more "modern" than Goodman, whose flirtation with a bebop combo was as dispirited as it was brief. Veteran Lionel Hampton worked Parker's *Ornithology* into his small group's version of *How High the Moon*. In 1950, wholesale changes in the once-constant Ellington personnel brought in modernists Clark Terry on trumpet and Louis Bellson on drums; both were showcased in the Ellington-Strayhorn revision of *Perdido*, with an arrangement for five reeds that foreshadowed *Supersax's* adaptations of Parker solos (*Hi-Fi Ellington Uptown*, Columbia CL 830).

True to the familiar pattern, the spread of bebop was accomplished by better-known white bands and combos: Woody Herman, George Shearing, Stan Kenton, Gerry Mulligan, Dave Brubeck, and the popular West Coast "cool" school. Formed at the start of the 1940s, the Stan Kenton Orchestra commanded a fanatical following of a large and exclusively white audience. Despite the Wagnerian pomposity that burdened much of Kenton's massed orchestral sound, paralleled by his periodic manifestos proclaiming the epochal significance of what he called "Progressive Jazz," his band carried Parker's message *via* a gifted platoon of bebop-oriented soloists—Lee Konitz, Conte Condoli, Frank Rosolino, Shelly Manne, and Stan Levey—and with the arrangements of Gerry Mulligan, Bill Russo, and Bill Holman. With messianic zeal Kenton subsidized and promoted jazz instruction in high school and college "clinics" all over the country. The more interesting Boyd Raeburn Band was likewise honeycombed with young disciples of Parker and Gillespie, at one time even including Dizzy himself, but this adventuresome outfit only engaged a cult following and was too short-lived to make the impact of Kenton or Herman.

The various Woody Herman "Herds" did more than any other white band to inject the sound of bebop, and its forerunner, Lester Young, into the mainstream. After fronting a successful Swing Era "Band that Plays the Blues," Herman, in one of his recurrent moves to keep abreast of changing styles, reorganized his "First Herd" in the mid-1940s, mixing

older modernists Red Norvo and Dave Tough with a wealth of high-energy
beboppers to generate an excitement on records that has stood the test of
time: the uptempo *Apple Honey*; Louis Jordan's raffish blues, *Caldonia*;
Neal Hefti's *Northwest Passage*; Ralph Burns's latin-tinged *Sidewalks of
Cuba*; and his extended work, *Summer Sequence*. Suddenly, at the end of
1946, Herman disbanded to regroup the next fall with the Second Herd,
tempering the frenzy of the First Herd with the relaxed spirit of Lester
Young in an early outcropping of the "cool" sound that was to dominate
modern jazz in the early fifties. Herman's shift from swing to bebop can be
plotted by comparing his million-seller hit of 1939, *Woodchopper's Ball*,

Stan Getz: An original member of Woody
Herman's "Four Brothers," Getz spread the
message of Lester Young to large audiences and
later popularized the fusion of Brazilian music
and jazz known as "bossa nova." (Photograph
by Grover Sales.)

with his 1947 adaptation of Ray Charles's *I've Got News For You.* Both pieces are blues; the listener will have no trouble distinguishing the steady four-four drumming on *Woodchopper's Ball* from Don Lamond's "bomb-dropping" on *I've Got News For You*, which features the strong bebop flavor of Shorty Rogers' arrangement for the sax section that is based on Parker's blues chorus on singer Earl Coleman's *Dark Shadows.*

One of the Second Herd's most widely-known records, a favorite of musicians and public alike, was *Four Brothers*, which might have been titled "Homage to Lester Young." Composed in 1949 by Jimmy Giuffre, later a fixture of West Coast "cool," *Four Brothers* featured tenor saxists Stan Getz, Zoot Sims, Herbie Steward, and baritone saxist Serge Chaloff. All of their phrasing, tone, and concept was Young-inspired, resulting in a remarkable unanimity of style and a felicitous blend that earned the Second Herd its permanent nickname as the "Four Brothers Band." The lush romantic ballad, *Early Autumn*, marked the meteoric debut of Stan Getz as the new tenor sax influence on younger musicians. Getz was to play a key role in establishing the first important offshoot of bebop, "cool," which dominated the jazz scene in the early 1950s and gave post-war college youths their first taste of authentic jazz. (All of the Herman records mentioned are included in the package *Woody Herman: The Thundering Herds*, Columbia C3L 25.)

ERROLL GARNER

Few jazzmen of the post-war period rivaled the success of Erroll Garner, an unslottable piano stylist adored by musicians of all persuasions as well as by the non-jazz public, whom he managed to ensnare at no detriment to his art. Garner's inability to read music made him unusual among "modern" jazz musicians, but his lack of formal training proved no more of a handicap than it did for the painter, Rousseau. Discovered by Mary Lou Williams, Garner hit the Fifty-second Street scene in the early 1940s as a bebopper—although a unique one—to record with the Slam Stewart Trio and with Charlie Parker on some of his finest early sides. Like Ellington and Armstrong, he caught the ear of a canny Jewish business agent, Martha Glaser, who took her young protégé out of the dives to showcase him in plush hotels and concert halls. In 1958 he became the first jazz artist ever presented by the leading concert impressario, Sol Hurok. His most famous composition, *Misty*, has remained a staple in both the jazz and pop repertoire since 1958 when an arranger first transcribed this piano improvisation to sheet music.

Garner's style ranged from the lush, florid romanticism of *Misty* to the bouncy jump-blues of *Fantasy on 'Frankie and Johnny'* (Smic 8/4). At medium and breakneck tempos he disported a firm melodic right-hand line backed by a chord-strumming left so far behind the beat that it courted rhythmic disaster, somewhat along the lines of Jelly Roll Morton's *New Orleans Joys* and Meade "Lux" Lewis's *Honky Tonk Train* (Smic 4/2). The result was an irresistible foot-tapping beat and a boisterous charm laced with puckish wit. With an obvious delight shared with his audience, Garner was fond of prefacing well-known, unannounced tunes like *S'Wonderful* and *April in Paris* with extended free fantasias of remarkable invention whose relationship to the familiar melody-to-come was known only to himself. To compare his happy rollicking *Indiana* (*Garner Gems*, Columbia CL 583) with Bud Powell's nervous agitated version of the same tune (Royal Roost RLP 2224) is to grasp why, more than any other musician of the bebop era save Miles Davis, Garner attracted a mass audience. Though the quality of his huge recorded output stayed consistently high, the popular LP, *Concert By the Sea* (Columbia CL 583), is representative of his best work. Widely copied, he put a firm stamp on a number of front-rank pianists including Jaki Byard and Roland Hanna. After a brilliant concert career throughout Europe, the Far East, Latin America, and the U.S., where he often performed with major symphony orchestras, Erroll Garner unexpectedly succumbed to pneumonia in 1977.

"Cool" Jazz

"Cool jazz for the cold war" may be a simplistic catch phrase, yet "cool" did not arise in a social vacuum and must be related to the peculiar political hothouse that nurtured it. In retrospect, cool jazz seemed well suited to the aesthetic needs of both its players and its audience, a fitting *obbligáto* to the cautious emotional climate engendered by the Korean War, bomb shelters, Sputnik, the Hiss and Rosenberg cases, HUAC (House Un-American Activities Committee) Hollywood pogroms, the matter of J. Robert Oppenheimer as a "security risk," government "loyalty" checks, the national paranoia over the "loss" of China, high-level "traitors" in the State Department, the purge of liberals, intellectuals, Eastern aristocrats, and homosexuals from government service, and other landmarks of the McCarthy era.

Overseas veterans who missed out on bebop during the war years came home to find that, with few exceptions, big bands had given way to small combos. In the post-war boom public interest in jazz reached unprecedented heights, catalyzed by mass media awareness, the birth of the long-playing record and hi-fi component industry, and the spread of FM radio and all-star concert packages like Norman Granz's "Jazz at the Philharmonic." Thanks to the G.I. Bill of Rights, entertainment-hungry veterans packed colleges and universities. Students unexposed to and emotionally unprepared for the exuberant demands of Parker and Gillespie gravitated toward a classically-oriented form of quiet chamber jazz: the George Shearing Quintet, the Red Norvo Trio, and later, the Modern Jazz Quartet, Dave Brubeck Quartet, Gerry Mulligan Quartet, and the Shorty Rogers-Jimmy Giuffre school of West Coast jazz.

A fusion of bebop harmonies with the shimmering impressionist timbres of Debussy and Ravel, plus some rudimentary baroque counterpoint, "cool" marked the shift from the belly-throbbing agitation of Coleman Hawkins to the relaxed, throaty wistfulness of Lester Young and Stan Getz; the sizzling intensity of Roy Eldridge gave way to the muted rock-skipping of Miles Davis, whose fleet stacatto putterings were likened by Paul Desmond to "a man constructing a mobile while riding a unicycle." Bud Powell's frantic keyboard steeplechase unnerved a public enchanted with the becalming behind-the-beat blend of George Shearing, the British pianist-composer whose quintet played bebop with a Debussy touch. Shearing's solo on the jukebox favorite, *East of the Sun*, was an obvious imitation of Charlie Parker (*You're Hearing George Shearing*, MGM E3216). The jubilant Afro-Cuban shouts of Dizzy Gillespie's big band in the 1940s were succeeded in the 1950s by the serene cerebrations of its former rhythm section, the Modern Jazz Quartet.

THE "BIRTH OF THE COOL"

A landmark series of twelve Capitol recordings in 1949 and 1950 by an experimental nine-piece band under the name of Miles Davis and his Orchestra struck young musicians with all the force of the Armstrong Hot Fives in the 1920s. These sessions that have come to be called "The Birth of the Cool" never sold well or got airplay, but their influence on the course of jazz was incalculable. (Only one side is included in the Smithsonian, *Boplicity*—Smic 9/1. Listeners are urged to get the entire set, *Birth of the Cool*, Capitol T 762.) The nucleus of this group was derived from the big band of Claude Thornhill of 1946 to 1949, a unique aggregation that employed voices new to jazz—the french horn, and the tuba played as a melodic rather than as a rhythm instrument. The quiet "snowfall" arrangements of Gil Evans scored for unusual timbres set the Thornhill sound apart from all other bands. Gil Evans, alto saxist Lee Konitz, bassist Joe Schulman, baritone saxist Gerry Mulligan, and tubist Bill Barber, all from the Thornhill Band, were joined by a confederation of sympathetic musicians who had been meeting in Evans's apartment to rehearse and exchange new ideas. This was the start of the long and fruitful collaboration of Evans and Miles Davis, who put together a "dream" band that money could not buy and keep on the road ten years later when most had become household names in jazz. A glance at the lineup of the "Birth of the Cool" reads like a blueprint of jazz-to-come:

Miles Davis	trumpet
J. J. Johnson	trombone
or	
Kai Winding	
Lee Konitz	alto sax
Gerry Mulligan	baritone sax
Gunther Schuller	french horn
or	
Junior Collins	
or	
Sandy Siegelstein	
Bill Barber	tuba
John Lewis	piano
or	
Al Haig	
Kenny Clarke	drums
or	
Max Roach	
Joe Schulman	bass
or	
Al McKibbon	
or	
Nelson Boyd	
Gil Evans ("Cleo Henry")	arranger-composers
John Lewis,	
John Carisi,	
Gerry Mulligan,	
Miles Davis	

Fresh from his apprenticeship with the Parker Quintet, Miles Davis went on to dominate new jazz developments and uncover fresh talent for the next twenty years. Gil Evans was to emerge as the premier composer-arranger-leader of his day, often compared to Ellington. J. J. Johnson was the first to adapt the trombone to a bebop style and later developed into a composer of note. Gerry Mulligan formed a pianoless quartet in the 1950s that made an impact on musicians and public alike. Lee Konitz, a pupil-disciple of "cool" pianist-composer Lennie Tristano, became a major post-Parker pacesetter whose exploratory freshness remains undiminished today. John Lewis was to found the Modern Jazz Quartet, the paramount small group for over three decades. Al Haig, whom Lewis called "the best bebop pianist I ever heard," was a veteran of the Parker-Gillespie quintet. Kenny Clarke was the father of modern bebop drumming and, like his disciple, Max Roach, is one of the most innovative and listenable drummers in jazz. Roach went on to found the famous quintet in the mid fifties with Clifford Brown, and he continues to be a force in music today. Gunther Schuller, a new breed of musician-critic-composer equally at home with jazz and classical, was to found the working alliance with John Lewis and J. J. Johnson called Third Stream, a fusion of modern jazz with contemporary European concert music.

The "Birth of the Cool" brought a fresh and distinct sound to jazz that can be heard by comparing *Boplicity* (Smic 9/1) to other sounds that preceded it: Parker's *Klactoveedsedstene* (Smic 8/1) and *Little Benny* (Smic 8/2) and Tadd Dameron's *Lady Bird* (Smic 9/2). An even more startling contrast can be heard between the group's only blues, *Israel*, and any other blues that had gone before: Parker's *Parker's Mood* (Smic 8/3), Dexter Gordon's *Bikini* (Smic 9/3), or Charlie Christian's *Breakfast Feud* (Smic 6/3).

Like Morton's Red Hot Peppers, "Birth of the Cool" solo voices are subordinate to the group, but all similarity ends there. The mood is cerebral, reflective, and understated. Timbres are blended and indistinct, floating in and out on quiescent waves. The trumpet, alto sax, and trombone are void of vibrato, more akin to the symphonic sound cultivated by Gunther Schuller's French horn. Gil Evans's arrangement of the pop tune, *Moon Dreams*, appears to waft on swirling mists; the low rumbling brass in *Move* and *Godchild* evokes the good-natured romps of a German marching band. Impossible to describe, these sounds are the work of schooled and experiment-minded young turks who cast the mold of jazz throughout the early Eisenhower years.

Concurrent with the "Birth of the Cool", another series of Capitol records in 1949 under the leadership of Lennie Tristano helped establish the dominance of "cool" among the musicians, though not the public. A reclusive, mystical figure, the blind Tristano founded a Platonic academy of devoted pupils: Lee Konitz; the poll-winning guitarist, Billy Bauer; and tenor saxist Warne Marsh, later an original member of *Supersax*. A superb pianist and avant-garde composer, Tristano blended bebop and the new "cool" sound with the atonality of Schoenberg. The intricate unison passages on *Crosscurrent* (Smic 8/8) testify to the iron discipline Tristano imposed on his students and himself. Years before the advent of Cecil Taylor, Ornette Coleman, and other "free jazz" pioneers, "Tristano," wrote Martin Williams, "was experimenting with free improvisations performed with no preconceptions as to melody, chords, mood or tempo." (*Smithsonian* booklet.) He was one of the first to overdub separate piano lines, playing duets and trios with himself. Too radical for public acceptance, he remained a cult figure throughout his career, but an influence on better-known avant-gardists, as well as on Bill Evans.

More accessible than the forbidding experiments of Tristano, though hardly in the best-selling bracket of the Shearing Quintet, was the Red Norvo Trio with guitarist Tal Farlow (later Jimmy Raney) and bassist Charlie Mingus (later Red Mitchell). An advanced musician from the time he surfaced in the early 1930s, Norvo was the first to play genuine jazz on a mallet keyboard, the xylophone. The fleet, subdued interplay of his trio was definitely of the cool persuasion.

The Modern Jazz Quartet was perhaps the most versatile and, beyond question, the most durable of all small combos to emerge from the cool tradition. Their approach to music, business, performance, and living signaled the arrival of a new style of black jazz artist personified by John Lewis, the MJQ's founder, leader, pianist, composer, and theorist. A complete cosmopolite, Lewis combines a wide-ranging intellect with fanatical discipline, an unshakable resolve to get his own way, and a grounding in

The Modern Jazz Quartet: Standing are drummer Connie Kay (left) and pianist/leader John Lewis. Seated are bassist Percy Heath and vibraphonist Milt Jackson. The suits are from Saville Row, London. Said John Lewis: "We don't want to go on stage looking like a bunch of tramps." (Photograph from the Ralph J. Gleason Collection.)

older jazz forms that is rare among musicians of his era. Skilled in both classical and jazz, with master's degrees in both music and anthropology, he imposed his quiet but unbending will on responsive cohorts to achieve a unique blend of vibraphone (Milt Jackson), bass (Percy Heath), and drums (Kenny Clarke, soon replaced permanently by Connie Kay). All four voices play equal rather than dominant or supportive roles. For all of Lewis's tireless rehearsals, meticulous concern with structure, and mixing of Bach and Renaissance music with jazz, the MJQ swings and has never lost touch with the blues, or the lifeblood of spontaneous improvisation. This adroit merger of discipline and abandon shines through in his most popular piece *Django* (Smic 10/4), a bluesy homage to gypsy guitarist Django Reinhardt. Both Lewis and the MJQ's supreme soloist, Milt Jackson, came out of the Parker combos and the Gillespie big band of the 1940s, once more showing how "cool" grew out of bebop. Organized in 1952, the MJQ has stayed together without a personnel change longer than any group in jazz, periodically disbanding and reuniting into the 1980s. Had the MJQ never existed John Lewis would still be noted as a composer, prime mover, patron of new music, publisher, educator, and what Whitney Balliett calls "a unique and invariably moving pianist . . . his touch is sure and delicate, his ideas are disarmingly simple and honest. He has a rhythmic sense and enough technique to allow him easy freedom." (*New Yorker.*) Since 1959 Lewis has often served as musical director of the Monterey Jazz Festival where he annually proves himself a matchless accompanist for lyric vocalists and blues singers and a versatile anchorman in jam sessions.

WEST COAST COOL

Miles Davis's "Birth of the Cool" records spawned a working alliance of Los Angeles based musicians—the West Coast school—that nearly cornered the jazz market in the early 1950s. Predominately white, their records sold well among a post-war college crowd that scarcely knew any other type of jazz existed. Their schooled technical precision, versatility, and arranging skills were much in demand in Hollywood studios and "name" recording sessions that provided a steady source of well-paid work. Adapting the easy facility and vibratoless timbres of "The Birth of the Cool," the West Coast group was given to exercises in counterpoint and arhythmical improvisations infused with a spirit of emotional restraint. With rare exceptions—Shelly Manne, Art Pepper, Gerry Mulligan, Red Mitchell—few of these once-heralded poll winners emerged in the 1960s as figures of influence or major repute: Pete Rugulo, Shorty Rogers, Russ Freeman, Howard Rumsey, Stu and Claude Williamson, Lennie Niehaus, Marty Paich, Bob Cooper, Jimmy Giuffre, Bill Holman, Bob Enevoldsen, and André Previn, whose trio topped jazz record sales and became a major concert attraction before he developed into a front-rank symphony conductor.

For all their technical expertise, most of the West Coast group recordings for Contemporary and Pacific Jazz today strike us as bloodless museum pieces, a neatly packaged sound track for the cold war. However this group was neither wholly white nor "cool;" their ranks included some like-minded blacks—drummer Chico Hamilton, bassist Leroy Vinnegar, and reedman Buddy Collette, who so immersed himself in the movement that when Leonard Feather played his tenor solos for Miles Davis in a *down beat* "Blindfold Test," Miles snorted, "All those ofay (white) tenor players sound alike to me." Pianist Hampton Hawes and saxman Art Pepper, both fixtures in the West Coast scene, never succumbed to "cool" but forged ahead with a hard-driving blues format rooted in bebop. The Parker-inspired piano of Hawes seemed at variance with the laid-back approach of his western colleagues.

An eastern transplant, Gerry Mulligan formed an unusual pianoless quartet (Prestige 24016) whose records sold well and bear repeated hearings today. They still beguile us with his witty, inventive interplay with trumpeter Chet Baker, a Miles Davis spinoff with a ravishing tone and incisive attack reminiscent of Bix.

The Dave Brubeck Brouhaha

The Dave Brubeck Quartet, by far the most popular combo of the fifties, is a special case that demands a full airing if we are to understand the heated reaction that followed in the wake of its unprecedented success. A music major at Stockton's College of the Pacific, Brubeck studied on the West Coast with Darius Milhaud and Arnold Schoenberg before cutting his initial records in 1949 for the then-obscure Fantasy label. In 1951 Brubeck was joined by his long-time associate, Paul Desmond, a lyric alto saxist in the "cool" tradition of Lee Konitz, who became identified with Brubeck as an equal. Before its move up from Fantasy to the major Columbia label, the Brubeck Quartet suddenly became a smash attraction among a white college crowd that could identify with Brubeck's "classical" style, full of familiar quotations from Chopin and Wagner thundered out with romantic grandeur, and his engaging Bachian counterpoint with Desmond. A consistent winner of reader's polls throughout the 1950s and a huge draw on the college concert circuit, Brubeck peaked in 1954 when he became the second jazz musician after Louis Armstrong to make the cover of *Time* magazine, a signal honor reserved for the great and near-great (in contrast to later years when President Ford's would-be assassin, Squeeky Fromme, made the covers of *Time* and *Newsweek* in the same week). Brubeck's *Time* cover fanned the long-smoldering resentment within the black jazz community against the commercial dominance of white "cool" and its genteel restraint, which they scorned as "Brooks Brothers" or "faggot" jazz (in days well before the gay movement). Feeling *Time* should have honored Ellington, among others, black musicians were put out because they held Brubeck to be peripheral to important developments, outside the mainstream of modern jazz, a founder of no schools, and an inspirer of few disciples. When Brubeck swept *down beat* and *Metronome* reader polls in 1956, not one of the 120 top musicians polled by Leonard Feather included the Brubeck quartet among their three favorite combos. In a corrosive *down beat* interview Miles Davis said, "Brubeck can't swing—he doesn't know how." But within a year he was recording Brubeck's tunes, *The Duke*, and *In Your Own Sweet Way.*

The truth about Brubeck lies somewhere between the easy dismissal of his detractors and the lofty praise of the *Time* editor who found him cover-worthy. It is as a composer of fine ballads, rather than as an improvisor, that Brubeck's place in history seems most assured. His recordings show him to be a skilled musician and Paul Desmond, an inspired one. Though his followers were few, one of them, Cecil Taylor, was destined for importance in the free jazz movement. Brubeck gave millions their first exposure to any form of jazz; he pioneered the use of time signatures unusual to jazz like the 5/4 of Desmond's hit, *Take Five*. He provided a long-time platform for Desmond and the superb drum technician, Joe Morello. Against strong opposition, Brubeck toured the South with an interracial quartet at a time when this was neither common nor prudent.

The "Hard-bop" and "Soul-Funk" Reaction to Cool

> The last thing Charlie Parker said to me was he wondered when young people would come back to playing the blues. (Art Blakey in Art Taylor's *Notes & Tones*)

Suddenly in the mid-1950s black musicians, mainly working in the East, mounted a musical-ideological revolt that wiped out the polite cerebral sound of West Coast cool almost overnight. Disdaining "cool" as "white man's music" that had meandered far afield from the "soul" and the down-home body-based impulse of black music, these committed and often hostile musicians launched a self-conscious revival of the black gospel roots and "funky" blues ("funk" being immemorial slang for the unwashed rutting odor of working-class blacks).

"Soul" and "funk" were joined in battle by "hard bop," a return to the basics of the Parker-Gillespie quintet driven by the insistent beat of rhythm'n'blues but enriched with the complexities of bebop drumming.

An advance rumbling of the black uprisings of the 1960s, the "soul-funk" movement coincided with the widespread youth revolt against cold war conformity. Few commentators seemed to notice that the pulse of black music coursed through all of these uprisings, including the bold "new wave" of cabaret satire that began with Mort Sahl in the early fifties. This breed of social critics gave voice to the "Great Refusal" with unheard of attacks on a deified President Eisenhower; Vice President Nixon; F.B.I. Chief J. Edgar Hoover, long immune from public attack; and Senator Mc-Carthy, who lent his name to the era. ("I'm teaching my kids about Senator McCarthy at home," quipped Sahl, "because I don't want them to find out about him in the street.") Unlike older comics of the Bob Hope persuasion, these new satirists were jazz-oriented, on stage and off. Paul Krassner, editor of a new type of dissident journal, *The Realist*, said, "Lenny Bruce fought for the right to say on a nightclub stage what he felt free to say in his own living room." Sahl and Bruce expanded the national forum for venerable black comics—Moms Mabley, Pigmeat Markham, Nipsey Russell, Redd Foxx—whose racial jibes, once confined to ghetto theaters and clubs, were now heard for the first time by large white audiences in cabarets, concert halls, and on prime-time television. There Nipsey Russell said, "They already have integration in the South—the NAACP just wants them to have it in the *daytime*." They joined a new wave of young black comics—Dick Gregory, Godfrey Cambridge, and later Richard Pryor—in giving whites their first unmasked look at what black people thought: Dick Gregory's six-year-old son told him on Christmas Eve that he didn't believe in Santa Claus, "because you know damn good and well, Pop, that no white man's gonna come into *this* neighborhoood after midnight."

It should not be surprising that the new comics of dissent—culminating in Lenny Bruce—hung out with jazz musicians and often performed in jazz clubs. They were discovered not by established theater critics but by jazz writers Ralph J. Gleason, Gene Lees, and Nat Hentoff, and they were recorded on the jazz label, Fantasy.

Bebop was a shared passion among the fifties' new wave of "beat" poets and writers whose work and lifestyle loomed in flagrant opposition to the literary establishment and academics: Jack Kerouac, Allen Ginsberg, Gary Snyder, Robert Creeley, Philip Whalen, Lew Welch, Lawrence Ferlinghetti, and their elder statesman, Kenneth Rexroth, who urged it was "time to take poetry out of the hands of the professors and the squares." The phono label of Parker-Gillespie's *Groovin' High* adorned the paperback of Kerouac's "beat" classic, *On the Road*. Lew Welch wrote:

> Thelonious Monk is making jazz out of the same music that I'm making poetry out of. Phil Whalen sees his (poetry) this way too; I know this from conversation. We wanted to put a little more bebop into our poetry. Bop didn't come from nowhere,

it comes out of the mouths of all Americans. And you can sing bop right on top of bluegrass banjo picking and it fits perfectly. And bluegrass is very close to the way we talk. (Welch, *How I Work as a Poet*.)

Many of these jazz comics and anti-establishment writers settled or worked in San Francisco's bohemian colony of North Beach, where a visible tribe of white middle-class dropouts, dubbed "beatniks" by *Chronicle* columnist Herb Caen, mushroomed in the mid-1950s. This loose, chaotic army of foot soldiers in the "Great Refusal" donned the rebellious uniform of tangled beards, matted hair, and army surplus hand-me-downs to signify their sneering rejection of respectability and the nine-to-five "gig." They aped the cool, disengaged stance and laconic speech of the original hipster, Lester Young; their "pads" (apartments) resounded with the intense trumpet of a new anti-hero, Miles Davis, whose glowering hostility on stage and off seemed a pointed put down of the black entertainer's customary minstrel stance. Beatniks embraced that anathema of the square world, the "killer weed" marijuana, used as a casual pleasure-giving device by jazzmen since the twenties. They copied black speech and movement while digging black music. Interracial alliances between black men and white women were part of the passing parade on North Beach's "beat" thoroughfare, Grant Avenue, site of endless jam sessions. "The beatniks," wrote Eldridge Cleaver in *Soul On Ice*, "like Elvis Presley before them, dared to do in the light of day what America had long been doing in the sneak-thief anonimity of night—consorting on a human level with blacks."

Like the Presley generation, those avid readers of *Mad Magazine*, which lampooned all that their parents held sacred, the beatniks found in black music and dance a ready language of defiance, just as their grandparents did in the Roaring Twenties.

THE REBIRTH OF
BLUES AND GOSPEL

It is ironic that Miles Davis, a founding father of "cool," was among the first to drive a nail into its coffin with a 1954 recording of *Walkin'*, a twelve-bar blues whose straight-ahead funkiness loomed in contrast to the cerebral restraint of West Coast jazz. Thirteen minutes long thanks to the mixed blessing of the LP, *Walkin'* was embraced by musicians as a welcome return to "soul" (*Miles Davis Tune Up*, Prestige P-24077). Miles takes seven choruses in a passionate vein, which marked a break from the dancing-around-eggshells style he unfolded a few years earlier in "Birth of the Cool." Propelled by the hypnotic behind-the-beat "bomb-dropping" of drummer Kenny Clarke, *Walkin'* reaches a rousing climax on a note of high emotional intensity. This well-copied disc also showcased another leader in the new "soul-funk" movement, pianist-composer Horace Silver, a high-energy player whose frenetic approach to the keyboard loomed in contrast to the unflappable decorum of John Lewis. Silver composed and recorded, for Blue Note, one of the first gospel-jazz hits of the 1950s, *The Preacher*, and the aptly titled *Señor Blues* (Blue Note 1539), a long variation of a minor blues with a latin beat. Both discs became standard fixtures in beatnik "pads."

The so-called "hard bop" groups of Horace Silver, Art Blakey and the Jazz Messengers, and the Max Roach-Clifford Brown Quintet revived the instrumentation and form created a decade earlier by the Parker-Gillespie Quintet in, for example, *Shaw Nuff* (Smic 7/6). The "front line" of trumpet

Horace Silver: A leader of the "soul-funk" reaction against west coast "cool," Horace Silver's hard-driving gospel-rooted music, like his demonic approach to the keyboard, seemed the very antithesis of "cool." (Photograph from the Richard Hadlock Collection.)

and sax, backed by piano, bass, and drums, states a theme in unison, either an original or an involved refashioning of a standard pop; the front line instruments take turns in soloing, followed by solos from members of the rhythm section. Often the soloists "trade" or exchange four or eight bar "chases" before concluding with a restatement of the unison opening theme. The pianist does not play steady 4/4 rhythm but "feeds chords" in the irregular style of Bud Powell and Al Haig. The drummer tends to assume a dominant role, keeping time on the top cymbal and punctuating with "bombs" on the bass drum. More and more, the drums are coming into their own as an independent musical instrument, turning over their timekeeping function to the string bass. The emotional charge is kept at peak levels save for occasional respites with slow pensive ballads in the manner of Parker's *Embraceable You* (Smic 7/8, 7/9).

Sonny Rollins's *Pent-up House* (Smic 11/1) (actually the Max Roach-Clifford Brown Quintet) is the essence of "hard bop," with choice examples of Rollins's hard-edged urgency and the amazing trumpet of Clifford Brown, a towering eminence in modern jazz whose repute has increased since his tragic death in 1956 at age 25. "Brownie" was well on his way to carving out territory unclaimed even by Gillespie or Fats Navarro. In both his playing and his exemplary personal life he showed an authoritative maturity that belied his years. Whether on slow ballads or blinding uptempo challenges, his tone glowed with a richness and warmth, set off by a technical mastery yet to be surpassed by anyone with the possible exception of his young admirer, Wynton Marsalis. Brownie's improvisations at high speed seemed like logically structured compositions written out in advance. During his four-year recording career, he cut a number of records with Max Roach that remain a source of awe for musicians; these include his own composition, the standard *Joy Spring* (*Jordu*, Trip Jazz TLP-5540), *Cherokee* (*A Study in Brown*, Emarcy MG 36037), and *What is This Thing Called Love?* (Emarcy EXPR-1031). His final recording with a pick-up group in 1956 contains solos on *A Night in Tunisia* and *Donna Lee* that are as galvanizing as any trumpet playing in jazz (*Clifford Brown*, Columbia C 32284).

The auto crash that ended his life also claimed that of his cohort in the Max Roach Quintet, Richie Powell, a superb pianist in the style of his older brother Bud, whose immense repute among musicians tended to overshadow Richie's. The premature death of the revered, almost saintly "Brownie" sent a shock through the jazz world that took years to subside. Sonny Rollins said, "Clifford got me off hard drugs and showed me that a musician could lead a clean and responsible life." His passing moved Benny Golson to compose the standard *I Remember Clifford*, a yearning ballad with lyrics by Jon Hendricks.

Before the dramatic arrival of John Coltrane, Sonny Rollins was the undisputed "hard-bop" tenor influence. His unusual approach to the blues on *Blue 7* (Smic 10/3) is but one of Rollins's striking exercises in that seeming contradiction, "organized spontaneity," which moved Gunther Schuller to call him "another juncture in the constantly unfolding evolution of improvisation . . . the equal of Charlie Parker and Lester Young." Schuller analyzed in minute detail *Blue 7*'s "thematic (or motivic) and structural unity," while musically notating examples of "the ideational thread running through Rollins's improvisation that makes this particular recording so distinguished and satisfying." Rollins's reaction to such praise made a revealing contrast between the thought process of a critic and an improvisor. Rollins told Martin Williams of the *Jazz Review*: "Until I read Gunther Schuller, I really didn't understand what I was doing. This thing about the thematic approach, I guess it's true, but I never thought about it, I was just playing it."

After some reflection Rollins grew upset with Schuller's analysis and vowed never to read his notices again. Despite his claim that he was "playing without thinking about it," Rollins's entire career has been marked by restless experiments and frequent long leaves of absence from the performing scene for the avowed purpose of reexamining his approach, extensive private practice, and "agonizing reappraisals." In a moving tribute to Rollins, Gary Giddins's *Riding on a Blue Note* mentioned experiments in "modes, free jazz, unaccompanied tenor solos, soprano sax . . . overdubbing, electric accoutrements, a rainbow of tones and a diversity of song structures." A compelling example of Rollins's later work, unencumbered by his periodic flirtations with jazz-rock electronic fusion, is the title song of his 1977 album *Easy Living* (Milestone M-9080). It opens with a long unaccompanied cadenza and closes with cries of exquisite agony in the upper registers where few saxophonists had ventured.

The Age of Self-Conscious Innovation

Though Rollins's long withdrawals from the bandstand into the closet realm of "woodshedding" (practice) were extreme aberrations for a jazz musician, his willful attempts at innovation and the compulsion to find "something new" were typical of his contemporaries. This is not to claim that Armstrong, Hines, Young, and Parker functioned on purely intuitive levels, arriving at natural styles without experiment or reflection. Still, their approach to improvising seemed marked by a spontaneity and lack of deliberation that one is hard put to find in much of the work of Cecil Taylor, the early Archie Shepp, Albert Ayler, Anthony Braxton, Miles

Davis in his "fusion" days, and John Coltrane during his *Ascension* period. One cannot imagine Lester Young, a fully matured artist when he first recorded, taking Rollins-like sabbaticals to embark on some lone pilgrimage for a "new sound." Nor can we envision Armstrong instructing his Hot Five to forget about chord changes and improvise on scales, as did Miles Davis, or Bird telling his bass player to "forget about the changes in key and just play within the range of the idea," as did Ornette Coleman, anymore than we would expect Mozart to compose twelve-tone rows in the style of Schoenberg.

With the era of soul-searching innovation, jazz once more recapitulated the pattern of European classical music. In the late nineteenth century Wagner dominated Western music in the same way that Parker came to dominate jazz. Working within traditional forms, the early Schoenberg, to his self-confessed anguish, sounded too much like Wagner for his own comfort. His first experiments with "atonal expressionism" (1908–1913) arose in part from a determination to flee the Wagnerian nest by contriving a radical system wholly outside Wagner's framework. This quest for innovation culminated in Schoenberg's "serial" compositions of 1921 and 1922 that abandoned the entire concept of "home" keys and assigned each of the twelve notes in the chromatic scale an equal voice and weight.* This serial system opened new vistas for future generations of composers, like Berg and Webern, and to some exploratory jazzmen of the post-Parker period, like Cecil Taylor and Lennie Tristano.

Aside from serial compositions, the 1920s marked the beginning of brash experiments in aleatory (chance) sounds, tone clusters, and electronic music: George Antheil, Henry Cowell, Edgard Varèse (with whom bird wished to study), and later, John Cage, Lukas Foss, and Karlheinz Stockhausen.

The ghost of Bird fluttered over the jazz landscape populated with fledglings determined to soar into vistas never viewed by the master, giving rise to a period of self-conscious innovation that assumed many and diverse forms.

THE ASCENDANCY
OF MILES DAVIS

In the mid-1950s Miles Davis emerged as the dominant influence on a number of levels: as a trumpet stylist, as a best-selling recording star who broadened the audience for authentic jazz, as a leader with an uncanny gift for launching important new trends, and for introducing innovative

---

*The American, Charles Ives, working independently and without knowledge of Schoenberg and other European avant-gardists, composed fully formed twelve-tone rows twenty years earlier.

Miles Davis/1964: Miles's chameleon-like career was marked by radical changes in his music—along with his clothing and hairstyle—to flow with the changing times (see photo opposite). (Photograph by Grover Sales.)

musicians who were to help shape the future course of jazz. Among these were John Coltrane, Bill Evans, Ron Carter, Wayne Shorter, Chick Corea, Herbie Hancock, Joe Zawinul, Keith Jarrett, and Tony Williams.

Davis's chameleonlike career can be divided into many periods, the first starting at age twenty as a member of the Parker quintet, followed by the epochal "Birth of the Cool" recordings for Capitol in 1949 and 1950. After a fallow period ended by his triumph over hard drugs, Davis led or took part in a series of small combo recordings for Prestige whose personnels almost comprise a who's who of the era: Sonny Rollins, Thelonious Monk, Kenny Clarke, Philly Joe Jones, Charlie Parker, Milt Jackson, John Lewis, Art Blakey, Horace Silver, Max Roach, Charlie Mingus, J.J. Johnson, and John Coltrane. (*Miles Davis: The Complete Prestige Recordings*, Prestige Limited Edition). The Prestige series included the 1954 blues *Walkin'*, which announced the return of "funk" to unseat "cool."

In 1955 Miles regrouped his quintet to include John Coltrane, whose torrential outpourings, dubbed "sheets of sound" by critic Ira Gitler, heralded the arrival of a new gun in town. It was thought that Coltrane's ascendancy triggered Sonny Rollins's abrupt resolve to take the first of his long sabbaticals to search for the "new sound." In 1958 Miles added alto saxist Cannonball Adderley to form the sextet and replaced pianist Red Garland with Bill Evans, who immediately succeeded Bud Powell as the prime piano influence.

Miles Davis/1970 (Photograph courtesy of Columbia records.)

Evans introduced a Debussy-like lyricism and reflective romantic delicacy that had long been missing from jazz piano and spawned an entire school of disciples, many of them Davis alumni-to-be: Herbie Hancock, Keith Jarrett, Joe Zawinul, and Chick Corea. Evans is heard briefly on *So What* (Smic 11/3) and recorded often with his own trio, which boasted a succession of spectacular bassists: Scott La Faro, Eddie Gomez, Chuck Israels, Michael Moore. His finest work of the fifties, proving that "cool" had not been killed outright, included *Peace Piece* (Milestone 47024) and *Conception* (Milestone 47063). Just before his untimely death in 1980 he swung harder without sacrificing his early lyricism, as on *Montreux III* (Fantasy F-9510), and his duets with singer Tony Bennett (Fantasy F-9489) were especially rewarding as Evans expanded his audience to include young listeners with no previous exposure to jazz. His admirers included symphonic conductors like George Cleve, with whom he performed. Bill Evans's merger of bebop, cool, and French impressionism, coupled with an instantly recognizable style despite a legion of imitators, made him a universally celebrated artist who crossed all boundaries of age, background, and taste.

It must be emphasized that white Bill Evans was acknowledged as the major keyboard influence by overwhelming consensus at a time when the jazz world was rent by the phenomenon of "crow-jim," a reverse form of prejudice that forewarned of black uprisings to come. Black critic LeRoi Jones (Amiri Baraka) and white Third World polemicists like Frank Kofsky filled the jazz press with angry manifestos, insisting jazz to be the

177

Bill Evans/1950s: Evans became the undisputed piano influence during the turbulent 1960s, despite widespread "crow-jim" reverse prejudice against white musicians. (Photograph from the Ralph J. Gleason Collection.)

black music of protest and denouncing all whites as copyists at best and rip-off exploiters at worst. Miles Davis's reaction to the oft-voiced complaints about Bill Evans's color was, "I don't care if he's purple, blue, green or polka dotted—Bill has the piano sound I want in my group." Most of the musicians, if not the critics, shared Miles's view; during the most virulent period of "crow-jim," in the tense 1960s, white sidemen could be found in the black-led combos of Charlie Mingus, Archie Shepp, Cecil Taylor, Ornette Coleman, as well as that of Miles Davis, all among the most racially outspoken black artists of the day.

MODAL JAZZ

As part of a movement to explore new avenues untraveled by Bird, the Miles Davis Sextet in 1958 recorded pieces like *Milestones* that abandoned standard chord changes and used a series of scales as the framework for improvising. This technique, which had a profound impact on the future of jazz, is called "modal."

Bill Evans/1970s (Photograph from the
Ralph J. Gleason Collection.)

Modes (seven-tone scales) served as the basis of most Western music through the
17th Century. Between 1700 and 1900 the modes—from which our major and minor scales emerged—were seldom used. However, 20th Century composers . . .
have returned to the use of modal scales. Many songs of the Beatles are modal as
well as music of Bartók, Debussy and others. (Lindeman, *Piano Lab*.)

For example, all of the black keys on the piano are akin to the pentatonic
scale, or "mode," in use among the ancient Greeks and primitive cultures
(See Figure 10).

Figure 10: The pentatonic
scale.

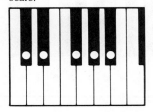

The Dorian mode is based on the pattern of all white keys starting with D (See Figure 11).

It was typical of Miles Davis's career that he did not originate modal jazz but popularized it, as Collier points out in *The Making of Jazz*:

> By 1951 or 1952 John Coltrane was familiar with Nicholas Slonimsky's *Thesaurus of Scales and Melodic Patterns* which he (Coltrane) had learned about from his teacher Dennis Sandole . . . Perhaps more influential was composer George Russell who by 1953 had worked out his "Lydian Concept of Tonal Organization," a complicated modal theory that could be used to justify the employment of almost any note in any context.

Modal jazz made its largest impact with the 1959 release of the LP *Kind of Blue* by the Miles Davis Sextet with Coltrane and Bill Evans, moving up from Prestige to the major Columbia label (Columbia PC 8163). The influence of *Kind of Blue* would be hard to exaggerate; for once, critics and musicians concurred with the public that made this the largest-selling record in the history of jazz up to that time. Unlike Armstrong or Waller, Miles made this breakthrough into the mass market without singers, gimmicks, horseplay, or commercial concessions of any kind, the first seminal jazz artist to do so. Bill Evans's thoughtful liner notes on the LP are worth reprinting:

> *So What* (Smic 11/3) is a simple figure based on 16 measures of one scale, 8 of another and 8 more of the first, following a piano and bass introduction in free rhythmic style . . . *All Blues* is a 6/8 12 measure blues form that produces its mood through only a few modal changes and Miles Davis' free melodic conception. *Flamenco Sketches* is a series of five scales, each to be played as long as the soloist wishes until he has completed the series. [Note: In Evans's descriptions of *All Blues* and *Flamenco Sketches*, their titles were inadvertently transposed on the album jacket notes.]

> Miles conceived these settings only hours before the recording dates and arrived with sketches which indicated to the group what was to be played. Therefore, you will hear something close to pure spontaneity in these performances.

Figure 11: The dorian mode.

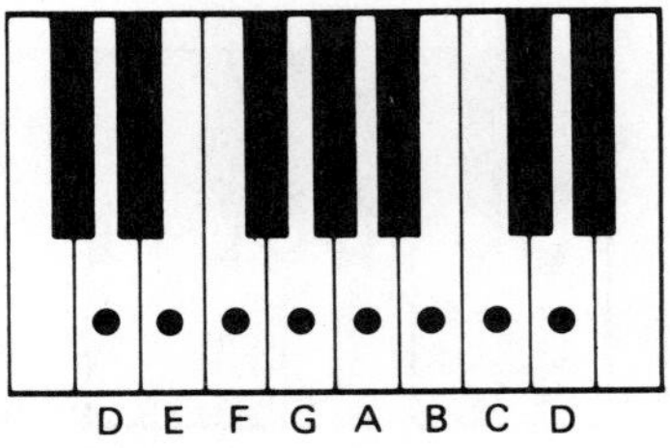

D E F G A B C D

All Blues, a hypnotic moody waltz, became a jazz standard as well as a popular hit among the young counterculture that purchased it in massive quantities.

As the Miles Davis Sextet became the most influential small group, its leader's revised trumpet style became the most widely copied of the period; the jazz scene abounded with often tiresome Davis clones. His lean spare broodings in the low and middle registers lent themselves to imitation in a way that the technical feats of Gillespie, Fats Navarro, and Clifford Brown did not. Chet Baker, the popular trumpeter with the Gerry Mulligan Quartet, openly modeled his style after Miles, who even began to affect the work of older trumpeters like Cat Anderson, Ellington's supersonic highnote specialist. I once caught Anderson in an after-hours jam session sounding surprisingly like Miles. When I mentioned this to him he said, "Duke hired me to play the high notes—that's my job, how I make my living—but *this* is the way I really enjoy playing."

Two years before *Kind of Blue* Miles made his first impact on the public with his initial Columbia collaboration with Gil Evans, *Miles Ahead: Miles Davis + 19* (Columbia CL 1041), featuring Miles as the only

Miles Davis and Gil Evans: Miles said, "I can read Gil's mind and he can read mine. We could not be closer if we were brothers." Gil named his son Miles. (Photograph from the Ralph J. Gleason Collection.)

soloist backed by a hand-picked crew of all-stars in lush versions of Kurt Weill's *My Ship*, Dave Brubeck's *The Duke*, and Delibes's *The Maids of Cadiz. Miles + 19* introduced jazz to thousands for the first time and was embraced with equal fervor by musicians and critics who hailed Evans as a worthy successor to Ellington. Max Harrison, jazz and classical critic for the London *Times*, found these scores to be "the full expression of Evans's powers. In elaboration and richness of resource they surpass anything previously attempted in big band jazz and constitute the only wholly original departure in that field outside of Ellington."

With that special brand of crass insensitivity of which only record companies seem capable, the original cover of *Miles + 19: Miles Ahead* sported a lithe blond woman sailing in a yacht; following howls from Miles, among others, subsequent issues replaced this gaffe with a pensive photo of Miles at work.

Jubilant over the sales of *Miles + 19*, Columbia quickly followed it in 1958 with an epic Evans-Davis production of *Porgy and Bess* (Columbia CS 8085), prompting speculation—or rather an idle dream—of a revival of Gershwin's great musical with Ray Charles and Carmen McRae, and Gil Evans's hand-picked band in the pit. The album found a ready market among Gershwin lovers who discovered new vitality in the re-mining of classics like *Summertime* (Smic 10/2) and *It Ain't Necessarily So*. An emotional high point in the album was the lesser-known *Fisherman, Strawberry and Devil Crab* that Gershwin adapted from a Charleston street cry. Miles's trumpet evocation of "I got blaaaaaaaaaackberries! Straaaaaaaaaaawberries! Raht off de vine!" dramatized the inseparable link between the jazz instrumentalist and the human voice in one of the most eerie, spine-tingling performances ever put on record. This linkage was repeated in 1959 with another Gil-Miles success, *Sketches of Spain* (Columbia CL 1480), that proved even more popular than its predecessors. The album came about when Miles heard a recording of Rodrigo's *Concierto de Aranjuez*:

> I couldn't get it out of my mind. Then when Gil and I decided to do this album, I played him the record and he liked it. As we usually do, we planned the program first by ourselves for about two months. I work out something; Gil takes it home and works on it some more . . . He can read my mind and I can read his. (Nat Hentoff liner notes: *Sketches of Spain*.)

Gil and Miles adapted the *Saeta*, the flamenco "arrow of song" in ancient Andalusian religious music, from the recording of La Niña de los Peiños, the Bessie Smith of classic flamenco singers, whose "heart pierced by grief" found an echo in Miles's piercing wails.

By the late 1950s Miles had no equal as a trendsetter whose LPs, concerts, and public utterances were mythic events eagerly awaited by his audience. A special mystique enshrouded his elusive temperament that appeared to capture the restless spirit of a nation in turmoil. He piqued the fancy of groupies titillated by the antisocial asides in his candid *Playboy* interview and in Leonard Feather's *down beat* "Blindfold Test," which evoked the following responses.

Miles Davis's reaction to Freddie Hubbard's *On the Que-Tee:*

> I don't dig that kind of shit, man . . . they shouldn't even put that out.

Reaction to the Thad Jones-Mel Lewis Big Band:

> Those guys don't have a musical mind—just playing what's written. They don't know what the notes mean.

On avant-garde "free jazz" tenor saxist Archie Shepp:

> You're putting me on with that! I don't understand that jive at all. People are so gullible . . . they go for something they don't know about. Ornette (Coleman) sounds the same way. That's where Archie Shepp and them got that shit from.

On Ellington's *Stormy Weather:*

> Oh God! You can give that twenty-five stars! I *love* Duke . . . all the musicians should get together on one certain day and get down on their knees and thank Duke—especially Mingus.

Ten years after *Kind of Blue*, Miles's perennial career as bellwether and propagandist of new trends reached its climax with his "fusion" of jazz-rock (the wide-ranging importance of which will be covered later in this chapter).

Charlie Mingus:
The Gargantua of Jazz

Charlie Mingus emerged in the 1950s as a major force as string bass virtuoso, avant-garde composer, and leader. His experience with groups as diverse as Kid Ory's New Orleans revival combo, Lionel Hampton's powerhouse big band, and Red Norvo's impeccably cool trio developed a versatility unusual among musicians of the time. Mingus's early background and temperament equipped him for a crucial role in the gospel-

Charlie Mingus: Never was there a more dramatic link between a man's personality and his music. (Photograph by Grover Sales.)

funk revival; his first exposure to music was in the black sanctified churches of Arizona, followed by a chance hearing of an early Ellington radio broadcast that he described as a religious experience: "I screamed." Gospel, Ellington, and Charlie Parker formed the grist poured into Mingus's creative mill. It was a rare Mingus recording or performance that failed to acknowledge his gospel-blues roots, his lifelong adoration of Ellington, and his immediate debt to Bird. Given to fanciful titles, Mingus named one composition, *Gunslinging Bird, or, If Charlie Parker Were a Gunslinger, There'd Be a Whole Lot of Dead Copycats.*

Mingus grew up in the Watts ghetto studying solfeggio (sight-singing), and trombone before settling on cello. Reedman Buddy Collette convinced him to switch to bass: "You're black. You'll never make it in classical music no matter how good you are. If you want to play, you've got to play a *Negro* instrument." (Ullman, *Jazz Lives.*) He studied bass at sixteen with Red Callendar (who joined him 25 years later as tubist for Mingus's triumphant debut at the Monterey Jazz Festival) and continued his studies with a bassist from the New York Philharmonic, determined to "scare all other bass players to death." His playing on *Hora Decubitus* (Smic 10/5)

shows how well he succeeded, opening this up-tempo blues with an elec-
trifying solo packed with the risk-taking defiance that made him the wonder of the bass world. His massive booming tone sounds as though the
strings were not plucked but seized six inches away from the bridge. The
fabulous technique that permitted him to play glissandi (left hand slides
up and down the strings) at wild tempos and his monumental swing that
could fire up a band can be heard throughout *Hora Decubitus*. A prime
example of his solo work can be heard on *I Can't Get Started* (Prestige
MPP-2506), and his sensitive backing of Ellington's piano on *Les Fleurs
Africaine* seems to have been plucked by Segovia. (United Artists Jazz
S15017).

Mingus's composing career began in the late 1940s when he did
Mingus Fingus for the Lionel Hampton band. Before his exposure to
Parker the teenaged Mingus had written promising works—*Half-mast In-
hibition* and *Bemoanable Lady* (another bow to Duke), featured on an
unusual LP, *Pre-Bird: Charlie Mingus* (Mercury TMP 5513). By the mid-
1950s he had developed into that rarity—a genuine jazz composer with
his own distinct voice.

No more striking example can be found of a jazzman's music as a
blueprint of his personality. Mingus—the man and the music—was larger
than life, unpredictable, paranoid, tender, angry, romantic, declamatory,
and violent. Many of his best works sprang from passions of the moment;
the death of Lester Young prompted the agonizing dirge of *Goodbye Pork
Pie Hat* (later called *Theme for Lester Young* on *Mingus, Mingus, Mingus*
Impulse A-54). Segregationist Arkansas Governor Faubus was lampooned
in *Fables of Faubus*, whose farcical theme was punctuated with Mingus's
savage cries of, "Why is he so sick and ridiculous?" He claimed he could
not play his *Haitian Fight Song* without thinking of racial prejudice. His
terrifying, violence-prone anger at the plight of black Americans spilled
into pieces entitled *Meditations on Integration*, *Prayer for Passive Resis-
tance*, and *Put Me in that Dungeon*. Mingus aimed to make every performance an emotional blood bath. His flirtations with atonality and clashing
dissonance sought to extend the frontiers of jazz, to the discomfort
of more conservative ears. During the brief fling of "Third Stream" fusion
of jazz and classical, Brandeis University commissioned Mingus to write
his turbulent *Revelations*, issued on a singular LP along with works by
Milton Babbitt, Gunther Schuller, and Harold Shapiro (Columbia C2S 831,
C2L 31).

As with Ellington, much of Mingus's music was worked out in a symbiotic alliance with members of his combos; drummer Danny Richmond
and white trombonist Jimmy Knepper were longtime residents in the

Mingus family, an ever-changing clan due to the patriarch's mercurial flights, uncompromising standards, and fits of violence. He once knocked out Knepper's front teeth and decked a stoned alto saxist on stage with one punch to the midriff. Still, the open-ended Mingus workshop harbored, at various times, an honor roll of innovative talent: Thad Jones, Jaki Byard, John Handy, Booker Ervin, Charles McPherson, Ted Curson, Max Roach, Johnny Coles, Mal Waldron, Roland Hanna, and two reedmen destined for greatness and early death, Rahsaan Roland Kirk and Eric Dolphy.

Mingus shunned the clichés of the hard-bop quintet; his personnel and instrumentation were as unpredictable as his behavior and appearance. One engagement in San Francisco's Jazz Workshop saw an octet of two trumpets, a fluegelhorn, an alto sax, a trombone, a french horn, a tuba, and drums, with Mingus alternating between bass and piano, sometimes playing both at once. He started the opening set with a twenty-minute arrangement of Billy Strayhorn's *Lush Life*, took a brief intermission, shuffled the scores (giving the alto sax the french horn part and so on), and repeated the work. During another gig at the same club he played piano exclusively, to the disgruntlement of bass players who had traveled far to observe the master. One year Mingus might appear in a club slimmed down to less than 200 pounds and elegantly turned out in a Saville Row bowler hat, spats, ascot tie, and gold-headed cane; the next year he would show up ballooned to a mountainous 350 pounds and decked entirely in leather. Few Mingus performances were without "incident." Unlike jazzmen of old he would brook no audience distraction; his verbal assaults on unruly nightclub crowds became legendary:

> You, my audience, are all a bunch of poppaloppers, a bunch of tumbling weeds tumbling 'round, running from your subconscious, unconscious minds . . . you come to me, you sit in the front row, as noisy as you can be. I listen to your millions of conversations, sometimes pulling them all up and putting them together and writing a symphony. But you never hear that symphony—that I might dedicate to the mother who brought along a neighbor and talked three sets and two intermissions about the old man across the hall making it with Mrs. Jones's son in the apartment below where the school teacher lives with Cadillac Bill. . . . (Dorr-Dorynek, *The Jazz Word.*)

Mingus documented the chaotic maelstrom of his life in a disappointing book, *Beneath the Underdog*, short on matters musical and long on vain sexual gymnastics. The real legacy of Mingus is the profusion of his recorded work: *Tijuana Moods* (Victor LSP-2533), *Mingus Dynasty* (Columbia CL 1440), *Mingus Ah Um* (Columbia CL 1370), and the "live" *Mingus at Monterey* (Fantasy F-JWS 1/2) where a crowd of 7200 rose as one to give him a standing ovation before this had become an overworked audience cliché. Long before his death in 1979 Charles Mingus was recognized as an undisputed giant whose innovations sprang from an original mind, not from some abstract urge to make a splash with "something new."

Ornette Coleman:
The "New Bird"?

Even before the passing of Bird the jazz press was abuzz with speculation on his successor, a fitting pastime for an era obsessed with experiment and change. Because jazz musicians and journalists tend to form a cloistered in-group, they naively anticipated a Mozartian fertility god like Parker to pop up every spring like some new welterweight. Where, they wondered, was the "New Bird"? Was it tenorman Johnny Griffin who was "faster than Bird"? Sonny Rollins? John Coltrane?

Suddenly, in 1958, word got out that the Messiah had arrived in the person of Ornette Coleman, a strange, intense young Texan who wrote bizarre tunes declaimed on a plastic alto sax in a radically new and disturbing way. Few would deny that Ornette Coleman is the most controversial musician in all of jazz. Even more than Parker and Gillespie in the bebop era, Coleman's ascension split the jazz world into two hostile camps. Nor was this breach soon to heal, for unlike Parker, the controversy over Coleman rages to this day.

Coleman's earliest champions included Gunther Schuller, Nat Hentoff, and Martin Williams who assigned him no less than three lengthy cuts in the Smithsonian Collection (Smic 12/1, 12/2, 12/3). His most prestigious support came from the Modern Jazz Quartet's John Lewis who claimed "Coleman is doing the only really new thing in jazz since the innovations of Parker, Gillespie and Monk." (Spellman, *Black Music: Four Lives.*) Many young soloists who were already notable and were to become more so—Rollins, Coltrane, Roland Kirk, Eric Dolphy—were profoundly changed by Coleman's concept of "free jazz." Tenorman Joe Henderson told Leonard Feather in 1966: "Ornette inspired me to move from the canal-like narrow-mindedness of the 40s through the latter 50s to the Grand Canyon-like harmonic awareness of the 60s." (Feather, *Encyclopedia of Jazz in the Seventies.*) Shelly Manne, the drummer on Coleman's second LP and one of the few older musicians to endorse his new style, offered a rare insight when he told Nat Hentoff:

> Ornette sounds like a person crying or a person laughing when he plays. And he makes *me* want to laugh and cry. The real traditional players will do those things to

you. Although he may be flying all over the horn and doing weird things metrically, the basic feelings are still there. . . . He makes you listen so hard to what he's doing that he makes you play a whole other way. . . . somehow I became more of a person in my own playing. He made me feel freer." (Hentoff, *The Jazz Life.*)

But most of the established players regarded Coleman's departures from bebop with skepticism at best. Roy Eldridge told Hentoff in *The Jazz Life*:

I listened to Coleman high, and I listened to him cold sober. I even played with him. I think he's jiving, baby. He's putting everybody on. They start out with a nice lead-off figure, but then they go off into outer space. They disregard the chords and they play odd numbers of bars. I can't follow them. I even listened to him with Paul Chambers, Miles Davis' bass player, "you—you're younger than me—can you follow Ornette?" Paul said he couldn't either.

Thelonious Monk, once stigmatized as a far-out cultist, sounded a lofty note of orthodoxy when he told Hentoff, "there's nothing beautiful in what he's playing. He's just playing loud and slurring his notes. Anybody can do that . . . I think he has a gang of potential though, but he's not all they say he is right now." (Hentoff 1975.) Leonard Feather's *down beat* "Blindfold Tests" drew similar responses when Ornette first burst on the scene:

Charlie Byrd: (1960) "Coleman's a sweet and sincere guy . . . but I resent his being touted as a great saxophonist . . . as for people making an analogy of Parker and Coleman, that's kind of ridiculous."

André Previn: (1961) ". . . an unmitigated bore . . . turning your back on any tradition is anarchy."

Benny Carter: "From the very first note he's miserably out of tune."

Miles Davis: "Hell, just listen to what he writes and how he plays. If you're talking psychologically, the man is all screwed up inside."

Alto saxist Paul Desmond told Gene Lees that "listening to Ornette is like being imprisoned in a room painted red with your eyes pinned open."

Coleman's painful struggle for acceptance and the barest livelihood is well covered in A. B. Spellman's *Black Music: Four Lives*. A native of Fort Worth, he toured the Southwest territory with rhythm 'n' blues bands that left a lasting mark on his urgent style. For all his drastic departures from tradition, Ornette, claim his advocates, remains basically a blues-man. By the late 1940s he was already forming the eccentric, unpredict-able style that aroused the anger of fellow bandsmen. Leaders fired him or paid him not to play. Tenor sax giant Dexter Gordon rudely ordered him off the bandstand. He supported himself, poorly, with a succession of me-nial daytime jobs—the kind that jazzmen call "slaves." These humiliations were compounded by ugly brushes with racial violence that left him guarded and touchy but no less determined to follow his own bent. Moving to Los Angeles, Coleman began to attract a coterie of young players like the dextrous drummer, Ed Blackwell, who told Spellman:

> Ornette sounded a lot like Parker back then, and he was still hung up with one-two-three-four time. I had been experimenting with different kinds of time and cadences . . . Ornette's sound was changing too, and a lot of musicians used to think he played out of tune. He never used to play the same thing twice, which made a lot of guys think that he didn't know how to play.

Coleman's first break came in 1958 when Lester Koenig, producer of the Los Angeles jazz label, Contemporary, gave him his first record date, *Something Else!* (Contemporary S7551) with Don Cherry on trumpet, Walter Norris on piano, Don Payne on bass, and Billy Higgins on drums. For all the fuss this record kicked up, its departures from standard bebop hardly seem radical compared to the records Coleman was to make within a few years. The instrumentation and basic structure of *Angel Voice* was similar to the *Bird's Nest* of Parker a decade earlier. Both pieces are based on *I Got Rhythm*; both begin and end with trumpet and alto sax unison statements of a "head" that sandwich a succession of solos. Coleman's pianist and bassist are still working along conventional bebop lines. What is most striking about *Something Else!*, besides Coleman's slide-whistle conception of pitch, is the originality of compositions like *Invisible* and *The Disguise.*

    Coleman soon made drastic changes in his group to urge it closer to the "free" concept he had been hearing all along. Though the pianoless quartet did not originate with him, Coleman's exclusion of a keyboard instrument was grounded on a different rationale than Gerry Mulligan's. His playing, and that of his disciples, was freeing itself from the pianistic "prison" of the chromatic scale in order to explore off-pitch notes and quarter tones, common in African and other ethnic musics, that would clash with a "properly" tuned keyboard. "There are some intervals," said Coleman, "that carry the *human* quality if you play them in the right pitch. I don't care how many intervals a person can play on an instrument; you can always reach into the human sound of a voice on your horn if you're actually hearing and trying to express the warmth of the human voice." (Spellman, *Black Music*.) Coleman's most gifted followers—Coltrane, Dolphy, and Kirk—adapted his notion of "crying" through a horn.

    The absence of a piano also helped to free Coleman and his group from improvising on chord progressions. Coleman told Nat Hentoff,

> What I'm trying to do is to make my playing as free as I can. The creation of music is—or should be—as natural as breathing. . . . Jazz is growing up. It's not a cutting contest anymore . . . if you put a conventional chord under my note, you limit the

number of choices I have for my next note. If you do not, my melody may move freely in a far greater choice of directions. (Liner notes, *The Best of Ornette Coleman*, Atlantic SD 1558.)

Coleman's discovery of bassist Charlie Haden proved a major breakthrough; at last he had found the "free" bassist he sought all along. Coleman instructed the flexible, receptive Haden to

forget about changes in key and just play within the range of the idea. . . . so after a while of playing with me it just became the natural thing for Charlie to do . . . it doesn't mean because you put an F7 (chord) down for the bass player he's going to choose the best notes in the F7 to express what you're doing. But if he's allowed to use any note that he hears to express F7, then that note's going to be right because he hears it, not because he read it off the page. (Spellman, *Black Music*.)

Coleman allied himself with drummers Billy Higgins and Ed Blackwell, who developed a freer style not tied to playing steady time but to making the drums more of an independent melodic instrument. As with bebop, Coleman's unorthodox rhythm section was the high hurdle most traditional players could not clear. Coleman's biographer, A. B. Spellman, confessed his reaction to the first LP was skeptical: " . . . typical of the general critical reception, I thought the saxophonist was some oddball imitator of Parker, but I can see now that this was more because of the rhythmic placement of his notes than because of the actual melodic material that he was using."

Aside from Coleman's "rhythmic placement of notes," his pitch threw many listeners off. Spellman wrote: "On first hearing, I actually did not recognize the melodic content of Ornette's music (because) . . . these melodies, simple as they are, are difficult to sort out if one is offended by the sound of Ornette's instrument."

Lonely Woman (Smic 12/1) is Coleman's best-known and most accessible piece for the uninitiated. This haunting ballad begins and ends with a trumpet and alto sax unison statement of a theme that, for all its originality, lies so much within the tradition of the popular song that singer Carmen McRae performed it with her own lyrics. What lies between, however, is Coleman's and Charlie Haden's unconventional sliding in and out of pitch and drummer Higgins's "free" concept of time. Listeners who approach *Lonely Woman* with open ears and steel themselves against the abrasive "off" pitch of Coleman's plastic horn may find themselves strangely moved by the naked emotions of this declamatory outcry. His oblique approach to Gershwin's *Embraceable You* (Atlantic SD 1558) shows how far he departed from the relative orthodoxy of Parker's treatment (Smic 7/8, 7/9). On the same album *Ramblin'* offers a good example of Coleman's way with a funky blues, bristling with wit and high spirits as does much of his work.

With his celebrated package, *Free Jazz* (Smic 12/3), Coleman cut his few remaining ties to bebop. The ten-minute excerpt in the Smithsonian Collection was taken from a 36 minute performance on Atlantic (S-1364). Thanks to the long playing record, free jazz advocates could now stretch out as they did in nightclubs with uninterrupted 45 minute sets devoted to a single composition (to the alarm of club owners anxious to push drinks). Here, stereo recording technique plays a crucial role because Coleman spatially divided his disciples into a double-quartet for the 1963 waxing of *Free Jazz:*

> alto sax (Coleman)
> trumpet (Don Cherry)
> bass (Charlie Haden)
> drums (Ed Blackwell)

and

> bass clarinet (Eric Dolphy)
> trumpet (Freddie Hubbard)
> bass (Scott La Faro)
> drums (Billy Higgins).

Stereo allows the listener to separate these voices of an unusually dense octet that is improvising collectively. As Martin Williams indicates in his Smithsonian notes, this session took place "with no preconceptions as to themes, chord patterns or chorus lengths. The guide for each soloist was a brief ensemble part which introduces him and which gave him an area of musical pitch."

Today, twenty-five years after Coleman's hotly-debated debut, how does his work stand up? Do his records stand the test of time or will they survive only as historical curiosities? Is his legacy permanent? Just what kind of a musician is he?

In *The Making of Jazz* James Lincoln Collier makes a sound case for Coleman as that anomaly in modern jazz, a primitive musician. Nothing derogatory is implied here. As Collier points out, primitive artists, like the painter Rousseau, function largely on instinct without the benefit (or, as some may insist, the hindrance) of formal academic training. While Coleman Hawkins and Charlie Parker were well schooled in harmony and could "think ahead" any number of chord changes at high speed, Coleman, unencumbered by such theories, felt "free" to pour out anything summoned up by his raw emotional state of the moment. This notion of Coleman-as-primitive is buttressed by his naive, self-taught playing of trumpet and violin, on which, his admirers claim, "he sounds amazingly like himself." (It was said that after hearing Coleman play violin in a club, Thelonious Monk admonished him at intermission: "Why do you bullshit the people? Do you have any idea how much discipline and training it takes to play the violin? Stick to the alto—you can *play* that.")

Coleman inspired a number of front-rank players whose work shows greater promise of survival than his own—Coltrane, Rollins, Rahsaan Roland Kirk, and the extraordinary Eric Dolphy who has yet to be given his due two decades after his early death. History seems to recall not those who did it first but those who did it best. Franz Lizst was an early influence on Bartók, but few would deny Bartók was the better composer.

While Coleman opened new exploratory fields for Coltrane, Eric Dolphy, trombonist Roswell Rudd, soprano saxist Steve Lacy, and even former detractors like Cannonball Adderley, his notoriety emboldened lesser talents to drape themselves in "free jazz" or the "new thing" to cloak a lack of inspiration and originality. Charlie Mingus saw this early in his 1959 liner notes to *Mingus Dynasty* (Columbia CL 1440):

> When the musicians hang on to a few rhythmic phrases Coleman has been able to create—when they realize they have a new camouflage of atonality, no time bars, no key signature—when they simultaneously begin to jabber in this borrowed style in all the nightclubs all over America—then the walls of all the nightclubs will probably crumble. . . .

Mingus's foresight bordered on clairvoyance. In the sixties, as "free jazz" began to alienate much of the jazz audience, coinciding with the ascendancy of rock among the young, leading jazz clubs from New York to San Francisco closed their doors forever.

Cecil Taylor:
The Schoenberg of Jazz

Pianist-composer Cecil Taylor's experiments in "free jazz" predated Coleman's, though his impact on young musicians was slower in coming. Taylor's approach to free jazz was the polar opposite of Coleman's primitivism. A music conservatory graduate, he employs a percussive concert hall technique to merge Ellington, Bach, Stravinsky, and Bartók "who showed me what you could do with folk material." Brubeck was an early influence, unusual for jazz people but in Taylor's case understandable since Brubeck was also a classically trained composer-pianist bent on fusing jazz with European concert music and time signatures rarely used in jazz. He later came under the spell of avant-garde classical composers John Cage and Karlheinz Stockhausen and began to use random sounds, aleatory (chance) techniques, atonality, and other devices common to concert music since the 1920s.

Like Ornette Coleman, Taylor's life and theories have been admirably covered in A. B. Spellman's *Black Music,* and like Coleman, his battle for paid work and recognition was all uphill. He took menial daytime jobs to support himself but never softened his uncompromising stance toward his own work and that of others: "Miles Davis plays pretty good for a millionaire." Despite raves from influential critics, Taylor still has trouble finding steady work while his audience remains limited to a small but hyperactive cult. Those who write anything less than praise are certain to be bombarded with ten-page manifestos from cupbearers who follow Taylor across the nation when on tour.

Joined by sympathetic sidemen—Sam Rivers on reeds, Jimmy Lyons on alto, Andrew Cyrille on drums—Taylor presents an intimidating figure on stage. Entering without a cursory nod to the audience, often decked in a white T-shirt and peaked cap, he attacks the piano from first to last with a furious demonism that never slackens. His 1969 concert in St. Paul de Vence, *The Second Art of A*, occupies six LP sides of unrelenting, dissonant fury with no more dynamic variation than a player-piano roll (*The Great Concert of Cecil Taylor,* Prestige P-34003).

In attempting to fuse jazz with contemporary European concert music, Taylor sounds closer to the compositions issuing from university music departments than he does to jazz, and like most academic composers, Taylor's audience is limited to a small in-group of musicians and critics laboring in the same vineyard. As Dr. Louis Gottlieb said of Stockhausen, "I've been in music all my life—Bach and before, Bartók and after, and then Lester Young and Bird, and I can't even begin to make sense out of a Stockhausen score."

Regardless of the volatile views of his idolators and detractors—and they are many—Cecil Taylor shares honors with Ornette Coleman and John Coltrane as fountainhead of a musically active, if financially unrewarded, avant-garde "free jazz" movement that exerted a major force among such proficient and uncompromising figures as the early Archie Shepp, Marion Brown, Dewey Redman, Steve Kuhn, Chick Corea, Pharoah Sanders, the Art Ensemble of Chicago, John Tchicai, Andrew Cyrille, Sam Rivers, and the multi-reed virtuoso Anthony Braxton.

With the "free jazz" movement as embodied in Cecil Taylor and Ornette Coleman, jazz once again, for better or worse, has recapitulated the history of European classical music.

John Coltrane:
Jazz Guru of the Tumultuous Sixties

When John Coltrane died at 41 in 1967, he was beyond question the dominant influence of his time, a sanctified figure of near-Gandhian proportions who had no parallel in jazz history. One cannot separate Coltrane the musician from Coltrane the religious philosopher-teacher who emerged as a guru during the Watts riot, the Selma-to-Montgomery civil rights march, and the assassination of Malcolm X. Black activist author Julius Lester named his son Malcolm Coltrane. The Coltrane combos took on all the trappings of a monastic order whose long-tenured brethren Elvin Jones and McCoy Tyner accorded the leader a reverence unheard of in the annals of jazz. Coltrane's best-known works of his final years bore such transcendental titles as *A Love Supreme*, *Ascension*, and *The Father and the Son and the Holy Ghost*.

In the 1950s Coltrane passed through hard-bop, the modal experience with Miles Davis's *Kind of Blue*, and his brief but indelible stint with Thelonious Monk, finally emerging as a leader with the LP *Giant Steps* devoted entirely to his own compositions. The title track (Atlantic LP 1311) made a stunning impact on the jazz community, a summation of his development up to 1959. The extravagant technique lavished upon *Giant Steps* was the result of Coltrane's obsessive marathon practice sessions that assumed legendary status. "This was the time," Cannonball Adderley told this writer, "that 'Trane was living like an animule, didn't bathe, change clothes, or do anything to take him away from the saxophone. When he wasn't on the stand he was practicing. Sometimes he even fell asleep with the horn in his mouth."

Giant Steps' torrential downpour of notes was based on a few carefully chosen chords whose potential for variation was exhausted at a punishing tempo. Musicians were fascinated by its structure because, says Collier, "the chord changes came along steadily, every two beats." For students this exercise provided a basic rule book for practice. But the proof of the pudding is in the listening, and *Giant Steps* captivated listeners because it sounded good; it's engaging melody swirled through loop-the-loop changes with an excitement that never let up during its jam-packed five-minute duration.

Of even wider appeal was Coltrane's modal treatment of Richard Rodgers simple, folksy *My Favorite Things* (1960) wailed on his new-found love, the soprano sax; this best-selling record got lots of airplay, surprising in view of its fourteen-minute length—with no vocal. It established Coltrane as the premier jazz player of the day and even made him something of a minor deity among the hippie culture.

John Coltrane: The guru of the 1960s ranks with Charlie Parker and Ornette Coleman as the most influential figures among today's musicians. (Photograph courtesy of Prestige-Fantasy Records.)

As his interest in Eastern religions and philosophy increased, Coltrane and his disciples began to explore Middle Eastern and Indian modes at a time when jazz was melding with all forms of ethnic music. Multi-reed player Yusef Lateef (born William Evans), a veteran of the Gillespie big band, took to Oriental-Middle East music played on the oboe and the clay Chinese globular flute. All this predated The Beatles' much-publicized study of Indian music and stringed instruments. The rejection of Western song form paralleled the swift growth of the Black Muslims with their perennial cry to abandon Christianity as the "white man's religion."

Coltrane magnetized a tight core of gifted players who revered him as a saint; drummer Elvin Jones and pianist-composer McCoy Tyner were among the top level of "high energy" soloists demanded by their leader. Long pieces like *Chim Chim Cheree* and *The Promise* were calculated to propel audiences as well as players into hypnotic trances bordering on religious exaltation (*The Best of John Coltrane*, Vol 2, Impulse AS-9223-2). Flailing away with ever-mounting volume and tension, the saxophone, piano, bass, and drums would reach almost unbearable climaxes. Coltrane never gave himself completely to such furious excursions; like all seminal jazz players, he remained a superb improvisor of slow romantic ballads throughout his career. His inspired mating with Ellington's piano on *In a Sentimental Mood* and Strayhorn's *My Little Brown Book* in 1962 resulted in one of the loveliest records in all of jazz (*Duke Ellington and John Coltrane*, Impulse A-30). The same can be said for Coltrane's group on McCoy Tyner's lyrical *Aisha* in 1961; with characteristic generosity, Coltrane turned over most of the solo space to Tyner, trumpeter Freddie Hubbard (in his pre-"crossover" days), and alto saxist Eric Dolphy (*The Art of John Coltrane*, Atlantic SD 2-313).

While the troubles of the mid-1960s culminated in the Watts riot, Coltrane's intensive study of African music found its fullest expression in the eighteen-minute *tour de force, Kulu Sé Mama*, an emotional merger of African percussion and chanting with free jazz (Impulse A-9106). In 1965 the Coltrane cadre, augmented by other *sympaticos*, carried free jazz to the point of no return with *Ascension* and *The Father and the Son and the Holy Ghost* (*The Best of John Coltrane*, Vol. 2, Impulse AS-9223-2). Aside from Coltrane's brief blues utterance near the start of *Holy Ghost*, anarchy rules the day in this every-man-for-himself explosion of frustration and outrage. Despite their sacramental titles, the message of "Burn, baby, burn!" sounds clear in these screams of anger that could serve as the ideal soundtrack for a film documentary on the Watts riot of the same year. Two decades later a large school of young musicians is still doggedly committed to worrying the bones of *Ascension*; drummer Philly Joe Jones told Art Taylor:

> Trane opened the door to a whole bunch of what I call bag carriers. They've been carrying their horns around for a year, jump up on the bandstand and don't know anything about the horn and just make a bunch of noises. Trane and Dolphy know their horns from top to bottom . . . the things they were doing were beautiful and well constructed. (Taylor, *Notes & Tones*.)

Coltrane's unexpected death sent a shock wave through the jazz community. His widow and collaborator Alice Coltrane, who shared his religious-musical bent, kept the flame alive after his passing. Today John Coltrane remains an all-pervasive influence as a hard-bop, modal, ballad, Afro-fusion, high-energy, or free jazz innovator. No one questions that his place in the forefront of jazz history is assured.

Rahsaan Roland Kirk
and Eric Dolphy

The early 1960s saw the arrival of two unclassifiable geniuses fated for early death, Rahsaan Roland Kirk and Eric Dolphy. A complete original, blind Roland Kirk's multi-reed playing pulsed from the early New Orleans style of Bechet to the farthest-out avant-garde of Coleman and Coltrane. The name "Rahsaan" came to him in a dream, as did the idea of playing three instruments at once, a feat once deplored as a gimmick by many who now accept it as a valid expression of one of the most fertile imaginations ever to grace the world of jazz. An incredible display of his one-man

"Rahsaan" Roland Kirk: This photograph was no gimmick. As Charlie Mingus said, "Roland might spin a bass on top of his head—but that bass is in tune." (Photograph courtesy of the Rutgers Institute of Jazz Studies.)

reed section can be heard on the pop ballad *Once in a While* (*Roland Kirk Quartet*: Limelight LS 86027). Listeners are reminded that no overdubbing or other electronic tricks are involved; as his one-time boss Charlie Mingus said, "Roland might spin a bass on top of his head, but that bass is in *tune*." Kirk in performance was an audio-visual experience unlike any other. A profusion of obsolete pawnshop offshoots of the sax family draped his bulky frame like some Baghdad peddlar's. Suddenly he would cram three horns in his mouth at once, playing two and three part harmony with a fingering that defied description. Spewing out an unpredictable pastiche of dirty blues, gospel, bebop, big band swing, and free extravaganzas peppered with whistles and sirens, Kirk enriched his unique stew with generous helpings of broad humor and parody. *Once in a While* was a sly take-off on a burlesque bump-and-grind band; *Shine on Me*, a good-natured spoof of old-time smeary clarinet playing (*Pre-Rahsaan* Prestige P-24080), and from the same LP, *Parisien Thoroughfare* was an impressionistic traffic jam abetted by Kirk's fellow-eclectic, pianist Jaki Byard, a consummate master of every style from Jelly Roll to Cecil Taylor. Like Kirk, Byard uses a formidable technique in the pursuit of pure listening delight rather than random sound. Overcoming some initial skepticism among reviewers, Kirk won critics polls and built a devoted following throughout Europe before his death from the complications following a stroke in 1977 at age 41.

ERIC DOLPHY:
THE UNDERCOVER BIRD?

Of all the players allied with free jazz, Eric Dolphy was perhaps the most listenable and overlooked. As Feather wrote in *The Encyclopedia of Jazz in the Sixties*: "Although Dolphy earned the unqualified admiration of the musicians with whom he associated, his contributions to jazz and his importance as a soloist have yet to be understood by a majority of listeners."

Feather could have added that his contributions have yet to be understood by a majority of critics; Dolphy barely gets mentioned in Collier's *The Making of Jazz* or Martin Williams's *The Jazz Tradition*. Little of the fanfare or notoriety showered on Ornette Coleman fell Dolphy's way. Two decades after his death a case can be made that Dolphy, rather than Coleman, may have been the long-awaited "new Bird." He recorded often with a variety of diverse talents: Mingus, Coltrane, John Lewis, Freddie Hubbard, Andrew Hill, Ron Carter, Oliver Nelson, Jaki Byard, Bill Evans, Gunther Schuller, and as leader of his own group featuring his compositions. Most of these records are still available, inviting an overdue reevaluation of his extraordinary career.

Dolphy had no "main" instrument but gave equal time and proficiency to the alto sax, flute, and bass clarinet, endowing each with an articulated fluency and massive tone reminiscent of Parker. Though much of his playing is accessible in an immediate way that most free jazz is not, a painless introduction to his alto sax style is the lovely *Afternoon in Paris* from *The Wonderful World of Jazz* (Atlantic 1375) under the direction of composer John Lewis, an early Dolphy patron and co-publisher (MJQ Music). Dolphy's solo comes as a shock since he is not teamed with his usual avant-garde cohorts but with more conventional players—pianist John Lewis, tenor saxist Benny Golson, and trumpeter Herb Pomeroy. Another easy-to-take Dolphy alto solo is on Mingus's Ellington-tinged *Bemoanable Lady* (*Pre-Bird: Charlie Mingus*, Mercury SR 60627). A stunning slow blues, *245* firms up the case for Dolphy on alto as a genuine extension of Bird (*Eric*, Prestige PR 24008). An alternate take of this eight-minute display of avant-garde funk shows Dolphy to be as resourceful and varied on the blues as Bird himself (Prestige MPP-2517). His uptempo alto on *Refuge*, under the leadership of the neglected pianist-composer Andrew Hill, stretches the bonds of credulity (*Andrew Hill: Point of Departure*, Blue Note ST-84167). Dolphy is heard briefly but with overwhelming impact on Mingus's fast blues *Hora Decubitus* (Smic 10/5). On flute he disported the most huge and sumptuous tone in jazz, ranging from the pensive romanticism of *Sketch of Melba* to the sprightly inventions of *17 West* (both on Prestige PR 24008 and Original Jazz Classics, OJC-023). A duet between Dolphy and Ornette Coleman enlivens Gunther Schuller's "Third Stream" experiments on *Jazz Abstractions* (Atlantic SD 1365). Dolphy early abandoned the B-flat clarinet for the notoriously difficult bass clarinet, heretofore rarely used as a solo voice. Showing the same easy fluency and power as on alto sax and flute, Dolphy started a surge of interest in the bass clarinet among younger players, notably Chico Freeman. *Something Sweet, Something Tender*, from Dolphy's *Out to Lunch* (Blue Note BLP-84163), and *God Bless the Child* (*Copenhagen Concert*, Prestige 24027) offer prime examples of his mastery over this treacherous, unwieldy instrument.

By the early 1960s Dolphy was firmly allied with the avant-garde, recording with Tony Williams, Ed Blackwell, Coltrane, Mingus, Coleman, and other leaders in the free jazz movement. He shared the obsession with practice and perfection that became the hallmark of Coltrane and Cecil Taylor. Utterly devoid of malice—of what Mingus called "the need to hurt"—Dolphy's patient gentility made him a figure of veneration among his peers. With a fatalism untainted by bitterness, he resigned himself to the neglect and pointed critical abuse of his native land, spending his final years in Europe before a more sympathetic audience. He died in Germany in 1964 at the age of 36 under somewhat cloudy circumstances that were later described as "pulmonary malfunction." Today few of Ornette Coleman's followers, or Coleman himself, seem as consistently rewarding as Eric Dolphy.

Jazz Agitprop: The Shotgun Wedding of Music and Politics

Coinciding with the black nationalist movement of the 1960s, some free jazz players introduced a strident note of "agitprop," new to jazz save for Mingus's occasional outcries in *Fables of Faubus*. A contraction of the Soviet "agitation and propaganda," agitprop, from the time of Lenin, has regarded art in any and all of its forms as valid, or even officially sanctioned, only when it is a weapon in the class struggle; the concept of "art for art's sake" was anathema incarnate. (These notions were later adopted without change by the Chinese communists.) With the possible exception of the theater of Brecht, little agitprop art—jazz included—has weathered well. In the 1960s tenor saxist Archie Shepp mixed "new thing" exercises with the chanting of his revolutionary poetry. "The Black Panther Party," wrote Ben Sidran in *Black Talk*, "turned to the music industry as an agent in the revolutionary struggle." In 1969 Elaine Brown signed a contract with Vault Records for an LP of "political songs . . . designed to give the Black Panthers a new avenue of communication to people." As Sidran points out in his excellent study, "this indicates a failure to understand that black music in America, by its very nature, is revolutionary and this quality is only submerged by highly sophisticated and rationalized (political) lyrics."

The Bossa Nova Reaction to Free Jazz

When anarchic imitators of Ornette Coleman and John Coltrane began to multiply in recording studios, jazz clubs, and concert halls, a hostile reaction set in among those who felt free jazz led to an artistic dead end. An obvious reaction was the sudden popularity in the mid-1960s of *bossa nova*, a native Brazilian fusion of samba rhythm and bebop with the folk and classical music of Brazil. *Bossa nova* (roughly colloquial for the "new thing") shined at the opposite end of the musical and emotional spectrum from free jazz; it was tuneful, romantic, body-based, danceable, and rooted in intriguing, complex chord progressions whose proper negotiations often eluded North American players taken with its infectious beat and lyric melodies. A large school of Brazilian jazz composer-players arose to produce an imposing body of work that survives today: Antonio Carlos Jobim, Oscar Castro-Neves, Carlos Lyra, João Gilberto, Baden Powell, and Luiz Bonfa. Bonfa and Jobim collaborated on the musical score of *Black Orpheus*, a perennial cult film from Brazil that did much to spread *bossa nova* northward. Introduced to American audiences by Dizzy Gillespie and his Argentine pianist-composer Lalo Schifrin, *bossa nova* and its creators escalated overnight in 1963 with the release of an album uniting Jobim on piano and singer-guitarist João Gilberto with tenor sax star Stan Getz (*Getz-Gilberto* Verve V6-8545). It became one of the largest selling jazz albums of all time, even among those who rarely listened to jazz. Getz's liner notes are worth quoting since they framed the most articulate attack written by a front-rank player against free jazz to date:

> The songs of João Gilberto and Antonio Carlos Jobim came to America like a breath of fresh air. Their music arrived here at a time when anemia and confusion were becoming noticeable in our music to anyone who knew enough to be concerned. The desperate craze for innovation had been overextending itself.

As with many music trends—ragtime and boogie woogie—*bossa nova* was nearly destroyed by commercialism and overplay, but the charm of this music and its broad appeal made it unkillable. Today the compositions of Jobim show every sign of survival; *Wave*, *Corcovado*, and *Desafinado*, among others, have taken their place in both the jazz and pop repertoire. Authentic *bossa nova* can be heard on the magnificent LP *Brasil '65 (In Person at El Matador* Atlantic SD 8112). (Listeners are cautioned against the debasements of *Brasil 65*'s unworthy successor, *Brasil 66*, which naturally outsold *Brasil 65* ten to one.)

The Ascendancy of Rock and the "Fusion" of Miles Davis

The ascendancy of rock during the 1960s took an ever-increasing toll on the jazz audience, largely a youthful one throughout history. Top jazz clubs went out of business; Erroll Garner, a round-the-block draw in the concert halls of Europe, could not fill a now-defunct 350-seat club in San Francisco. Dizzy Gillespie could not get booked into this same club without sharing a bizarre double bill with the Jefferson Airplane. Musicians fled to Europe and Japan to find steady work as many influential critics mounted the rock bandwagon. The late jazz columnist Ralph J. Gleason extolled the Jefferson Airplane and the Grateful Dead in superlatives once applied to Ellington and Parker. These were indeed the dog days of jazz.

Some bored rock artists had been gravitating toward jazz, while some jazz players dallied with rock to recapture their dwindling audience. Though Miles Davis was hardly the first to compound the jazz-rock mixture quickly dubbed "fusion" by the media, he was the first to attract universal notice with this inevitable brew. His 1969 LP, *In a Silent Way* (Columbia PC 9875), pointed the direction for a number of young musicians, giving the imminent fusion movement its initial kickoff. The album merged rock's repetitive electronic trancelike beat with a startlingly new Miles on trumpet—nervous, chattering—as Miles once again chose another protective color in his chameleon career. Though *In a Silent Way* fueled the fusion movement, it did not enjoy the massive sales envisioned by Columbia brass; this goal was realized by Miles's next album, *Bitches Brew*, in 1970, a heavily electronic rock creation that sold half a million copies in its first year. The album made Miles an overnight superstar for a vast new audience of young rock fans who had never paid the least attention to jazz in any form.

Into the jazz scene, already rife with contention and factions, the "new Miles" of *Bitches Brew* and *In a Silent Way* unloosed yet another controversy that has not abated to this day. While no one seriously questions the landmark importance of Miles's "Birth of the Cool" sessions or his collaborations with Gil Evans, *Bitches Brew* divided critics and musicians. There were those like Ralph J. Gleason who found it the latest innovation of the most creative mind in jazz and those who attacked it as, at best, a worthless fad, and at worst, a cynical attempt to grab a piece of the rock action in a calculated ploy—"if you can't lick 'em, join 'em."

Regardless of its quality—or lack of it—there is little doubt that *In a Silent Way* launched the fusion movement that remains very much alive today. A look at its personnel offers a portent of the future and once more displays Miles's remarkable gift for choosing sidemen destined to become major figures and trendsetters:

IN A SILENT WAY

Miles Davis, trumpet
Chick Corea, electric piano
Joe Zawinul, electric piano and organ
Herbie Hancock, electric piano
John McLaughlin, guitar
Dave Holland, bass
Wayne Shorter, tenor sax
Tony Williams, drums

The Austrian Joe Zawinul, once the hard-swinging funky pianist with the Cannonball Adderley Quintet, soon formed the influential group

Weather Report with Wayne Shorter, Czech bassist Miroslav Vitous, Brazilian percussionist Airto, and drummer Alphonse Mouzon. With consummate skill, *Weather Report* took the overall feeling of *In a Silent Way* to combine shimmering Debussian textures with latin rhythm, a strong electronic overlay, and an emphasis on collective improvisation that had all but disappeared from modern jazz. The bassist and drummers were freed from the function of keeping time to produce independent but interrelated melodic lines and textures with Shorter and Zawinul.

Herbie Hancock, both as pianist and composer, became one of the leading figures in 1970s fusion. Possessing a meticulous classical touch, though little individual style, Hancock seems more accomplished than inspired, a blend of Horace Silver, Lennie Tristano, Shearing, synthesizers, and, most of all, Bill Evans who put his indelible stamp on nearly all of his successors in the various Miles Davis groups.

Chick Corea, another Evans-inspired pianist with McCoy Tyner overtones, became a prime force in the 1970s with his group, *Return to Forever*, applying latin, hard-bop, and high-energy rock to the electric keyboard.

Britisher Dave Holland became one of the most sought-after bassists for his awesome technique and huge fat tone. In 1971 and 1972 Holland joined Chick Corea and avant-gardist Anthony Braxton as a member of *Circle*, which he followed with work with Stan Getz, Sam Rivers, Monk, and the Thad Jones-Mel Lewis big band.

Drummer Tony Williams began his much-talked-of six-year stint with the Miles Davis Quintet in 1963 at age seventeen and went on to form *Lifetime* with John McLaughlin, the guitarist from *In a Silent Way.* He remained in constant demand among the most advanced players of the 1960s and 1970s.

Keith Jarrett, who replaced Chick Corea in the Davis "fusion" group, cut the widest swath of all Miles's keyboard alumni. The move toward eclecticism—the merging of jazz with every form of music—is nowhere more evident than in Jarrett's marathon piano improvisations, a *bouillabaisse* of Bartók, boogie, Ravel, gospel, "soft rock," bluegrass, Alban Berg—with lavish helpings of Bill Evans. "The effect," wrote Stephen Davis in the New York *Times*, "is like Chopin and Art Tatum streaming together downriver in a canoe." Jarrett's becalming blend enjoys its special success in Europe and Japan. His *Köln Concert* of 1975 (ECM 1064/64) sold astonishingly well for an hour-long piano solo. Jarrett in a briefer vein can be heard in the Ravel-inspired *Introduction and Yaqui Indian Song*, which he considers among his best work (*Piano Giants*, Prestige P-24052). Unlike Corea, Hancock, and Zawinul, Jarrett is a militant foe of electric music, which he claims "is bad for you and for people listening."

Jarrett is given to extreme body contortions while playing—standing upright, lying on the floor—which seem to delight audiences and annoy critics. As with Miles's fusion, opinion on Jarrett is divided between those who consider him a genius and those who find him a monotonous bore.

As the jazz audience multiplied, it fragmented into many separate publics of widely differing tastes, a condition jazz shares with all other art forms today.

4

Jazz Today

(overleaf)
Wynton Marsalis: Equally gifted and
at home with Bach and bebop, at
age 21 trumpet virtuoso Wynton Marsalis
has set the jazz world on its ear.
He often joins forces with other
young player-composers like the highly
regarded multi-reed specialist Chico Freeman.
(Photograph by Brian McMillen.)

$\mathbf{A}$s jazz approaches the mid-1980s one striking fact is evident: In an art form long beset by the obsession with "something new," no major new development of lasting consequence has surfaced since jazz-rock fusion in the late 1960s. All current jazz movements are well rooted in the past. These categories, anything but hard and fast, overlap more often than not:

1. *Jazz-rock fusion* embraces rock players dabbling in jazz, like the Jeff Lorber Fusion, and jazz musicians mixing rock with classical and free jazz like *Weather Report, Return to Forever*, Bennie Maupin, and Herbie Hancock. Some versatile talents like guitarist Larry Coryell are equally adept at country, jazz, and rock.

2. *Free jazz* lives on with Coltrane alumni McCoy Tyner, Elvin Jones, and Pharoah Sanders as well as Anthony Braxton, Cecil Taylor, Sam Rivers, The Art Ensemble of Chicago, Ornette Coleman, Don Cherry, Dewey Redman, and Marion Brown, all of whom continue to attract large numbers of younger players like alto saxist Arthur Blythe.

3. *Bebop* still thrives in the hands of those who have played it throughout four decades: Gillespie, Stan Getz, the Modern Jazz Quartet, Zoot Sims, Oscar Peterson, Jimmy Rowles, Dexter Gordon, Art Blakey, Horace Silver, Phil Woods, Roy Haynes, Max Roach, Barney Kessel, Herb Ellis, and Joe Pass. Bebop currently enjoys a modest but ever-growing revival that is enlisting a new generation: Gillespie disciple Jon Faddis, guitarists Emily Remler and Bruce Forman, alto saxist Richie Cole. It is not uncommon to find musicians in their twenties thoroughly familiar with the work of Christian, Parker, Gillespie, Bud Powell, and Monk.

4. *Mainstream swing* of the 1930s continues to lure an older crowd yearning for the nostalgic sounds of their youth. Still played by Buddy Tate, Harry Edison, Benny Carter, and Count Basie, mainstream also attracts numbers of young white players like the Armstrong-influenced Warren Vaché, and tenor saxist Scott Hamilton who models his style after Ben Webster's.

5. *Ragtime, Dixieland, and Harlem Stride revivals*: Though the vogue for Dixieland jamming diminished as its veterans died off, there remain remnants of the old Eddie Condon gang, Max Kaminsky, Wild Bill Davison, and Bud Freeman to keep the memories aglow. The ragtime revival of the 1970s is still underway as many young concert pianists like Joshua Rifkin include Joplin rags in their public repertoire. Following the success of the movie *The Sting*, a strong ragtime "repertory" movement burgeoned that continues today with the excellent ensembles of Ralph Grierson's Southland Stingers and Gunther Schuller's New England Conservatory Ragtime Ensemble. Max Morath, longtime exponent and popularizer of ragtime, rediscovered and recorded the work of women ragtime composers unjustly neglected.

The Harlem "stride" style of James P. Johnson and Fats Waller survives in the work of pianists Ralph Sutton, Dick Wellstood, Dick Hyman, and 31-year-old Judy Carmichael whose grasp of James P. Johnson's work has won praise from seasoned musicians. "Stride" also flavors the eclectic piano styles of Jaki Byard, Sir Roland Hanna, and Jimmy Rowles. The Smithsonian Institute, among others, sponsored concerts and recordings of ensembles re-creating the classic discs of Jelly Roll Morton, Ellington, and Big Band swing, involving many superb players like Bob Wilber, Kenny Davern, Dick Hyman, Ruby Braff, and Doc Cheatham. Young rock guitarist Ry Cooder recorded evocative versions of Morton and Beiderbecke compositions, arranged and conducted by Joseph Byrd (*Ry Cooder: Jazz*, Warner Bros. BSK 3197).

6. *Rural and urban blues, and boogie-woogie*: The venerable tradition continues with veterans Big Joe Turner, Sammy Price, Albert King, B. B. King, and large numbers of white devotees—John Hammond, Mark Naftalin, and Charlie Musselwhite's Blues Band.

7. *"Crossover,"* closely akin to fusion, is the term applied to jazz players, like Donald Byrd (The Blackbyrds), George Benson, Freddie Hubbard, and sometimes Sonny Rollins, who have "crossed over" into the more lucrative area of pop-soul. Hubbard, a cohort of Ornette Coleman and Eric Dolphy before his defection, made this revealing comment to impresario Norman Granz: "I want to get back to playing some real jazz and not this shit I'm into now." Guitarist-singer George Benson, one of the most saleable of the crossover clan, told critic Gary Giddins that his latest pop recording would gross $6 million:

> Now, would you like to be the one to tell them (Warner Bros. Records) "this time George is going to make a record but we're not going to make as much money on it 'cause this is going to be a jazz record dedicated to the state of the art?" That's like

asking them to make a five million dollar donation to art music. . . . I've done that on records and they didn't sell. . . . If kids can't hear it, I don't care how good it is, you can't sell it to them. (Giddins, *Riding on a Blue Note*)

Despite the poor returns compared to rock and packaged "soul," ever-growing numbers of young people have entered the jazz life, so much so that keeping abreast of first-rate players who have surfaced since the early 1970s taxes the resources of full-time jazz scholars. Though much ground remains to be covered, jazz steadily pushes toward the frontiers of respectability. Every White House occupant since Johnson has played host to jazz greats at glittering front-page functions. A generation ago high school or college courses in jazz would be as unthinkable as courses in safecracking; today hundreds of public and private schools offer instruction in jazz history, theory, and performance.

As an adjunct to the largest surge of activism in the 150 year history of the women's movement, women have invaded what was once a nearly exclusive *macho* preserve, not only in their usually limited roles as singers and pianists, but as horn players, composers, and leaders. Toshiko Akiyoshi, whose career dates back to the early 1960s, currently conducts an all-male big band in her own compositions. Emily Remler, still in her twenties, is acclaimed for her bebop-flavored guitar. Pianist Shirley Horn won Miles Davis's not-readily-given enthusiasm; saxist Jane Ira Bloom, pianist Joanne Brackeen, trombonist Janice Robinson, and drummer Sue Evans may one day join the ranks of jazz's elder stateswomen—pianist Marian McPartland, pianist-composer Carla Bley, and trombonist-conductor Melba Liston. Women's jazz festivals and concerts have mushroomed in the eighties. Sally Placksin's scholarly and thorough *American Women in Jazz* was published in 1982.

With few exceptions, notably China, nearly every civilized country has spawned large numbers of accomplished musicians who have adopted jazz as a universal language: the Danish bassist Niels-Henning Orsted Pedersen, Polish pianist Adam Makowicz, Catalonian pianist Tete Montolieu, Brazilian guitarist-pianist-composer Oscar Castro-Neve, Filipino pianist Bobby Enriques, Argentinean tenor saxist Gato Barbieri, German trombonist Albert Manglesdorff, Japanese pianist Kai Akagi, Czech bassists George Mraz and Miroslav Vitous, Japanese clarinetist Eiji Kitamura, French violinist Jean-Luc Ponty, Hungarian bassist Aladar Pege, and French guitar wizard Bireli Lagrene who proved himself a worthy successor to Django Reinhardt at age thirteen!

Jazz continues to attract conservatory musicians, many from Europe, who have extended the technical frontiers of certain instruments well beyond the symphonic range. This is especially true of the string bass and percussion, whose importance in jazz have multiplied with each de-

Emily Remler: As an adjunct to the current
women's liberation movement, large numbers of
women are entering the jazz life. 24 year old
Emily Remler carries on the guitar traditions of
Charlie Christian and Wes Montgomery.
(Photograph by Charles Stewart.)

cade. Jazz today is blessed with countless string bass virtuosi: Cecil Mc-
Bee, David Friesen, Charlie Haden, Jim Hughhart, Brian Torff, George
Mraz, Red Mitchell, Michael Moore, Dave Holland, Marc Johnson, Ron
Carter, Richard Davis, Eddie Gomez, the veteran Ray Brown, and Niels-
Henning Orsted Pedersen who vies with Aladar Pege as the most technically accomplished bassist in the history of the instrument. Jazz drummers must cope with demands beyond those usually placed on
symphonic percussionists: marathon up-tempos and sudden shifts from
strict timekeeping to samba, Afro-Cuban, bebop, and free-form. Drum elders Jo Jones, "Philly" Joe Jones, Max Roach, Art Taylor, Roy Haynes,

Kenny Clarke, Shelly Manne, Art Blakey, and Elvin Jones have been joined by a host of younger masters—Tony Williams, Jack de Johnette, Billy Higgins, Ronnie Burrage, Billy Hart, Duffy Jackson, Barry Altschul, and Billy Cobham.

The "impossible dream" of outdoing Art Tatum haunts pianists whose techniques are developed to concert hall levels: Oscar Peterson, McCoy Tyner, Tete Montolieu, Denny Zeitlin, Adam Makowicz, Joanne Brackeen, Toshiko Akiyoshi, James Williams, Jim McNeely, and John Hicks. The tradition of jazz piano has never seemed richer. A vast confederation of distinctive keyboard stylists continues to flourish. Dubbed "the poets of the piano" by Count Basie, each is capable of playing unaccompanied concerts, and each is worthy of a special chapter: Jimmy Rowles, Tommy Flanagan, Dave McKenna, Hank Jones, Jaki Byard, Phineas Newborn, Ellis Larkins, Cedar Walton, Barry Harris, Albert Dailey, Jackie Wilson, Sir Roland Hanna, Randy Weston, Ray Bryant, Lou Levy, Mal Waldron, Roger Kellaway, and overlooked masters like Bobby Van Eps, and Walter Norris who currently lives in Germany.

The guitar offers no less fertile a field: Kenny Burrell, Jim Hall, Herb Ellis, Barney Kessel, Philip Catherine, Tal Farlow, Bucky Pizzarelli, Michael Howell, Emily Remler, Pat Metheny, Larry Coryell, Charlie Byrd, Pat Martino, Martin Taylor, Lorne Lofsky, the neglected Eddie Duran, the supreme virtuoso Joe Pass—"Art Tatum with a piano in his lap"—and the aforementioned gypsy kid, Bireli Lagrene.

Though few premier jazz artists command the income or audience of rock and pop superstars, the profusion of jazz concerts, festivals, new records, and ambitious programs of classic reissues testify that jazz has a promising future. But what *kind* of a future continues to be the nagging question.

5

Where Is Jazz Going?

(overleaf)
Chico Freeman
(Photograph by Brian McMillen.)

The amazing survival of jazz despite the exploitative onslaughts of half a century of commercial entrepreneurs is, in my opinion, due to its folk quality. And as the noble and the peasant understood each other better than either understood the bourgeois, so it seems significant that jazz is the only art form that appeals to both the intelligentsia and the common people. As for the others, let them listen to *South Pacific*. (Dwight Macdonald, *Against the American Grain*, 1960.)

To trot out the disc jockey's eternal query, "Where is jazz going?" is to ask "Where is America going?" Again and again we have found jazz to be a foolproof barometer of our national psyche and its players to be in the vanguard of the culture. Should the United States suffer a 1929-style depression or schedule a rerun of the Vietnam war or be caught up in a sweeping religious revival, these would be sounded in our music.

But no crystal ball is needed to foresee the quandary jazz faces in the future; hindsight will do. *In recapitulating the pattern of European concert music, jazz stands today where classical music has stood frozen for more than half a century.* This frankly argumentative concept is crucial to an understanding of contemporary music, jazz included, and demands elaboration.

Music critic Henry Pleasants kicked up an horrendous fuss in classical circles in 1956 with the publication of *The Agony of Modern Music*, followed in 1961 with *Death of a Music?* and in 1969 with *Serious Music— and All That Jazz*. The subtitle of *Death of a Music?—The Decline of the European Tradition and the Rise of Jazz*—encapsulates Pleasants's main argument: Jazz is the vital, creative music of our time that filled a void left by the classical tradition when its obsession with atonality and its abandonment of the communicative power of rhythm, song, and folk roots alienated modern audiences and led European concert music down a dead end to sterility where it has foundered for over fifty years.

Pleasants's books proved all the more upsetting because his classical credentials were as unassailable as the uneasy truths he forced upon a reluctant concert world—much the same truths the jazz world faces today:

1. What is still called "modern music"—Schoenberg, Berg, Stravinsky, Bartók—was already half a century old when Pleasants proposed his argument.

2. The atonal and arhythmic techniques that dominate much of today's "serious" music are addressed solely to a small coterie of composers, critics, and academics and have failed to communicate either musically or emotionally to contemporary audiences that stubbornly cling to the familiar music of the past.

3. "The composer's inability to provide viable new music has imposed upon the 'executive musician' the unwelcome role of an antiquarian specializing in music fifty to three hundred years old." No one can dispute Pleasants when today's most celebrated young virtuosi and conductors—Yo-Yo Ma, André Previn, Murray Pereiha, the Tokyo Quartet—follow the lead of their elders—Rubinstein, Heifetz, Furtwangler, Gieseking—to specialize in Bach, Mozart, Chopin, Mahler, Debussy, and the "modern(!)" music of Stravinsky and Bartók.

Though Pleasants assaults contemporary critics for "not recognizing the music of *their* time (jazz) when it was all around them," he was not the first classicist to sense the coming dominance of American music. Charles Ives, the yankee father of avant-garde music who freely used ragtime, barroom ballads, Protestant hymns, and other vernacular music in his thorny works, railed in print against European domination of American art music. Ives found the "serious" concert music of his time bloodless and effete when compared to the music of "rugged working men that was democratic, stirring and profound." In 1919 Swiss conductor Ernst Ansermet concluded his prophetic review of Sidney Bechet's improvisations as "perhaps the highway the whole world will *swing* along tomorrow [Italics mine]." British composer-critic Constant Lambert raised eyebrows in 1934 by comparing Ellington favorably with Ravel and Stravinsky. Henry Pleasants follows in his steps, dedicating *Serious Music—and All That Jazz* "to the memory of Constant Lambert (1905–1951) who in *Music Ho! A Study of Music in Decline* (1934) was twenty years ahead of any of us in discerning the new crosscurrents in the evolution of Western music in the twentieth century."

When *Death of a Music?* first saw print in the early 1960s, Cecil Taylor had inspired the coming generation to mix jazz with Schoenberg, John Cage, and Stockhausen, while Ornette Coleman and his followers were already obsessed with atonality and "breaking the tyranny of the beat." Pleasants sounded early warnings:

> If the jazz musician persists in the notion that respectability and status can be acquired by studied originality, eccentricity, defiance of his listeners and the composition of twelve-tone jazz, he will be ruined before his time has come.
>
> Jazz musicians sometimes talk of breaking the "tyranny of the beat" and sometimes even try to. In this they remind us of the serious composer rebelling against the restraints of tonality.

This point was made earlier by Ezra Pound: "Music begins to atrophy when it departs too far from the dance." Woody Herman said it another way: "When you stop swinging you're competing with Toscanini—and that cat can *cut* you!"

Pleasants concluded *Death of a Music?* on what we see now as a note of over-optimism:

> As jazz gains in status its composers will be less tempted to try symphonic writing as a bid for respectability. We may also hope they will be less susceptible to the empty fashions of serious music's avant-garde reactionaries. *There is no brighter future for the jazz musician in atonality . . . than there is for the serious composer* [Italics mine].

Many young musicians and critics still work under the spells of Coleman, Cecil Taylor, Anthony Braxton, and the Coltrane of *Ascension* that carried free jazz to its extreme of anarchic cacaphony. The atonal movement that backed European music down a blind alley now threatens jazz with the same prison. In seeking freedom from tonality, the "tyranny of the beat," chord progressions, and that unspeakable taboo—song—contemporary free jazz players, like their European forerunners, have, as Pleasants wrote, "got themselves into a fix where they are more dependent than ever upon just those technical elements from which they sought emancipation. . . . It was not until they had practically destroyed the implications of tonality that composers suddenly discovered that emancipation had brought them, not freedom of musical speech, but the inability to speak musically at all."

With Cecil Taylor and Anthony Braxton, American music has come full circle from the European tradition by producing intellectualized, non-rhythmic, nonmelodic hurricanes of sound that even the most cultivated audiences find unlistenable. This music speaks only to those who make it and to an intimidated clique of critics and agitprop writers more attuned to politics than to music. Braxton titles his pieces:

```
SIDE TWO:
Cut One:          Cut Two:   H   Cut Three:
489 M             BOR----    |       4038--NBS
   70-2--(TH-B)   N-K64     ( )          /  |
        M          (60)      |      |\      |
                    |     S  |      | \/|   |
                    |        |          |   6
                    M       373
```

He attempts to "explain" them in that nonlanguage borrowed, like his music, from academia at its most obscure: ". . . to really view progressionalism, especially with respect to restructuralism, is to see how each thrust moves at different cycles to connect to the world group." (*Jazz Times*, January 1983.)

No one disputes the instrumental skills or integrity of Anthony Braxton or Cecil Taylor, but technical prowess and good intentions alone will not produce an enduring and emotional music that speaks to us of our time.

The slowly mounting suspicion, which I have come to share, that the music of Taylor, Braxton, Coltrane during his *Ascension* period, and much of Ornette Coleman has a rendezvous with oblivion, runs counter to the conventional wisdom of the day. These musicians enjoy, if not large incomes, the plaudits of widely-read and influential critics. Without second-guessing the motives of such writers, one can see the familiar pattern of "once bitten, twice shy." Dogged by painful memories of the 1940s when nearly every established jazz writer except Leonard Feather dismissed Parker and Gillespie as fakes, critics later thought twice before rushing into judgement on the apostles of free jazz and atonality for fear of repeating past mistakes. As Pleasants wrote of their classical brethren: "Having seen what happened to critics who pointed out the faults in composers now remembered for their virtues, [late Beethoven, Berlioz, Stravinsky] the critic now looks for virtues in composers unlikely to be remembered for any virtue at all." This syndrome is not limited to music but infests all contemporary art forms, the most ready example being "modern art," long in the throes of one puffed-up fad after another, where the potential for critical gullibility, unintentional farce, and calculated fraud is seemingly inexhaustible.

Free jazz atonalists command fierce partisans among ultra-left critics Amiri Baraka and Frank Kofsky who brand opponents of this music as "reactionaries" motivated not by aesthetic considerations but by a "vested interest" in perpetuating the evils of racism and the economic status quo of black artists.

At the other end of the spectrum are those like this author, who agree with James Lincoln Collier's conclusion to *The Making of Jazz*: "Jazz needs, at the moment, a respite from experiments. It needs time to consolidate gains, to go back and to re-examine what is there." Gene Lees, author-publisher of *Jazzletter*, has framed the perfect reply to the perennial question: "Where is jazz going? Nowhere—it's *there*. Jazz has the capacity, not seen in classical music to nearly the same extent, to renew itself from its own past."

Today, when thousands of youths are fresh with the discovery of Django Reinhardt, Charlie Christian, Parker, Mingus, and Bill Evans, it is time to remine the riches of the past, making available to young audiences the long tradition from Morton to Coltrane that bypassed them throughout the 1950s and 1960s. Such a revival would also enlighten young musicians who often work in total oblivion to jazz before Parker or even Miles Davis. This oblivion helps explain why so much jazz after Parker sounds derivative and boring.

A Joplin revival of major proportions has scarcely touched Jelly Roll Morton. James P. Johnson is still the leading contender for the title of our most overlooked musical genius. Neither the public nor the musicians have begun to assimilate the half century of Ellington's achievement. Nearly three decades after his death Art Tatum is still the "musician's musician." Lester Young, Roy Eldridge, and other masters of the 1930s are overdue for revival. As Richie Cole and *Supersax* have found, there is enough in Parker's output to consume several generations of study and wonder.

Jazz spent the 1950s craning its neck to find the "new Bird" before it made time to study the Bird it already had. Monk, Mingus, Dolphy, and the Miles Davis Sextet with Coltrane and Evans will fuel musicians of the future, just as Bach and Haydn prepare conservatory graduates. And who knows? From a future generation steeped in the glories of the past, some "new Bird" may hover where no one's looking for him.

If this is not to be, if it is true, as some suspect, that the golden age of jazz is past and that this music has lost any further capacity to evolve, it will not be the first time such a fate has befallen an art form and it will not be the last. But even if jazz hardens into a stylized ritual like the Japanese Noh play, the legacy will endure as long as there are recordings and machines to play them.

One may hope, however idly, that the jazz revival and its eventual recognition in its own country as the art music of our time can happen with help from, rather than in spite of, the media whose past involvement ranged from bland indifference or tokenism to frank misrepresentation. More newspapers could follow the lead of the New York *Times, Village Voice*, San Francisco *Chronicle*, and San Francisco *Examiner* by opening their columns to jazz writers who are as informed and competent as the best classical critics.

Jazz has rarely been well served on television, save for the memorable CBS *Sound of Jazz* in 1959 and Ralph J. Gleason's *Jazz Casual* series for PBS two decades ago. These programs are still talked about because their producers showed a taste and restraint rare for television in selecting top musicians, pointing the camera at them, and leaving them alone. Most TV forays into jazz are gimmick-ridden spectaculars showcasing atrocious singers, like the 1983 "Ellington—The Music Lives On" for PBS that sullied the memory of Ellington and insulted all who love his music. A heartening and unusual exception to television's lackluster treatment of jazz was the 1983 *Jazz in America* series underwritten by Atlantic-Richfield for PBS that displayed front-rank musicians like Dizzy Gillespie, John Lewis, and Milt Jackson at work without the concessions, hokum, and distractions that normally plague "live" jazz programs on TV.

Though Hollywood turned out two honest films about country music—*Payday* and *Coal Miner's Daughter*—and one about rock—*The Buddy Holly Story*—the movie capital's grotesque attempts at jazz biography—*The Benny Goodman Story, Gene Krupa Story, Young Man With a Horn*—only proved Hollywood's corporate mentality incapable of dealing with an expression as personal, idiosyncratic, and free as the jazz experience. More recently, *Lady Sings the Blues*, a shameless exploitative travesty of Billie Holiday's art, showed that a black producer, Motown Records Berry Gordy, got no further afield from Hollywood clichés than did Louis B. Mayer. If the first honest jazz bio is to be filmed it will probably be done by the French director Louis Malle or by Woody Allen, both of whom have consistently used jazz to advantage in their work. Though much remains to be done, Hollywood often assigns film scores to jazz composers Quincy Jones, Lalo Schifrin, Denny Zeitlin, and Johnny Mandel.

While Hollywood's track record is largely unimpressive, it far outstrips the Broadway musical theater's since *West Side Story* in the mid-1950s. It is no coincidence that the decline and fall of American musical theater paralleled the exodus of jazz from Broadway since the 1920s and 1930s when Eubie Blake, James P. Johnson, and Fats Waller wrote tune-packed revues; when Goodman, Gene Krupa, Waller, and Armstrong sparked the pit bands of top Broadway shows; and when leading Broadway writers George Gershwin and Harold Arlen drew from the jazz and blues idiom.

Today, the Broadway musical is dominated by the sacred cow, Stephen Sondheim, who is alienated from the entire jazz experience. The flight of jazz from Broadway ushered in the era of tuneless musicals—*Company, Follies, Pacific Overtures, A Chorus Line, Cats, Annie, The Best Little Whorehouse in Texas, Godspell, Hair*, or at best, the one-tune musical: *Hello Dolly, A Little Night Music, Evita*. No one denies that the musicals of yesteryear like *Girl Crazy* had silly plots and lacked the urban veneer and smart lyrics of a Sondheim production, but they boasted tunes galore that promise to live forever. In 1930, not an unusual year for that fertile era, Broadway musicals introduced no less than *two dozen songs* that remain in the standard jazz and pop repertoire of all musicians and vocalists.* With the sole exception of *Send in the Clowns*, no Sondheim

---

*Memories of You, Love For Sale, Body and Soul, The Man I Love, What Is This Thing Called Love?, Soon, You're Drivin' Me Crazy, Time on My Hands, But Not For Me, Fine and Dandy, Bidin' My Time, I've Got a Crush on You, On the Sunny Side of the Street, Embraceable You, If I Could Be With You, Strike Up the Band, Dancing on the Ceiling, Would You Like to Take a Walk?, Something to Remember You By, Sing Something Simple, You're Lucky to Me, and the all-time jam session favorite, I Got Rhythm. The year before, 1929, Broadway musicals introduced 17 tunes that are still current, including Ain't Misbehavin, Black and Blue, I Guess I'll Have to Change My Plans, Can't We Be Friends?, Spring Is Here, and More than You Know. In 1932, 16 evergreens bowed on Broadway, including I Gotta Right to Sing the Blues, Alone Together, Night and Day, Who Cares?, April in Paris.

song has survived from one season to the next, hardly an impressive record for the author of over half a dozen musicals, a man showered with every Tony and Drama Critics Circle Award a grateful Broadway can bestow, pictured on *Time*'s cover, and hailed for fifteen years as Broadway's premier composer.

Recently Broadway hosted successful revivals of songs by Eubie Blake—*Eubie!*—Fats Waller—*Ain't Misbehavin'*—Ellington—*Sophisticated Ladies*—and George Gershwin—*My One and Only*. The public warmed to these shows because they were brim-full of what had been missing on Broadway for nearly thirty years—great songs. After countless dreary seasons of the sterile and instantly forgettable music of Sondheim and Stephen Schwartz (*Godspell, Pippin*), the timeless songs of Gershwin, Waller, and Ellington once more paved Broadway with gold.

Except for these occasional revivals, Broadway's current divorce from its once-thriving jazz tradition is complete. This curious alienation of our commercial theater from the lifeblood of American music was dramatized by the producer of the PBS television series *Musical Comedy at Home*, Sylvia Fine Kaye, when she called musical comedy "the only original, native, and indigenous art form this country has" while on the Merv Griffin Show. This was to the amazement of the program's regular band that includes a number of well-known jazzmen. Such blithe unawareness of the jazz idiom seems typical of today's Broadway community and is largely to blame for the era of tuneless musicals that marked the swift decline of American musical theater, which, Sylvia Fine Kaye to the contrary, is not an art form—but *could* be. Whoever creates an American *Threepenny Opera*—the first authentic jazz musical of the 1980s—will make history as surely as Kurt Weill and Bertolt Brecht did.

Campy black versions of *Hello Dolly* and *The Wizard of Oz* are not the answer. Black artists must create theater from their own rich experience. Instead of revamping wanton trivia like *No, No Nanette*, why not revive Ellington's socially advanced *Jump for Joy*, which closed in 1941 after four months in Los Angeles, never to surface again? Instead of musicals about Coco Chanel and Eva Peron, why not an authentic musical about Harlem in the 1920s? All this is possible if, through some miracle, Broadway rediscovers jazz and broadens its present function of providing idle distraction for expense-account squares. But it is more likely that independent film companies will venture where Broadway angels fear to spend.

No one looks for miracles; *Annie* and *Evita* will always outdraw jazz, just as they outdraw heavily subsidized arts like symphony, opera, and ballet. Because jazz developed and flourished in the face of grueling financial odds, many have feared that large-scale subsidies, with their attendant urge to confer "respectability" on what had long been an underground music, could well destroy jazz as an art form. Yet something must be done when the only nightclub in San Francisco that exclusively booked top jazz artists year-round went bankrupt in the Summer of 1983. The time must pass when concert-level pianist-composers Roland Hanna, Ray Bryant, Jimmy Rowles, and Jaki Byard count themselves lucky to get booked into the noisiest restaurants in Manhattan and when gifted musicians like Walter Norris must go abroad to make a living.

The time has come for our governments, multi-national corporations, and foundations to sponsor and underwrite our resident jazz talent—beyond those occasional jam sessions in the White House. As we approach the 1990s the nation must recognize and support jazz for what it has struggled against shameful obstacles to become—America's classical music.

When the face of Dizzy Gillespie peers at us from a postage stamp, it may no longer be possible for him to write, "Jazz is too good for Americans."

Chronology

	HISTORY	JAZZ
1899		Joplin's *Maple Leaf Rag* starts ragtime craze.
1914	World War I begins.	
1917	United States enters World War I. Bolshevik Revolution in Russia.	Decline of ragtime. Original Dixieland Jazz Band makes first jazz records.
1918	World War I ends.	
1920	Prohibition passed. First commercial radio broadcast.	"Jazz Age" begins.
1922	Sinclair Lewis's *Babbitt* published.	
1923		King Oliver's Creole Jazz Band makes first extensive records of black jazz. Jelly Roll Morton records first piano solos. James P. Johnson records *Carolina Shout*. Blues craze begins; Bessie Smith makes first records.
1924	Gershwin and Paul Whiteman pioneer "symphonic jazz."	Armstrong joins Fletcher Henderson's Orchestra.
1925		Armstrong Hot Five's first recordings, including the first "scat" vocal.
1926		Jelly Roll Morton's Red Hot Peppers first recordings.
1927	Electrical recording developed.	Ellington records *Creole Love Call* and *The Mooche*. Beiderbecke-Trumbauer record *Singin' the Blues*.
1928	Hoover elected.	Armstrong-Hines collaborations.
1929	Stock market crash; the Great Depression begins.	Armstrong makes breakthrough into white mass market.

	HISTORY	**JAZZ**
1930		Ellington records *Mood Indigo*, his first popular hit.
1931		Ellington records first extended jazz composition, *Creole Rhapsody.*
1933	Roosevelt takes office; New Deal begins; Prohibition repealed.	Henderson, Don Redman, and Benny Carter pioneer big band format.
1935	Rise of Hitler and Mussolini.	Goodman launches overnight Swing Era, Big Band craze. Teddy Wilson-Billie Holiday records. Goodman Trio are first interracial group in public. Roy Eldridge records.
1937		Basie Band with Lester Young records.
1938	Tape recording developed.	First Carnegie Hall jazz concerts.
1939 to 1940		Golden Age of Ellington Band with Blanton and Webster; Christian joins Goodman Band and Sextet; Boogie Woogie revival.
1941	Pearl Harbor bombed; World War II.	Christian, Monk, and early beboppers jam in Harlem; New Orleans revival; Louis Jordan's early R 'n' B.
1944		First bebop recordings with Parker and Gillespie.
1945	Atom bomb dropped; World War II ends.	Parker-Gillespie's *Groovin' High.*
1946	Cold war begins.	Big Band era ends; rise of R 'n' B and bebop.
1948	Truman elected; government "loyalty checks" begin; long playing records marketed.	Gillespie big band merges jazz with Afro-Cuban; some black musicians turn Muslim.
1950	Rise of Senator McCarthy; Korean War begins.	Miles Davis's Capitol "Birth of the Cool" sessions; Rise of "cool" and West Coast jazz: Brubeck, Mulligan, Shearing, Tristano.
1952	Eisenhower elected.	
1953	Korean War ends.	Modern Jazz Quartet organized.
1954	Vietnam War begins. Supreme Court desegregates schools.	Soul-funk and hard-bop reactions against "cool." Revival of blues and gospel. Stirrings of black nationalism in jazz. Rise of rock: Elvis Presley, *Hucklebuck.*
1956	Eisenhower reelected.	Clifford Brown-Max Roach Quintet.

HISTORY	**JAZZ**
1958 Stereo LP's marketed.	Miles Davis Sextet with Coltrane and Evans; rise of modal jazz. Mingus merges avant-garde with blues-gospel roots. Ornette Coleman launches "free jazz" controversy. "Third Stream" fusion movement. Monk wins belated recognition.
1959 Castro revolution in Cuba.	
1960 Kennedy elected. Civil rights movement.	
1963 Kennedy assassinated.	Coltrane merges African, Middle East music with free jazz and black protest music.
1965 Watts riot.	
1968 Martin Luther King assassinated.	
1969	Miles Davis's fusion of jazz-rock; rise of Davis alumni: Jarrett, Corea, *Weather Report*, Hancock electronic jazz; ragtime revival underway.
1974 Nixon resigns.	
1976 Carter elected.	
1980 Reagan elected.	Bebop has modest revival. Increasing numbers of women and non-Americans enter jazz, but no major new "movement" has surfaced. "Free jazz," though not profitable, continues to thrive and attract young musicians.

Discography

The following list is brief compared to the exhaustive discographies included in many jazz books. Rather than overwhelm beginning collectors, I prefer to limit the discography to a practical and affordable length. Even so, the purchase of all records listed may be beyond the means of most readers.

It is inevitable that readers will come to prefer one style or one musician over another and feel the urge to specialize. In that case they are directed to more extensive discographies—James Lincoln Collier's *The Making of Jazz* (Houghton Mifflin), and Marc C. Gridley's *Jazz Styles* (Prentice-Hall)—that does the yeoman's service in guiding the reader through the maze of multiple listings and the profusion of reissues, foreign and domestic, that have long been the hallmark of the jazz record industry. Readers are also advised to consult Len Lyons's *The 101 Best Jazz Records,* strong on bebop and after, though sketchy on earlier periods.

This list has been chosen on the basis of historical importance, breadth of coverage, lasting influence, and most of all, good listening. At this writing most are available.

COLLECTIONS AND ANTHOLOGIES

Archive of Jazz: The Blues, New Orleans Style, BYG G 529 068.

The Gospel Sound, Columbia G 31086.

Hammond, John. *Spirituals to Swing: Concerts 1938–39,* Vanguard VRS 8524/5 (later Vanguard 47/48).

The Riverside History of Classic Jazz, BYG 529.061, Vol. II.

Smithsonian Collection of Classic Jazz (by mail only):
Smithsonian Records
P. O. Box 10230
Des Moines, Iowa 50336

RAGTIME

Bolling, Claude. *Original Ragtime*, Columbia PC 33277.
Max Morath Plays Ragtime, Vanguard VDS 83/84.

EARLY CLASSIC JAZZ

Bechet, Sidney. *Master Musician*, RCA Bluebird AXM2–5516.
Bix Beiderbecke: Time-Life "Giants of Jazz."
Hawkins, Coleman. Victor Vintage LPV–501.
Jelly Roll Morton: Time-Life "Giants of Jazz."
Smith, Bessie. *Nobody's Blues But Mine*, Columbia G 30416.
Teagarden, Jack. Victor Vintage, LPV–528.

LOUIS ARMSTRONG AND EARL HINES

Armstrong, Louis. *The Genius of Louis Armstrong*, Columbia G 30416.
Louis Armstrong: Time-Life "Giants of Jazz."
Earl Hines: Time-Life "Giants of Jazz."

BIG BANDS

Basie, Count. *The Best of Count Basie*, Decca DXB–170.
Goodman, Benny. *Carnegie Hall Concert*, Columbia 814–6.
Henderson, Fletcher. *A Study in Frustration*, Columbia C4L 19.
Herman, Woody. *The Thundering Herds*, Columbia C3L 25.

HARLEM "STRIDE" PIANO

James P. Johnson: Time-Life "Giants of Jazz."
Fats Waller: Time-Life "Giants of Jazz."

DUKE ELLINGTON

Ellington, Duke. *At His Very Best*, Victor LPM 1715.
Ellington, Duke. *The Ellington Era, 1927–1940 Vols. 1 and 2*, Columbia C3L 27
and 39.
Ellington, Duke. *An Explosion of Genius*, Smithsonian package.
Ellington, Duke. *In a Mellotone*, Victor LPM 1364.

MASTERS OF THE THIRTIES

Christian, Charlie. *The Genius of Charlie Christian*, Columbia G 30779.
Eldridge, Roy. *The Early Years*, Columbia C2 38033.
Hawkins, Coleman. *Classic Tenors*, Flying Dutchman FD 10146.
Billie Holiday: Time-Life "Giants of Jazz."
Reinhardt, Django. *The Best of Django Reinhardt*, Capitol T–10458.

Art Tatum: Time-Life "Giants of Jazz."

Tatum, Art. *God Is in the House*, Onyx ORI–205.

Teddy Wilson: Time-Life "Giants of Jazz."

Young, Lester. *Classic Tenors*, Doctor Jazz FW 38446.

BEBOP-MODERN JAZZ

Brown, Clifford (with Max Roach). *Jordu 1955*, Trip Jazz TLP–5540.

Davis, Miles. *Birth of the Cool*, Capitol T–762.

Davis, Miles. *Kind of Blue*, Columbia CL 1355.

Davis, Miles (with Gil Evans). *Porgy and Bess*, Columbia CS 8085.

Evans, Bill. *Peace Piece and Other Pieces*, Milestone M–47024 (and Original Jazz Classics OJC–068).

Evans, Gil. *The Individualism of Gil Evans*, Verve V6–8555.

Garner, Erroll. *Concert by the Sea*, Columbia CL 883.

Gillespie, Dizzy. *The Development of an American Artist*, Smithsonian package.

Gillespie, Dizzy. *The Greatest Jazz Concert Ever*, Prestige PR 24024 (and Original Jazz Classics OJC–044).

Gillespie, Dizzy. *In the Beginning*, Prestige P 24030.

Kirk, Roland (with Jaki Byard). *Pre-Rahsaan*, Prestige P–24080.

Lewis, John. *Jazz Abstractions*, Atlantic SD–1365.

McRae, Carmen. *The Greatest of Carmen McRae*, MCA A2–4111.

Mingus, Charlie. *Better Git it In Your Soul*, Columbia CG 30628.

Mingus, Charlie. *Mingus, Mingus, Mingus*, Impulse AS-54.

Modern Jazz Quartet. *The Modern Jazz Quartet*, Prestige PR 24005.

Monk, Thelonious. *Genius of Modern Music Vols. I & II*, Blue Note 1510, 1511.

Thelonious Monk & John Coltrane, Milestone-Fantasy M–47011.

Parker, Charlie. *The Complete Charlie Parker*, BYG 529 129.

Parker, Charlie. *Yardbird in Lotus Land*, Phoenix Jazz LP 17.

Powell, Bud. *The Amazing Bud Powell*, Vols. I and II, Blue Note BLP 1503, 1504.

Rollins, Sonny. *Saxophone Colossus*, Fantasy-Prestige P–24050.

Silver, Horace. *6 Pieces of Silver*, Blue Note 1539.

Tristano, Lennie. *Crosscurrents*, Capitol M 11060.

FREE JAZZ

Coleman, Ornette. *The Best of Ornette Coleman*, Atlantic SD 1558.

Coleman, Ornette. *The Shape of Jazz to Come*, Atlantic 1317.

JOHN COLTRANE

Coltrane, John. *The Art of John Coltrane: The Atlantic Years*, Atlantic SD 2–313.

Coltrane, John. *Duke Ellington & John Coltrane*, Impulse A–30.

Coltrane, John. *Kulu Sé Mama*, Impulse A–9106.

ERIC DOLPHY

Dolphy, Eric. *Dolphy,* Prestige-Fantasy PR 24008 (and Original Jazz Classics OJC–022, –023).

Dolphy, Eric. *The Great Concert,* Prestige P–34002.

JAZZ-ROCK FUSION

Davis, Miles. *In a Silent Way,* Columbia PC 9875.

CONTEMPORARY TRENDS

Art Blakey & the Jazz Messengers with Wynton Marsalis. *Straight Ahead,* Concord Jazz CJ–168.

Chico Freeman with Wynton Marsalis. *Destiny's Dance,* Contemporary 14008.

Freeman, Chico. *The Outside Within,* India Navigation IN 1042.

Selected Bibliography

The following list is by no means complete since jazz books number well into the hundreds. I have included those of major importance, as well as those that offer conflicting points of view.

The Essential Works

Collier, James Lincoln. *The Making of Jazz: A Comprehensive History.* Boston: Houghton Mifflin, 1978. Also a Dover paperback. The best single volume history, despite minor omissions and flaws. Superbly organized and written, avoids heavy-handed pedantics as well as the hipster's argot that despoils too many jazz histories.

Feather, Leonard. *The New Encyclopedia of Jazz.* New York: Bonanza, 1960.

Feather, Leonard. *The Encyclopedia of Jazz in the Sixties.* New York: Horizon, 1966.

Feather, Leonard, with Gitler, Ira. *The Encyclopedia of Jazz in the Seventies.* New York: Bonanza, 1976.

The standard reference works with excellent brief historical surveys and Feather's "Blindfold Tests" of leading musicians plus Readers and Critics Polls.

Shapiro, Nat, and Hentoff, Nat. *Hear Me Talkin' To Ya.* New York: Dover, 1955. The story of jazz told in readable sequence by the musicians in their own words.

Taylor, Arthur. *Notes & Tones.* New York: Perigree Press, 1981. A unique series of interviews with leading black jazz musicians conducted by their peer, drummer Art Taylor, who got responses that were more frank than the usual interviews by white critics and non-players. Musically and racially, a one-of-a-kind insight into the private rarely-glimpsed world of the black artist.

General

Balliett, Whitney. *Improvising.* New York: Oxford paperback.

Balliett, Whitney. *New York Notes.* Boston: Houghton Mifflin, 1976.
Profiles and essays by the *New Yorker*'s venerable literary stylist who describes the sound of jazz like no one else.

Ellison, Ralph. *Shadow and Act.* New York: New American Library, Signet paperback, 1966. Evocative essays, some on jazz, by the author of *Invisible Man*, who takes issue with critic LeRoi Jones. His memoirs of jazz in his native Oklahoma City are brilliantly written.

Feather, Leonard. *The Book of Jazz.* New York: Horizon, 1961. Also a Paperback Library paperback. Excellent introduction, with a musically notated analysis of "The Anatomy of Improvisation." Useful for advanced music students as well as beginners.

Giddins, Gary. *Riding on a Blue Note.* New York: Oxford Paperback, 1981. The most stimulating young jazz journalist to surface in years, Giddins combines an exhilarating style with rare insight, standing nearly alone in relating jazz to the allied fields of pop and rock. Highly recommended.

Hammond, John, with Townsend, Irving. *John Hammond on Record.* New York: Summit Books, 1977. Also a Penguin Paperback. Stunning autobiography of jazz's great patron, publicist, critic, and prime mover who anticipated and changed the course of American music more than any other non-player. A little-known saga that deserves the widest possible audience.

Hentoff, Nat. *The Jazz Life.* New York: Da Capo Press, 1975.

Hentoff, Nat. *Jazz Is.* New York: Random House, 1976.
Solid interviews and reflections by a seasoned and versatile journalist and observer of the jazz scene.

Hitchcock, H. Wiley. *Music in the United States: An Historical Introduction.* Englewood Cliffs, New Jersey: Prentice-Hall, 1969. Excellent brief survey of all American music, jazz included, with a penetrating discussion of the conflict and distinction between "cultivated" concert music and the "vernacular" folk tradition.

Hodeir, André. *Jazz: Its Evolution and Essence.* New York: Grove Press, 1956. Also a Da Capo Press paperback. Technical, influential, and contentious as only the French convert can be. His valuable celebration of Ellington is offset by many perverse judgments, like an indefensible attack on Art Tatum.

Jones, LeRoi [Amiri Baraka]. *Blues People.* New York: William Morrow, 1963.

Jones, LeRoi [Amiri Baraka]. *Black Music.* New York: William Morrow, 1968.

The first black jazz critic of note offers a bitter, polemical, and highly influential overview of the sociology of jazz that reflects the black nationalist movement.

Keil, Charles. *Urban Blues.* Chicago: University of Chicago Press, 1969. A black sociologist contributes a fine, detailed study of the bluesman as culture hero. Essential for specialists in country and urban blues.

Murray, Albert. *Stomping the Blues.* New York: McGraw-Hill, 1976. A black journalist celebrates jazz and the blues as body-based affirmations of life, and the joys of black communal experience. Splendid writing throughout.

Newton, Francis [Eric Hobsbawm]. *The Jazz Scene.* New York: Da Capo Press, 1975. Brilliant appreciation by the noted British economist and jazz critic, written cleanly and with remarkable good sense.

Pleasants, Henry. *The Agony of Modern Music.* New York: Touchstone Press, 1977.

Pleasants, Henry. *Death of a Music?* London: Gollancz, 1961.

Pleasants, Henry. *Serious Music—And All That Jazz.* New York: Simon & Schuster, 1968.

A classical critic set off a bomb with these superlative essays that championed jazz as the vital, creative music of our time and indicted current European classical music as an art form in decline that has lost all contact with modern audiences. Highly recommended and provocative in the best sense.

Sidran, Ben. *Black Talk.* New York: Holt-Rinehart, 1971. Superb analysis by a Ph.D. jazz musician who sees jazz as a "radical alternative to the values of Western literary tradition."

Spellman, A.B. *Black Music: Four Lives.* New York: Schocken Books, 1970. Originally published as *Four Lives in the Bebop Business* by Pantheon Books, a Division of Random House, Inc. Bitter, revealing interviews with four black contemporary musicians who tell of their often futile struggle for recognition and survival.

Stearns, Marshall. *The Story of Jazz.* New York: Oxford University Press, 1956. Also a Mentor Paperback. Though its 1956 date renders it incomplete, this remains one of the best and most readable introductions to jazz, particularly its African and early roots.

Tirro, Frank. *Jazz: A History.* New York: W. W. Norton, 1977. A careful, condensed outline of major developments and innovators.

Specialized

Blesh, Rudi, and Janis, Harriet. *They all Played Ragtime.* New York: Oak Publications, 1971. The definitive work, lavishly illustrated, thoroughly researched, with many ragtime scores in full.

Feather, Leonard. *Inside Jazz* (originally *Inside Bebop*). New York: Da Capo Press, 1977. The first, and still the best, musical analysis of bebop and a lucid explanation of its departures from the Swing Era.

Gitler, Ira. *Jazz Masters of the Forties.* New York: Collier Books, 1970. Comprehensive treatment of the revolutionary bebop figures: Charlie Parker, Dizzy Gillespie, Bud Powell, Fats Navarro, and many others less well known.

Hadlock, Richard B. *Jazz Masters of the Twenties.* New York: Collier Books, 1974. The definitive work on this crucial period, with superb appraisals of the contributions of Armstrong, Henderson, Beiderbecke, Hines, Waller, Teagarden, and Bessie Smith.

Placksin, Sally. *American Women in Jazz.* New York: Wideview Press, 1982. Carefully researched work reflecting the recent impact of the women's movement on the jazz scene. Many unknown and forgotten musicians are covered.

Schuller, Gunther. *Early Jazz.* New York, Oxford University Press, 1968. Unique musical analysis of jazz until the early 1930s by the eminent composer, critic, conductor, musician, equally at home with classical and jazz. For the serious student and music major. The chapters on Morton and Ellington are essential.

Stewart, Rex. *Jazz Masters of the Thirties.* New York: Macmillan, 1972. The volatile and literate cornet star with Fletcher Henderson and Duke Ellington displays wit and total recall in these valuable remembrances of the Big Band Era and its stars.

Williams, Martin (ed.). *The Art of Jazz.* New York: Grove Press, 1960. Anthology of diverse essays, including Ross Russell's essential early discussion of bebop and its radical departures from big band swing.

Biography

Albertson, Chris. *Bessie.* New York: Stein and Day, 1972. Full-scale biography of Bessie Smith and her fabulous era, briefly marred by the author's preoccupation with her sexual exploits but valuable nonetheless.

Collier, James Lincoln. *Louis Armstrong: An American Genius.* New York: Oxford University Press, 1983. A thorough and readable assessment of the early Armstrong's massive and total transformation of all of American music, plus a perceptive psychological rationale for the commercial "sell-out" of his final years that is sure to be an affront to many Armstrong admirers. This promises to remain the definitive study of Armstrong for years to come.

Dance, Stanley. *The World of Duke Ellington.* New York: Charles Scribner's Sons, 1970.

Dance, Stanley. *The World of Earl Hines.* New York: Charles Scribner's Sons, 1977.

Dance, Stanley. *The World of Count Basie.* New York: Charles Scribner's Sons, 1980.

Few critics got as close to their subjects as this British veteran; memorable interviews throughout.

Ellington, Duke. *Music is My Mistress.* New York: Doubleday, 1973. Ellington's often chatty but still informative account of his career and the musicians who shaped it.

Lomax, Alan. *Mister Jelly Roll.* Berkeley: University of California Press, 1950. Frank, informative profile of Jelly Roll Morton mostly taken from Lomax's epochal 12 volume recorded interview for the Library of Congress in 1938.

Russell, Ross. *Bird Lives! The High Life and Hard Times of Charlie "Yardbird" Parker.* New York: Charterhouse Press, 1973. The finest, most exhaustive biography of a major jazz figure by Parker's former manager and record producer. The magnificent opening chapter, and much of what follows, is one of the few pieces of jazz writing that deserves to be called literature. Out of print.

Sudhalter, Richard M., and Evans, Philip R., with Dean-Myatt, William. *Bix: Man & Legend.* New Rochelle, New York: Arlington House, 1974. Exhaustive, almost day-by-day account of the tragic hero of the Roaring Twenties, Bix Beiderbecke. Thoroughly researched.

Autobiography

Gillespie, Dizzy, with Fraser, Al. *To Be, or Not to . . . Bop.* New York: Doubleday, 1979. Without question, the best and most informative of all jazz autobiographies. Essential to an inside understanding of the bebop era and full of the bust-out humor one expects from Dizzy Gillespie. As a thorough account of what the bebop revolutionaries were trying to accomplish, musically and socially, told by one of its major creators, this book stands alone.

Hawes, Hampton, and Asher, Don. *Raise Up Off Me.* New York: Coward, McCann & Geohegan Publishers, 1974. Scaldingly frank narrative of bebop piano giant Hampton Hawes, of his addiction and prison life, and his association with Parker and other jazz figures. Exquisitely written with the aid of novelist-jazz pianist Don Asher.

Mezzrow, Milton, with Wolfe, Bernard. *Really the Blues.* New York: Dell Publishers, 1946. The archetypal "white Negro" jazzman of the 1920's, Mezzrow tells the harrowing story of his drug addiction and prison life in this slang-ridden and entertaining account of the live-for-the-moment white Chicago jazz acolytes. Colorful, salty, sometimes suspect and self-serving, but an invaluable document for all that.

Fiction

Skvorecky, Josef. *The Bass Saxophone.* New York: Alfred Knopf, 1979. Most jazz fiction ranges from terribly written to forgettable. This is a glorious exception. The author is a Czech jazzman-writer who has composed two exquisite novellas bound together by the glue of jazz. His introduction on the impact jazz made on his native country under both the Nazis and the Soviets is a unique celebration of American music—the "sweet poison of Jazz" that the totalitarians cannot control. They therefore recognize the "men with the horns" as their natural enemies.

Jazz Magazines and Publications

Cadence
Route 1, Box 345
Redwood, New York, 13679

Coda
Box 87, Station J
Toronto, Ontario
Canada M4J 4X8

Contemporary Keyboard
GPI Publications, Box 615
Saratoga, California 95070

Crescendo
122 Wardour Street
London W1V 3LA
England

down beat
222 West Adams Street
Chicago, Illinois 60606

Jazz Journal International
35 Great Russell Street
London WCIB 3PP
England

Jazz Magazine
Box 212
Northport, New York 11768

Jazz Times
8055 13th Street, Suite 301
Silver Springs, Maryland 20910

Gene Lees' Jazzletter
P.O. Box 240
Ojai, California 93023

Annual Review of Jazz Studies
Transition Books
Rutgers University
New Brunswick, New Jersey 08903

Swing Journal
Tokyo, Japan

Index

Abba Labba, 74
Adderley, Cannonball, 123, 147, 176, 192, 194
African heritage, 33–34, 49–50
African rhythm, 27–28
Agee, James, 62
Agitprop, 200
Agony of Modern Music, The (Pleasants), 215
Airto, 203
Akagi, Kai, 209
Akiyoshi, Toshiko, 209, 211
Alexander, Willard, 107, 114
Allen, Henry "Red," 40, 62, 104
Altschul, Barry, 211
Ambush, 42
American Mercury, The, 94
American Society of Composers and Performers (ASCAP), 40
Ammons, Albert, 119, 120
Anderson, Cat, 181
André, Maurice, 30
Ansermet, Ernst, 53, 216
Antheil, George, 175
Arlen, Harold, 24, 220
Armstrong, Louis, 3, 11, 16, 19, 24, 29, 30, 33, 38, 44, 45, 52, 56, 58–73, 91, 99, 103, 131, 138, 153, 175, 220
Arnold, Kokomo, 154
Art Ensemble of Chicago, 193, 207
Aufderheide, May, 52
Auld, Georgie, 126
Avante-garde movement, 128–30
Ayler, Albert, 174

Bailey, Buster, 30
Bailey, Mildred, 70, 108
Baker, Chet, 168, 181
Bales, Burt, 58

Balliett, Whitney, 40, 147, 167
Bar, 19
Barber, Bill, 163, 164
Barber, Chris, 149, 150
Barbieri, Gato, 209
Barefield, Eddie, 114
Barker, Blue Lu, 154
Barker, Danny, 22, 34, 39, 40
Barnes, George, 126
Barnet, Charlie, 113, 140
Bartók, Bela, 113, 192, 215, 216
Basie, Count, 29, 36, 40, 41, 68, 84, 101–6, 109, 111, 114–16, 119–20, 126, 131, 139, 140, 207, 211
"Battle of the Bands," 38, 40
Bauer, Billy, 165
Beatles, The, 23, 24, 151, 156–58, 195
Beatnicks, 171
Bebop, 120–48, 154–55, 158–61, 169–74, 207
Bebop (Russell), 136
Bechet, Sidney, 3, 23, 61, 66, 119–20, 216
Beiderbecke, Bix, 3, 35, 39, 43, 63, 89, 90, 92, 95–98
Bellson, Louis, 84, 159
Benson, George, 103, 208–9
Berg, Billy, 140
Berigan, Bunny, 98, 106, 108, 109, 137
Bernstein, Leonard, 19, 24, 37
Berry, Chuck, 150, 157
Bigard, Barney, 80, 84, 110
Big band era, 100–18, 126, 131
Big Maceo, 154
Bix: Man & Legend (Sudhalter and Evans with Dean-Myatt), 96
Black Music: Four Lives (Spellman), 188, 193
Black Muslim movement, 133–34, 195
Black Talk (Sidran), 45

Blackwell, Ed, 189, 190, 191, 199
Blackwell, Scrapper, 154
Blake, Eubie, 74, 220
Blakey, Art, 34, 132, 147, 150, 169, 172–73, 176, 207, 211
Blanton, Jimmy, 83–84, 123
Bley, Carla, 209
Bloom, Jane Ira, 209
Bluegrass, 38
"Blue notes," 18–19
Blues, the, 16, 18–24, 49, 56–58, 138, 171–74, 208
Blues scale, 18
Blythe, Arthur, 207
Bonfa, Luis, 151, 201
Boogie-woogie, 118-20, 208
Book of Ragtime (Joplin), 53
Borneman, Ernest, 33
Bossa nova, 151, 160, 200–201
Boyd, Nelson, 164
Brackeen, Joanne, 209, 211
Bradley, Will, 120
Braff, Ruby, 208
Braud, Wellman, 80
Braxton, Anthony, 174, 193, 203, 207, 217–18
Break-the-rules attitude, 37–38
Brewer, Teresa, 44
Broadway musical theater, 220–21
Broonzy, Big Bill, 21, 120, 154
Broun, Heywood Hale, 149
Brown, Cleo, 120
Brown, Clifford, 30, 64, 135, 141, 150, 164, 172–73
Brown, Lawrence, 33, 85
Brown, Marion, 193, 207
Brown, Ray, 37, 83, 132, 210
Brown, Steve, 97
Brubeck, Dave, 43, 86, 159, 163, 168–69, 182, 193
Bruce, Lenny, 34, 158, 170
Bryant, Ray, 211, 222
Buchanan, Roy, 126
Buckley, Lord, 89
Bull, Sandy, 38
Bumblebee Slim, 154
Burns, Ralph, 160
Burrage, Ronnie, 211
Burrell, Kenny, 211
Burton, Gary, 38
Bushkin, Joe, 109
Byard, Jaki, 162, 186, 198, 208, 211, 222
Byas, Don, 130, 132
Byrd, Charlie, 126, 188, 211
Byrd, Donald, 208
Byrd, Joseph, 208

Caen, Herb, 171
Cafe Society Downtown, 120
Cage, John, 129–30, 175, 193, 216
Cakewalk, 50
Callendar, Red, 184
Calloway, Cab, 70, 133
Carisi, John, 164
Carmichael, Hoagy, 96, 98
Carmichael, Judy, 208
Carney, Harry, 40, 80, 85
Carr, LeRoy, 154
Carter, Benny, 105, 107, 131, 132, 188, 207
Carter, Ron, 176, 198, 210
Casa Loma Orchestra, 107, 109
Castro-Neves, Oscar, 201, 209
Catalysts of jazz, 38–43
Catherine, Philip, 211
Catlett, Big Sidney, 104
Challis, Bill, 98
Chaloff, Serge, 161
Chambers, Paul, 188
Charles, Ray, 70, 150, 157, 161, 182
Cheatham, Doc, 208
Checker, Chubby, 147, 155
Cherry, Don, 189, 191, 207
Chicagoans, 94–100
Chord changes or progressions, 13–17
Chords, 15, 16
Christian, Charlie, 43, 70–71, 103, 114, 120, 125–26, 130, 132, 141, 143, 207
Chromatic scale, 15
Chronology, 223–25
Clarke, Kenny, 89, 115, 126, 130, 132, 141, 150, 164, 167, 171, 176, 211
Clayton, Buck, 33, 116
Cleaver, Eldridge, 171
Cleve, George, 177
Cobham, Billy, 211
Cole, Nat "King," 44, 71, 72, 106, 111, 118, 132, 136, 140
Cole, Richie, 207, 219
Coleman, Bill, 89
Coleman, Earl, 161
Coleman, Ornette, 6, 14, 36, 56, 151, 175, 178, 187–92, 198–200, 207, 216-218
Coles, Honi, 154
Coles, Johnny, 186
Collette, Buddy, 168, 184
Collier, James Lincoln, 4, 5, 42, 139, 180, 191, 194, 198, 218
Collins, Cal, 126
Collins, Junior, 164
Coltrane, Alice, 196
Coltrane, John, 5, 11, 14, 37, 71, 146, 148, 151, 173, 175, 176, 180, 187, 189, 192, 194–96, 198, 199, 217–19

Condoli, Conte, 159
Condon, Eddie, 92, 95, 96, 100, 208
Conservatory musicians, 209–10
Cooder, Ry, 58, 98, 208
Cooke, Sam, 150, 157
Cool jazz, 117–18, 150, 159, 161–68
Coon songs, 50
Cooper, Bob, 167
Corea, Chick, 176, 177, 193, 202, 203
Coryell, Larry, 38, 126, 207, 211
Cotton Club, 79
Country music, 38
Cowell, Henry, 175
Craft, Robert, 75
Crawford, Rosetta, 154
Cream, 23
Crosby, Bing, 43, 44, 70
Crosby, Bob, 110, 120
Crossover, 208–9
"Crow-jim," 177–78
Curson, Ted, 186
Cutting contests, 38–43
Cyrille, Andrew, 193

Daddy-O Dailey, 155
Dailey, Albert, 211
Damerson, Tadd, 16, 130, 132, 139, 165
Dance, Stanley, 40, 78, 89
Dart, Bill, 152
Davern, Kenny, 208
Davis, Meyer, 92
Davis, Miles, 11, 13–14, 16, 33, 36, 43, 44, 49,
    64, 71, 97, 111, 114, 117, 124, 132, 137,
    141, 145–48, 150, 151, 162–64, 167–69,
    171, 174–83, 188, 193, 202, 209, 219
Davis, Richard, 210
Davis, Stephen, 203
Davison, Wild Bill, 208
Dean-Myatt, William, 96
Death of a Music? (Pleasants), 215–17
Debussy, Claude, 53
Delaunay, Charles, 89, 119, 152
Desmond, Paul, 163, 168, 169, 188
Diatonic scale, 14–15
Dickenson, Vic, 116
Diddley, Bo, 101, 150, 157
Discography, 227–30
Dixieland, 58–66, 73, 148–53, 208
Dodds, Baby, 60
Dodds, Johnny, 60, 64
Dolphy, Eric, 151, 186, 187, 189, 191, 192,
    196–200, 219
Domino, Fats, 157
Dorsey, Jimmy, 90, 99–100, 109
Dorsey, Tommy, 43, 86, 90, 91, 99–100, 109,
    111, 119, 120, 131
down beat, 39–40, 147
Drug use, 134–35
Duran, Eddie, 126, 211

Durham, Eddie, 125
Dutrey, Honore, 60
Dvořák, Antonin, 49
Dylan, Bob, 103, 158

***Early Jazz* (Schuller), 27, 49, 89**
Eckstine, Billy, 72, 126, 135, 136, 145
Edison, Harry, 116, 207
Eldridge, Roy, 33, 36, 43, 64, 67, 70–71, 110,
    113, 120–21, 145, 159, 163, 188, 219
Elements of jazz, 26–34
Ellington, Duke, 3, 5, 15, 22, 23, 33, 36–38, 40,
    44, 45, 52, 55, 58, 62, 68, 72, 74, 77–88,
    101, 111, 116, 123–26, 131–133, 145, 159,
    183, 184, 196, 208, 216, 219, 221
Ellis, Herb, 126, 207, 211
Ellison, Ralph, 127
Elman, Ziggy, 32, 109
Enevoldsen, Bob, 167
Enriques, Bobby, 209
Ervin, Booker, 186
Estes, Sleepy John, 154
European support of jazz, 86, 88–89
Evans, Bill, 35, 36, 148, 151, 165, 176–80, 198,
    203, 219
Evans, Gil, 16, 38, 150, 163, 164, 165, 181–82,
    202
Evans, Herschal, 116, 117
Evans, Philip R., 96
Evans, Sue, 209
Expatriate musicians, 89

Faddis, Don, 207
Faddis, Jon, 142
"False fingerings," 30
Farlow, Tal, 126, 165, 211
Farrell, Jack W., 149
Feather, Leonard, 36, 44, 55, 89, 111, 124, 131,
    134, 136, 145, 168, 169, 183, 187, 188,
    198, 218
Ferguson, Otis, 99
Films, 220
Fitzgerald, Ella, 41
Flanagan, Tommy, 211
Flatt and Scruggs, 38
Forman, Bruce, 207
Foss, Lukas, 175
Foster, Pops, 60, 68, 91
Fox, Charles, 89
France, 88–89
Franklin, Aretha, 103
Free jazz, 151, 187–93, 207, 218
Freeman, Bud, 95, 106, 109, 208
Freeman, Chico, 199, 206, 214
Freeman, Russ, 167
Friesen, David, 210
Frumbauer, Frankie, 97
Fusion:
    of Ellington, 80–81

jazz-rock, 49, 151, 201-3, 207
ragtime-blues, 56-58

Gaillard, Slim, 135
Garland, Red, 176
Garner, Erroll, 52, 161-62, 201
Gershwin, George, 182, 220, 221
Getz, Stan, 35, 89, 117, 132, 142, 151, 160, 161, 163, 201, 207
Giants of Jazz series (Time-Life), 6-7, 99
Gibson, Harry "The Hipster," 135
Giddins, Gary, 174
Gilberto, João, 20
Gillespie, Dizzy, 11, 12, 14, 30, 35-37, 42, 43, 64, 70-72, 76, 80, 86, 97, 111, 120-21, 123, 126, 130-33, 135-43, 146, 150, 152, 153, 159, 163, 187, 201, 207, 218-20, 222
Gitler, Ira, 176
Giuffre, Jimmy, 161, 163, 167
Glaser, Joe, 65, 68, 72, 91
Glaser, Martha, 161
Gleason, Ralph J., 35, 157, 170, 201, 202, 219
Goffin, Robert, 88
Golden Gate Quartet, 119-20
Goldkette, Gene, 40
Golson, Benny, 173, 199
Gomez, Eddie, 177, 210
Gonsalves, Paul, 85
Gonzales, Babs, 35
Goode, Mort, 108
Goodman, Benny, 30, 35, 44, 86, 91, 92, 95, 97, 98, 101, 103-14, 118, 120, 125, 126, 137, 220
Goodman Quartet, 111-13
Goodman Sextet, 125
Goodman Trio, 111-13
Gordon, Dexter, 89, 117, 132, 165, 188, 207
Gordy, Berry, 220
Gospel, 18, 150, 184
Gottlieb, Louis, 193
Gottschalk, Louis Moreau, 49, 51
Gramercy Five, 110, 159
Granz, Norman, 118, 208
Grappelly, Stephane, 122
Great Britain, 89
Green, Lil, 20, 108, 154
Greene, Bob, 58
Greene, Freddie, 115
Gregory, Dick, 170
Grey, Al, 31
Grierson, Ralph, 208
Grisman, David, 38
Grossman, William L., 149
Guitar, 33

Hackett, Bobby, 97, 109
Haden, Charlie, 190, 191, 210

Hadlock, Richard B., 62-63, 70, 98
Haggart, Bob, 110
Haig, Al, 132, 139, 142, 164, 173
Hakim, Sadik, 134
Haley, Bill, 23-24, 101, 150, 157
Hall, Adelaide, 80
Hall, Jim, 211
Hamilton, Chico, 168
Hamilton, Scott, 208
Hammond, John, 92, 101-3, 106, 107, 111, 113-15, 118-20, 125, 131, 208
Hampton, Lionel, 105, 111, 113, 126, 132, 159, 183
Hancock, Herbie, 176, 177, 202, 203, 207
Handy, John, 186
Handy, W. C., 54
Hanna, Roland, 162, 186, 208, 211, 222
Hard Bop, 150, 169-74
Hardin-Armstrong, Lil, 60-62, 64
Harlem Hamfats, 154
Harlem stride, 74-77, 208
Harmony, 15, 26
Harris, Barry, 211
Harris, Benny, 139
Harrison, Jimmy, 99
Harrison, Max, 73, 89, 182
Hart, Billy, 211
Hart, Clyde, 132
Hawes, Hampton, 168
Hawkins, Coleman, 3, 31, 38, 40, 62, 99, 104, 116-17, 123, 124, 131, 132, 137, 163, 191
Haynes, Roy, 132, 207, 210
Heart of Jazz, The (Grossman and Farrell), 149
Heath, Percy, 166, 167
Hefti, Neal, 160
Henderson, Fletcher, 3, 40, 62, 64, 77, 84, 99, 101, 103-4, 106-8, 116, 117, 126
Henderson, Horace, 104, 107
Henderson, Joe, 187
Henderson, Stephen "the Beetle," 74
Hendricks, Jon, 18, 35
Hentoff, Nat, 12, 42, 170, 187-90
Herman, Woody, 110, 111, 132, 136, 159-61
Heroin, 135
Hicks, John, 211
Higginbotham, J. C., 104
Higgins, Billy, 189-91, 211
Hill, Andrew, 198
Hines, Earl "Fatha," 3, 5, 29, 66-68, 72-74, 89, 99, 111, 122-23, 135, 136, 149, 152
Hodeir, André, 127, 147
Hodges, Johnny, 11, 80, 84
Holiday, Billie, 20, 26, 70, 89, 103, 111, 113-14, 117, 120, 220
Holland, Dave, 202, 203, 210
Holly, Buddy, 150, 157
Holman, Bill, 159, 167
Horn, Shirley, 209

Horne, Ellis, 152
Horne, Lena, 113
Hot Fives, 64, 65
"Hot" players, 97
Howard, Rosetta, 154
Howell, Michael, 211
Hubbard, Freddie, 141, 183, 191, 196, 198, 208
Hughes, Spike, 85
Hughhart, Jim, 210
Humes, Helen, 115
Hunter, Alberta, 21, 64
Hurok, Sol, 161
Hyman, Dick, 58, 208

Iamb, 19
Iambic pentameter, 19
Improvisation, 11–12, 16, 56, 174–75
Inside Jazz (Feather), 136
International musicians, 209
International support of jazz, 86, 88–89
I Paid My Dues (Gonzales), 35
Israels, Chuck, 177
Ives, Charles, 53, 216

Jackson, Duffy, 211
Jackson, Jesse, 34
Jackson, Mahalia, 18
Jackson, Milt, 132, 166, 167, 176, 220
Jackson, Preston, 60, 61
Jack the Bear, 74
Jamal, Ahmad, 133
James, Clive, 147
James, Harry, 100, 109
Jam sessions, 38–39
Jarrett, Keith, 176, 177, 203–4
"Jazz age" of the roaring twenties, 92–94
Jazz-rock fusion, 49, 151, 201–3, 207
Jazz Style in Kansas City and the Southwest (Russell), 115
Jazz Tradition, The (Williams), 198
Jazz writers, 219
Jefferson, Blind Lemon, 21
Jewell, Derek, 84–85
Jobim, Antonio Carlos, 142, 151, 201
Johnette, Jack de, 211
John Hammond on Record (Hammond and Townsend), 101
Johnson, Budd, 132
Johnson, Bunk, 149, 150, 153
Johnson, J. J., 37, 132, 147, 151, 164, 165, 176
Johnson, James P., 3, 28, 29, 42, 74–76, 78, 208, 219, 220
Johnson, Lonnie, 154
Johnson, Marc, 210
Johnson, May Wright, 74
Johnson, Pete, 119, 120
Johnson, Robert, 21, 23, 154, 157
Johnson, Walter, 104

Jones, A. W., 27
Jones, Elvin, 194, 195, 207, 211
Jones, Hank, 211
Jones, Jo, 39, 115, 126, 141, 210
Jones, LeRoi (Amiri Baraka), 35, 45, 101, 177–78, 218
Jones, Maggie, 21, 64
Jones, Philly Joe, 176, 196, 210
Jones, Quincy, 220
Jones, Thad, 183, 186
Joplin, Scott, 28, 51–54, 239
Jordan, Barbara, 34
Jordan, Louis, 136, 150, 154, 155, 160
Josephson, Barney, 120

Kaminsky, Max, 96, 208
Kassel, Art, 92
Kay, Connie, 166, 167
Kaye, Sylvia, 221
Keepnews, Orrin, 147
Keil, Charles, 41
Kellaway, Roger, 211
Kemp, Hal, 109
Kenton, Stan, 22, 80, 86, 132, 159
Keppard, Freddie, 93
Kern, Jerome, 24
Kessel, Barney, 110, 126, 132, 159, 207, 211
King, Albert, 208
King, B. B., 208
King, Martin Luther, Jr., 34
Kirk, Andy, 105, 125
Kirk, Rahsaan Roland, 186, 187, 189, 192, 197–98
Kitamura, Eiji, 209
Knepper, Jimmy, 185–86
Koenig, Lester, 184
Kofsky, Frank, 218
Konitz, Lee, 117, 147, 159, 163–65
Krassner, Paul, 170
Krell, W. H., 51
Krupa, Gene, 58, 91, 95, 100, 106, 107, 109, 111, 113, 220
Kuhn, Steve, 193
Kyle, Billy, 72
Kyser, Kay, 44, 108

Lacy, Steve, 192
La Faro, Scott, 177, 191
Lagrene, Bireli, 209, 211
Lamb, Joseph, 52
Lambert, Constant, 216
Lamond, Don, 161
Larkins, Ellis, 211
Latref, Yusef, 133, 195
Leadbelly, 21, 154
Lee, Peggy, 108
Lees, Gene, 97, 125, 147, 170, 188, 218
Le Jazz Hot, 40

Leonard, Harlan, 105
Levey, Stan, 132, 159
Levy, Lou, 211
Lewis, George, 149, 150, 153
Lewis, Jerry Lee, 101, 150, 157
Lewis, John, 11, 13, 36, 117, 132, 135, 138, 148, 151, 164–67, 176, 187, 198, 199, 219–20
Lewis, Meade "Lux," 27, 119, 120, 162
Lewis, Mel, 183
Lewis, Sinclair, 94
Liston, Melba, 209
Little Richard, 157
Lofsky, Lorne, 211
Lofton, Cripple Clarence, 119
Lomax, Alan, 57
Lombardo, Guy, 92, 107–8
Lorber, Jeff, 207
Lowe, Mundell, 82
Lunceford, Jimmy, 40, 101
Lynn, Loretta, 38
Lyons, Jimmy, 85, 193
Lyra, Carlos, 201

Macdonald, Dwight, 127, 128, 215
Machismo, 41–42
Major scale, 14–15
Making of Jazz, The (Collier), 4, 5, 139, 191, 198, 218
Makowicz, Adam, 209, 211
Mandel, Johnny, 220
Manglesdorff, Albert, 209
Manne, Shelly, 132, 159, 167, 187–88
Marching band music, 28, 51, 59–60
Marijuana, 134–35
Marmarosa, Dodo, 110, 132, 134, 142, 159
Marsalis, Wynton, 43, 141, 173, 206
Marsh, Warne, 165
Martino, Pat, 126, 211
Masscult & Midcult (Macdonald), 127
Maupin, Bernie, 207
Mayall, John, 120
McBee, Cecil, 210
McHugh, Jimmy, 26
McKenna, Dave, 211
McKenzie, Red, 95
McKibbon, Al, 164
McKinney's Cotton Pickers, 104
McLaughlin, John, 202
McNeely, Jim, 211
McPartland, Jimmy, 92, 95
McPartland, Marian, 209
McPherson, Charles, 186
McRae, Carmen, 182, 190
Melody, 26
Mencken, H. L., 94
Meryman, Richard, 59, 61, 64, 69–71
Metcalf, Louis, 90

Metheny, Pat, 126, 211
Metronome, 39–40
Mezzrow, Milton "Mezz," 91, 94–95
Miley, Bubber, 79
Milhaud, Darius, 168
Miller, Big, 138
Miller, Glenn, 44, 86, 97, 99–100, 109, 131
Millinder, Lucky, 146
Mills, Irving, 79
Mills Brothers, 70
Mingus, Charlie, 13, 36, 37, 114, 132, 148, 150, 151, 165, 176, 178, 183–87, 192, 197–99, 219
Minor scale, 14–15
Minton's playhouse, 130
Mitchell, Red, 165, 167, 210
Mitchell's Christian Singers, 110, 119–20
Modal jazz, 151, 178–83
Modern jazz, 120–48, 150, 158–68
Modern Jazz Quartet, 147, 150, 163, 166–67, 207
Mole, Miff, 62, 98
Monk, Thelonious, 43, 126, 127, 130, 132, 143–47, 150, 170, 176, 187, 188, 192, 194, 207, 219
Monroe's Uptown House, 130
Montgomery, Little Brother, 119
Montgomery, Wes, 126
Montolieu, Tete, 209, 211
Moody, James, 26
Moore, Michael, 177, 210
Morality issue, 52
Morath, Max, 208
Morgan, Lee, 142
Morrison, George, 89
Morton, Bennie, 98
Morton, Jelly Roll, 24, 28, 54–59, 67, 162, 208
Moten, Bennie, 29, 105, 114
Mouzon, Alphonse, 203
Mraz, George, 209, 210
Mulligan, Gerry, 117, 124, 135, 159, 163, 164, 167, 168
Mundy, Jimmy, 107
Murphy, Turk, 149, 150
Musical Courier, 52
Music Ho! A Study of Music in Decline (Lambert), 216
Musselwhite, Charlie, 208
Mutes, 32–33

Naftalin, Mark, 208
Nanton, Joseph "Tricky Sam," 32–33, 79, 85
Nathan, George Jean, 94
Navarro, Fats, 132, 141, 146
Nelson, Oliver, 198
Nelson, Romeo, 119
Nesbitt, John, 104–5
Newborn, Phineas, 211

New Orleans jazz, 58–66, 149–53
New Orleans Rhythm Kings, 95
Nicholas, Albert, 89
Nichols, Red, 62, 92
Niehaus, Lennie, 167
Noble, Ray, 140
Noone, Jimmy, 106
Norris, Walter, 189, 211, 222
Norvo, Red, 98, 131, 132, 160, 163, 165–66,
    183

O'Day, Anita, 113
Okeh Records, 64–65
Oliver, Joe "King," 23, 59–61, 67
Oliver, Sy, 109
Original Dixieland Jazz Band (ODJB), 92–93, 98
Ory, Kid, 61, 64, 98, 150, 153, 183
Osborne, Mary, 126

Page, Walter, 105, 115
Paich, Marty, 167
Panassié, Hugues, 88, 149, 152
Paris, Wilbur de, 150, 153
Parker, Charlie, 5, 11, 13, 22, 26, 32, 34, 37,
    39, 43, 47, 48, 56, 70–72, 77, 80, 89, 109,
    122, 126, 127, 129, 130–33, 135–40, 143,
    147–48, 150, 154, 156, 158, 159, 161, 165,
    169, 175, 176, 184, 187, 191, 207, 218,
    219
Pass, Joe, 126, 207, 211
Payne, Don, 189
Pedersen, Niels-Henning Orsted, 35, 37, 209,
    210
Pege, Eiji, 209, 210
Pepper, Art, 167, 168
Perry, Doc, 78
Peterson, Oscar, 72, 111, 122, 207, 211
Pettiford, Oscar, 113, 123, 132
Piano, 33, 118–20
Pizzarelli, Bucky, 126, 211
Placksin, Sally, 209
Pleasants, Henry, 215–17
Pollack, Ben, 92, 106
Pomeroy, Herb, 199
Ponty, Jean-Luc, 209
Popular music vs. jazz, 43–45
Popular songs, 24–25
Postif, Francois, 117
Powell, Baden, 142, 201
Powell, Bud, 73, 111, 132, 142–43, 146, 150,
    162, 163, 173, 207
Powell, Richie, 173
Presley, Elvis, 24, 101, 150, 156–58, 171
Previn, André, 80, 167–68, 188, 216
Price, Sammy, 208
Pritchard, Herman, 39
Pryor, Richard, 18, 34
Purvis, Jack, 91

Race and jazz, 34–36
Raeburn, Boyd, 132, 136, 159
Ragtime, 28, 50–54, 56–58, 208
Rainey, Ma, 21, 64
Ramey, Gene, 39, 41
Raney, Jimmy, 165
Really the Blues (Mezzrow), 94–95
Recordings, notes on, 6–7
Red Hot Peppers, 57–58
Redman, Dewey, 193, 207
Redman, Don, 40, 104
Reinhardt, Django, 33, 35, 121–22, 167
Remler, Emily, 126, 207, 209–11
Return to Forever, 207
Rexroth, Kenneth, 170
Rhythm, 26–29, 33
Rhythm 'n' blues, 149–50, 153–55, 157
Richmond, Danny, 185–86
Rifkin, Joshua, 54, 208
Risk, improvisational, 12
Rivers, Sam, 193, 207
Roach, Max, 115, 123, 132, 140, 141,
    142, 150, 164, 172–73, 176, 186, 207,
    210
Roberts, Luckey, 74
Robinson, Janice, 209
Rock, 201
Rock-jazz fusion, 49, 151, 201–3, 207
Rock 'n' roll, 150, 156–58
Rodgers, Jimmy, 38
Rodney, Red, 132
Rogers, Shorty, 161, 163, 167
Rolling Stones, The, 23, 24, 151, 156–58
Rollins, Sonny, 124, 147, 173–74, 176, 187,
    192
Rose, Wally, 152
Rosolino, Frank, 159
Rowles, Jimmy, 207, 208, 211, 222
Rudd, Roswell, 192
Rugulo, Pete, 167
Rushing, Jimmy, 115–16, 154
Rumsey, Howard, 167
Russel, Luis, 68
Russell, George, 151, 180
Russell, Nipsey, 170
Russell, Pee Wee, 95, 96, 149
Russell, Ross, 115, 131, 136
Russo, Bill, 159

Sahl, Mort, 170
St. Cyr, Johnny, 60, 64
Sampson, Edgar, 107
Sanders, Pharoah, 193, 207
Sandole, Dennis, 180
Savoy Sultans, 40
Saxophone, 30–32
Schifrin, Lalo, 201, 220
Schoenberg, Arnold, 168, 175, 215, 216

Schuller, Gunther, 27–28, 34, 36, 49, 67, 89, 147, 151, 164–65, 174, 185, 187, 198, 199, 208
Schulman, Joe, 163, 164
Scobey, Bob, 152
Scott, James, 52
Scott, Raymond, 125
Sedric, Gene, 76–77
Serious Music—and All That Jazz (Pleasants), 215, 216
Shaw, Artie, 86, 100, 110, 113–14, 131, 132, 159
Shearing, George, 132, 139, 146, 150, 159, 163, 203
Shepp, Archie, 36, 114, 174, 178, 183, 193, 200
Shertzer, Hymie, 108
Shihab, Sahib, 133
Shorter, Wayne, 176, 202, 203
Sidran, Ben, 45, 200
Siegelstein, Sandy, 164
Silver, Horace, 150, 172, 176, 203, 207
Simeon, Omer, 55
Simon, George T., 140
Sims, Zoot, 132, 161, 207
Sinatra, Frank, 43–44, 100, 109
Singleton, Zulty, 96
"Smashed notes," 18
Smith, Bessie, 16, 18, 19–24, 64, 75
Smith, Clara, 21
Smith, Floyd, 125
Smith, Joe, 63, 104
Smith, Pinetop, 119
Smith, Trixie, 21, 64, 157
Smith, Willie "The Lion," 42, 74, 78
Smithsonian Collection of Classic Jazz, 6, 23–26
Sondheim, Stephen, 220–21
Soul, 150, 169–71
Sousa, John Philip, 51, 53
Spanier, Francis "Muggsy," 91, 95
Speckled Red, 119
Spellman, A. B., 188, 189, 190, 193
Spivey, Victoria, 21
Stacy, Jess, 95, 98
Stark, John Stillwell, 51, 54
Stearns, Marshall, 49
Steward, Herbie, 161
Stewart, Rex, 30, 40, 62, 84, 97
Stitt, Sonny, 132
Stockhausen, Karlheinz, 175, 193, 216
Story of Jazz, The (Stearns), 49
Stravinsky, Igor, 53, 129, 131, 192, 215, 216
Strayhorn, Billy, 81–82, 84, 132
Stride, 74–77, 208
Studies in African Music (Jones), 27
Styles, 11
Sudhalter, Richard M., 96
Sullivan, Joe, 95, 96
Sutton, Ralph, 58, 98, 208

"Sweet" players, 97
Swing, 27–29, 100–18, 126, 131, 207–8
Symphony Sid, 155
Syncopation, 27–29
Szegeti, Josef, 113

Tampa Red, 154
Tate, Buddy, 116, 207
Tate, Erskine, 64
Tatum, Art, 13, 29, 37, 43, 44, 120, 122–23, 132, 142, 211, 219
Taylor, Art, 196, 210
Taylor, Billy, 96
Taylor, Cecil, 6, 14, 151, 169, 174, 175, 178, 192–93, 199, 207, 216–18
Taylor, Martin, 211
Taylor, Montana, 119
Tchicai, John, 193
Teagarden, Charles, 99–100
Teagarden, Cub, 90, 91
Teagarden, Helen, 90, 91
Teagarden, Jack, 35, 68, 90–92, 95, 98–100, 106, 149, 152
Teagarden, Norma, 90, 91
Television, 219
Terry, Clark, 84, 98, 141, 159
Teschemacher, Frank, 95, 106
Third Stream jazz, 151, 165, 185
Thornhill, Claude, 150, 163
Thornton, "Big Mama" Willie Mae, 24, 101
Timbre, 26, 29–34
To Be or Not to Bop (Gillespie), 142
Tone color, 26, 29–34
Torff, Brian, 210
Tough, Dave, 95, 109, 141, 160
Townsend, Irving, 101
Tristano, Lennie, 132, 150, 164, 165, 175, 203
Trombone, 32–33
Trouble With Cinderella, The (Shaw), 110
Trumpet, 32–33
Turner, Big Joe, 103, 119, 120, 154, 208
Tyner, McCoy, 194–96, 207, 211

Ulanov, Barry, 131
Urban Blues (Keil), 41

Vaché, Warren, 208
Van Eps, Bobby, 211
Varése, Edgard, 175
Vaughn, Sarah, 72
Venuti, Joe, 106
Vinnegar, Leroy, 168
Vitous, Miroslav, 203, 209

Waldron, Mal, 186, 211
Walker, T-Bone, 101
Wallace, Sippi, 21, 64

Waller, Fats, 11, 14, 26, 29, 42, 44, 45, 67, 74–77, 89, 115, 139, 208, 220
Waller, Maurice, 77
Wallington, George, 132, 142
Walton, Cedar, 211
Washington, Booker T., 34–35
Waters, Ethel, 44, 70, 75
Watson, Doc, 38
Watters, Lu, 149, 150, 152
Weather Report, 203, 207
Webb, Chick, 40, 41, 107
Webster, Ben, 39, 43, 81–84, 98
Welch, Lew, 170–71
Wells, Dicky, 116
Wellstood, Dick, 58, 208
West Coast cool, 150, 159, 161, 167–69
Weston, Randy, 211
Wettling, George, 60
Wheatstraw, Peetie, 154
White, Georgia, 154
Whiteman, Paul, 92, 97, 98
White musicians, 35–36, 89–92, 101, 134, 149, 150, 167–68, 177–78
Wilber, Bob, 208
Wiley, Lee, 70
Willett, Chappie, 107
Williams, Cootie, 33, 63, 79, 84, 85, 125
Williams, Hank, 38
Williams, Jabbo, 119

Williams, James, 211
Williams, Joe, 102
Williams, Martin, 6, 55, 165, 174, 187, 191, 198
Williams, Mary Lou, 105, 107, 120, 125, 131, 132, 145, 161
Williams, Tony, 176, 199, 202, 203, 211
Williamson, Claude, 167
Williamson, Stu, 167
Wilson, Jackie, 211
Wilson, Teddy, 26, 67, 72, 97, 103, 111–13, 117, 120, 132, 142
Winding, Kai, 37, 164
Witherspoon, Jimmy, 20, 21, 154
Wolfe, Tom, 129
Women, 21–22, 209
Woods, Phil, 207
Wright, Richard, 89

Yancey, Jimmy, 119
Yerba Buena Jazz Band, 149, 152
Young, Lester, 2, 11, 30–32, 35, 39, 43, 70–71, 97, 103, 111, 116–20, 123, 125, 127, 132, 136, 160, 163, 171, 175, 185, 219
Young, Trummy, 113

Zawinul, Joe, 176, 177, 202–3
Zeitlin, Denny, 211, 220
Zurke, Bob, 120